D0004364

DON'T CALL ME GOON

HOCKEY'S GREATEST ENFORCERS, GUNSLINGERS, AND BAD BOYS

GREG OLIVER & RICHARD KAMCHEN

ECW PRESS

At ECW Press, we want you to enjoy this book in whatever format you like, whenever you like. Leave your print book at home and take the eBook to go! Purchase the print edition and receive the eBook free. Just send an email to ebook@ecwpress.com and include:

- the book title
- the name of the store where you purchased it
- your receipt number
- your preference of file type: PDF or ePub?

A real person will respond to your email with your eBook attached. And thanks for supporting an independently owned Canadian publisher with your purchase!

Published by ECW Press
665 Gerrard Street East
Toronto, Ontario, Canada M4M 1Y2
416-694-3348 / info@ecwpress.com

We acknowledge the financial support of the Government of Canada through the Canada Book Fund for our publishing activities, and the contribution of the Government of Ontario through the Ontario Book Publishing Tax Credit and the Ontario Media Development Corporation.

LIBRARY AND ARCHIVES CANADA
CATALOGUING IN PUBLICATION

Oliver, Greg, author
Don't call me goon : hockey's greatest
enforcers, gunslingers, and bad
boys / Greg Oliver, Richard Kamchen.

ISBN 978-1-77041-038-1 (PBK.)
ALSO ISSUED AS: 978-1-77090-420-0 (PDF)
978-1-77090-421-7 (EPUB)

1. National Hockey League—History.
2. Hockey players—Attitudes.
3. Violence in sports. I. Kamchen, Richard,
1974–, author II. Title.

GV847.8.N3069
2013   796.962'64   C2013-902464-6

Editor for the press: Michael Holmes
Cover design: David Gee
Front cover photos: AP Photo (top: Francis Specker; bottom: Paul Vernon)
Back cover photo: Icon Sports Media
Text design: Tania Craan
Typesetting: Kendra Martin
Printing: Marquis   5   4   3

PRINTED AND BOUND IN CANADA

To that old-time hockey!

TABLE OF CONTENTS

OFTEN OVERLOOKED AMONG the beautiful end-to-end rushes, pretty passes, explosive slap shots, and glorious glove saves are the hockey enforcers who ensure the most talented players are allowed to shine.

Before the enforcer came into being, players of all sizes and skills were on their own and were expected to take care of themselves. All-Star defenceman Eddie Shore, who routinely excited crowds with his rushes and scoring prowess generations before Bobby Orr would do the same, accumulated 978 stitches before retiring from the game. And before him, many a player was cut down with fouls that left a gash on his head and a pool of blood in his wake. Those who refused to get back up to fight another day were quickly drummed out of the sport.

The game of those early days makes today's hockey seem tame. The players were ruthless and brutal, many seemingly on a mission to stop the opposition by any means necessary. And often those means included a heavy stick, which they used with little or no restraint, chopping one another down with crushing blows that would earn them lifetime suspensions—and perhaps even lengthy prison terms—today.

Then along came the enforcer, who would instill fear into opponents who previously had no qualms about belting smaller, more talented players into submission. "The first one to come along to protect people was [John] Ferguson," said Hall of Fame defenceman Pierre Pilote. "There were other fighters in the league, but all of a sudden we noticed Ferguson was going to be protecting the guys."

Thanks to the muscle Ferguson provided for his Canadiens

teammates, hockey's most gifted would be given a better chance to demonstrate their talents without fearing for their health or being forced to respond in kind to the wild men who would otherwise have squashed them, dragging them to the penalty box in an unequal exchange of talent.

By the expansion era, the game had regressed to an earlier period of brutality as the new franchises, thin on talent, promoted the toughest and most desperate to escape the bush leagues in order to intimidate their way to victories. Other teams responded and, eventually, balance was again restored as every winning club had deterrents on their benches. No longer could any team rule by sheer force alone.

Enforcers—protectors who'd let the opposition know that transgressions against their stars would not be tolerated—remained prominent in the 1980s. With heavies like Dave Semenko looking out for him, a lanky superstar by the name of Wayne Gretzky would rewrite the record books and last 20 years in what was once the most violent professional sport on Earth. Gretzky knocked Gordie Howe off in the record books, but it is unlikely he could ever have knocked him off on the ice, though they did faceoff against each other at the beginning of the Great One's career and at the end of Howe's. After all, the Gordie Howe Hat Trick—a goal, an assist, and a fight—is still referenced today.

Howe is just one of numerous stars in the league's history to have demonstrated a flair for fisticuffs to go along with his scoring prowess.

Besides owning the Norris Trophy, Bobby Orr was a tough guy who had no problem throwing down. Orr would be tested in his rookie season as veterans looked to see if the new golden boy would back down. He wouldn't, mixing it up with Montreal's Terry Harper and New York's Reg Fleming. Orr's fights wouldn't be confined to his first pro year, and he'd prove himself handy, even holding his own against the likes of the Rangers' Orland Kurtenbach.

Typically he'd raise his hands in retribution, flashing his temper

Dave "Tiger" Williams of the Toronto Maple Leafs lands a left on the jaw of Guy Lapointe of the Montreal Canadiens while being held by the linesman during a game in December 1975. (AP Photo/DMB)

if he'd been wronged on the ice. He went wild after Toronto's Brian Conacher accidentally clipped him on the nose, steaming through teammates to get at Conacher and then mauling him. After Pat Quinn of the Leafs knocked him out with an elbow, Orr gave him his receipt, dropping the gloves and pounding away on Quinn after he fell to the ice. Opponents took notice of such vengeful attacks. Also not lost on them would be the severe retribution the Big Bad Bruins or Lunch Pail Gang would inflict on anyone taking liberties with Orr.

Besides being an All-Star defenceman for the New York Rangers, Brad Park showed up for any challenges thrown his way and engaged in numerous fights. But when he went to Boston, Don Cherry told him to turn the other cheek since his value was greater on the ice than in the penalty box: "Deep down, I loved it when Brad fought, but I had my designated fighters, and he wasn't one of them," Cherry wrote in *Grapes*.

Opponents recognized Park's value to the Bruins and would try to goad him into fights. Cherry had had enough when Detroit's Dennis Polonich drove Park to go after him, which resulted in Park getting thrown out of the game. Afterwards, Cherry told reporters Park was forbidden to fight and if he did, he'd get fined. "I told the entire league, in effect, that Park was no longer permitted to fight so he, therefore, no longer felt obliged to display his toughness and we were all the better for it," Cherry wrote.

Another '70s All-Star, Larry Robinson, was feared for his size and big open-ice hits. And although he didn't get in many fights, his pugilistic acumen deterred most from bothering this particular member of Montreal's Big Three. At 6-foot-4, Robinson towered over his peers and was one dandy fighter, typically mopping the ice with anyone he faced, even a heavyweight specialist like Dave "Hammer" Schultz.

Power forwards also hurt other teams, with their scoring touch and physical intimidation.

Wendel Clark of the Leafs came into the NHL with all guns firing, hitting and fighting everything that moved, no matter how big. He had no qualms about taking on enforcers like Bob Probert, Behn Wilson, and Marty McSorley.

"Talk about giving 100% in a fight, that's what he did. It's not always the biggest dog in the fight," said Todd Ewen. "There's lots of guys who can throw a punch but not a lot of guys who can *really* throw a punch. A lot of people think that you throw a punch with your shoulders and arms, and Wendel threw with his legs. It came from his toes all the way through his hands and when he threw he had bad intentions—he was awesome and that's why he did so well."

"Wendel Clark had a huge impact on the game. He could play any way you wanted to play," added Dave Manson. "He wasn't the biggest guy in stature, but he played a big man's game. Plus he could score, plus he could hit, plus he could fight, plus, plus. Wendel was the epitome of a power forward back in the day."

But given that Clark was by far the best Leaf on the ice, he sometimes needed reining in. When the Red Wings assigned Joe Kocur to shadow Clark in the 1987 Norris Division Final, John Brophy forbade Clark from duking it out with his cousin. Even a legendary minor-league roughneck like Brophy could see no upside in Toronto losing its best man in exchange for a role-player like Kocur.

Clark's style also forced him to cut back on his fighting. His first two years of vigorous play took their toll, giving him back problems that nearly caused him to retire and forced him to miss most of three straight seasons. When he returned as a regular, his fight card wasn't nearly as full as it had been during his first two years.

But he made his point in those early years, and as he was still able to throw a devastating hit or get into a fight—like that with Marty McSorley in Toronto's 1993 series with the Los Angeles Kings—other teams were wary of him. Clark could still put the fear into other teams. After warning Pavel Bure in a playoff contest the following year that he'd take his head off if Gino Odjick didn't lay off Doug Gilmour, Odjick got Bure's message to leave Gilmour alone.

"Look at the amount of respect guys gave him going in the corner fighting for the puck after he went out there and made a statement or two," said Ewen. "That's a tribute to the four skills of hockey, not three—skating, shooting, passing, and checking. The physical contact is a major part of hockey."

Milan Lucic is the modern-day prototype of the power forward.

An amateur boxer in his teens, the 6-foot-4, 220-pounder jumped out of the Bruins gates with fists flying. A glimpse of the total package he had to offer came early in his first season, in an October 2007 game against the Kings, during which he recorded a Gordie Howe Hat Trick, with his first goal, an assist, and a fight against enforcer Raitis Ivanāns. He made an impression, racking up 13 majors in his rookie season.

The following year, Lucic played on the first line with Marc Savard and Phil Kessel, and his coach, like Brophy with Clark, tried to rein him in. In a late November 2008 contest against the Canadiens, coach Claude Julien ordered Lucic not to take the bait of tough-guy Georges Laraque. "There was no way it was going to happen," Julien said at the time. "[Shawn] Thornton was there, ready for Georges. Nothing happened. My tough guy was ready for their tough guy. Simple as that. I told him not to fight. It was me."

Although concentrating more on scoring, Lucic continued to stand up and be counted, duking it out with top heavies like Matt Carkner, Colton Orr, John Erskine, Jay Rosehill, and Chris Neil.

In 2011–2012, the NHLPA and CBC's *Hockey Night in Canada* released a joint poll of over 250 NHL players, and Lucic was named the NHL's toughest player.

Lucic's teammate Zdeno Chara was the runner-up in that same poll, but he was also overwhelmingly voted the defenceman hardest to play against.

Chara is something of a throwback to when talented leaders on defence didn't shy away from the rough going. He's menacing at 6-foot-9, 260 pounds, and he's had his run-ins with numerous superheavyweights, including Peter Worrell, Georges Laraque, and Donald Brashear, and his bloody pounding of David Koci was replayed over and over. His fights are few and far between, in no small part thanks to his imposing size and freakish strength. The images of Chara rag-dolling Toronto's 220-pound defender Bryan McCabe and sending Montreal's Max Pacioretty into a Bell Centre stanchion are imprinted on opponents league-wide. As a result, Chara is rarely challenged.

But the skilled players who can fight are a rare breed, more so than the enforcer, many of whom will only have a cup of coffee in the big league.

Tough guys have the hardest job in hockey, and perhaps all sports, coming off the bench for only brief periods during most games to throw their weight around and occasionally correct what they perceive as opposition malfeasance with a punch to somebody's head. Despite shouldering this heavy burden, the enforcer also has to deflect or absorb continuous calls from the press for his permanent removal from the game, endure endless barbs, and denouncement as a "goon."

"I hate that word," seethed former Winnipeg Jet Jimmy Mann. "I tell people [who say], 'Jimmy, you're a goon,' I tell 'em, 'I just despise that.' I think that's an insult. Anybody who could spend [years] in the National Hockey League, they have to have something else than just being a goon."

"Everybody tried to group you into that goon status and you try not to ever be a goon. It's hard," said Dave Manson, known better for his "spirited" play in Chicago and elsewhere than for his booming slap shot and two All-Star Game appearances.

Chris Nilan, a fighter who elevated his game to became a solid checker who could also score 20 or so goals a year while with the Montreal Canadiens, finds the term offensive. "I don't feel too good about it. I don't like it, actually. I guess you could say my role was to be an enforcer," said Nilan, who won a Stanley Cup in 1986, to the *Montreal Gazette*. "Anyway, people who call you 'goon' are basically idiots themselves."

Jay Miller, however, simply dismissed the pejorative term and those who insisted on using it. "Didn't care; I was getting paid," he said. "You call me dickhead . . . I played with a 'B' and an L.A. Kings label on my shirt. Got to hang around with the best players—about

30 Hall of Famers. What do I care what they call me? I go in a city, they wanted me to be on their team. I meet a rock star, he wants to be me, I want to be him. What's the difference? It's only words."

Despite the fact that enforcers often see little ice time and rarely share in the glory of the goals that are scored, they are often as popular—if not more so—than the slickest stars among the fans who pay to see the games.

No one scored more points in Maple Leafs history than Mats Sundin, and yet during a typical home game in his Toronto heyday, there would be as many Tie Domi sweaters in the crowd as fans with No. 13 on their backs.

Hartford fans voted Whaler tough-guy Jim McKenzie their favourite in 1990–91, despite the fact that he appeared in only 41 games. Even though he only scored two goals during his five years in Minnesota, Derek Boogaard's Wild jersey was the team's bestseller. Tony Twist was the only St. Louis Blue who had his own television show. And just before Georges Laraque left Edmonton, he staged a goodbye autograph session that lasted 10 hours.

"I'm at a hockey game and a fight breaks out. I look at the crowd. It's going bananas," Canada's highest-profile promoter of rock 'em, sock 'em hockey, Don Cherry, told the *Toronto Star*. "Next day, I read in the papers that the game was marred by a fight. Who decides it was marred? The people who paid to get in didn't seem to think so."

Cherry, a former coach turned broadcaster for CBC's *Hockey Night in Canada*, has often pointed out he never heard of anybody heading for the concession stands when a fight started. He isn't saying anything new. In a November 1962 *Hockey Illustrated* story, linesman George Hayes said, "Let's face it, a good fight helps put people in the building. I've worked many games that were dull until a fight broke out. Then, it turned out to be a heck of a game."

But the price of the fans' adulation is heavy, both physically and mentally. "Patrick Côté led the league in majors in the Predators' first season, 1998–99, with 30," recalled Pete Weber, the Preds' play-by-play announcer. "Patrick fell victim. His hands couldn't keep up. He had to have surgery on his knuckles."

"The stress of having to score a goal every night is one thing, but the stress of going into a game knowing you're going to have to fight is something totally different," retired Buffalo Sabres enforcer Rob Ray told the *Waterloo Region Record*. "I try to explain that to people and they have a hard time understanding."

"The night before you didn't sleep very much," said Jimmy Mann, who would read the opposition lineup after morning practices to scout whom he'd be facing. "Probably the hardest, most tiring part of the job to do was the mental part of it. The physical part of it, not a problem."

"It's not the most glamorous role, it's a very hard role to play, some have said it's the toughest role in all of pro sports," said Stu Grimson, who accumulated over 2,000 penalty minutes for seven different NHL franchises.

CHAPTER 1

PIONEERS OF MAYHEM

HOCKEY'S FOUNDING BRUISERS have more in common with Western outlaws than they do with today's comparatively mild-mannered unionized brotherhood of skaters.

Those behind the uproar that followed Marty McSorley striking fellow enforcer Donald Brashear in February 2000 probably knew little about "old-time hockey," when helmetless players routinely parted each other's hair with their sticks. McSorley's own stick swing to Brashear's head resulted in a conviction for assault with a weapon and 18 months probation; he avoided jail time. Compare that to the actions of two players of the early 20th century who stood trial for manslaughter for vicious and fatal attacks on opposing players; they were acquitted.

Whenever multiple fights break out in a modern-day game, the media is quick to bring up the brawl-filled 1970s of the Big Bad Bruins and the Broad Street Bullies. While the action then could be vicious, it wasn't the at-times murderous game that existed in pro hockey's early days.

JOE HALL

When "Bad" Joe Hall arrived in Montreal after carving out a name—and reputation—for himself in Manitoba, he wanted to show that his nickname was not fitting. "I have been reinstated," Hall said in 1906, "and I am going to show the Montreal people that I am not half as bad as I have been painted in the matter of rough play. I had two tickets waiting for me from Pittsburgh, but I thought I would rather stay in Canada, and take a hand in the struggle in this part of the country."

Hall balanced out the violent incidents that made headlines over the next 12 seasons (such as cutting up a referee's pants, driving "Newsy" Lalonde's head into the fence at the end of the rink, and being charged by police for disorderly conduct for an on-ice fight in Toronto) with three Stanley Cups with the Kenora Thistles (1907) and Quebec Bulldogs (1911–12, 1912–13) and a Hall of Fame–worthy career. His sudden death on April 5, 1919, during the Stanley Cup Final in Seattle from influenza only helped to grow his legend. Yet Hall always felt there was a target on his back, and the newsmen of the day tended to agree. "The whole trouble is that no referee thinks he is doing his duty unless he registers a major or a minor against the Brandon man," reads one lament. "There are far dirtier players in the NHA [National Hockey Association] today but they get away with it, though the referees know that they are handing out the rough stuff, even though the crowd does not always tumble to it right away."

Joseph Henry "Joe" Hall was born on May 3, 1881, in Milwich, England, and moved to Winnipeg in 1884. Having served his junior years in Winnipeg, Hall headed to Brandon in 1900 to play senior hockey, and he would later suit up for the Rat Portage/Kenora Thistles and the Winnipeg Rowing Club. Before leaving for his first pro club, in Houghton, Michigan, friends and fans gathered at the Brandon CPR station to say farewell. "A number of boys lifted him shoulder high and bounced him about in the air, during which proceeding Joe blushed and smiled," reads the recap, going on to praise Hall's contributions: "He has always been a valuable member of the local puck-chasing septette, a straight, honest hockeyist, who played the game with a vigor that sometimes laid him open to criticism. But when the season gets into swing, it is pretty safe to predict that Houghton will show no more valuable defenceman on its line-up than Joe Hall."

Going east was a big deal for the 5-foot-10, 175-pound Hall. While he signed with the Montreal Hockey Club for a "fairly good contract," it was said that the other squads in town, the Shamrocks and the Wanderers, had been after him as well. Seeing Hall accompanied by his wife, the newspaper admitted that Hall "does not look at all like the terrible hockey ruffian which the Western papers tried to make him out; and, according to his own story, he was more sinned against than sinning. He showed one or two marks which certainly went far towards corroborating that theory."

Art Ross, who had played with Hall in Brandon and against him as well, encouraged Hall to head east in 1907, pleading Hall's case after a suspension:

He is a fast, clever player, and all right when he is left alone. Unfortunately for himself, he has earned the reputation of being rough, and when he steps on the ice for a game he is a marked man for every player on the other side. I have heard 'Dirty Hall' called out by a crowd for a piece of work which happened at the other end of the rink from where Hall was at the moment. His temper, I suppose, gave under repeated provocations in the Winnipeg match, but to show you that he put up with a lot himself, I can say that he came out of the game with two cuts on his head, each of which required four stitches. He was told by Winnipeg players that they would get to him. He is a gentlemanly fellow off the ice, and he played good, clean hockey against us in our two matches. I would like to see him playing in the east, and I am sure it would not take long for him to wipe out the impression that he is a rough player, and to build up a reputation for what he is, a fast and a clever one!

That reputation would stay with Hall, right until his final season. In the seven-position game, Hall played rover and switched to defence when the game trimmed down, allowing him more room to roam—and roar. In short seasons, he piled up the penalty minutes: 98 PIM in 20 games in 1905–06; 78 PIM in 18 games in 1912–13; 100 PIM in 21 games in 1917–18; and 135 PIM in 16 games in 1918–19. Hall could score too, netting 15 and 13 goals during seasons in Quebec. "On the defence Joe Hall is an artist. He is not a heavy defenceman as they go but [he] has the knack," reads one story. "He knows to the full how to make the best use of himself and he makes the best use of his knowledge."

The most famous clash involving Hall came on January 22, 1910, when, as a member of the Montreal Shamrocks, he slashed a hole in the pants of referee Roddy Kennedy. Perturbed that he had been skewered continuously by Frank Patrick of Renfrew without any penalty, Hall had lost it on the ref as well as his opponent. "Every time I went down the ice I received the stick on the head from F. Patrick," Hall said in the dressing room about the affair, which included a bloody fight between Patrick and Hall. "After receiving this continual punishment for a certain length of time I could not stand it any longer, nor could any man with any sort of heart. F. Patrick fairly drove me to hit him, and I do not consider it my fault that the scrap occurred."

It had looked like Hall would be fined $100 and suspended, perhaps for life, but his genuine good nature prevailed. He went to visit Kennedy, who forgave him and gave him a bill for mending the hole in the trousers. When Hall died, Patrick praised his foe: "Off the ice he was one of the jolliest, best-hearted, most popular men who ever played."

The Jekyll-and-Hyde aspect of Hall, who was also a gun

enthusiast and a champion trap-shooter, is perhaps best demonstrated by his feud with Newsy Lalonde. As a playmaker, Lalonde of the Canadiens would have to brave Hall's position on the Quebec Bulldogs blue line to make any attempt on the goal. In 1913, Hall was given a match penalty for charging Lalonde and knocking him so that his head came in contact with the fence at the end of the rink. Emmett Quinn, the boss of the National Hockey Association, addressed the attack. "According to the report of the referees, Hall charged Lalonde deliberately from behind. While a bodycheck in front is allowed, Hall's actions constituted a serious foul," said Quinn, who also proposed modifying the rinks. "I think that a change in the arena fence would aid in preventing at least such accidents as last night. The place where Lalonde struck is a very dangerous corner."

"I never really had anything against Newsy," Hall said in 1916. "He began the whole thing by keeping up a running fire of insulting and sarcastic remarks to me once during a game. I became sore and always handed back the same line of conversation. I bodied him hard on every occasion and literally goaded him on to hitting me—and I struck back."

Despite the on-ice animosity, Hall's son, J.C. Hall, said that his father had a heart: "After giving Newsy a real going over, he learned Mrs. Lalonde had given birth to a daughter that morning. Father went with Newsy to the hospital and apologized to his wife for cutting him up. That's the sort of guy he was," J.C. Hall told Bob Pennington of the *Toronto Telegram* in 1969, adding, "When Dad moved to Montreal somebody thought it would be fun to make them roommates. They finished up the best of friends and it was Newsy who gave me my first hockey stick."

Lalonde and Hall were key members of the 1918–19 Canadiens squad that travelled west to Seattle, Washington, to take on the Pacific Coast Hockey Association–champion Metropolitans in a five-game Stanley Cup Final. With the series tied at two games apiece, health officials were forced to cancel the deciding game because of an influenza epidemic, which had hospitalized players on both teams.

All recovered but Hall, who died in the Columbus Sanitarium in Seattle of pneumonia. He was buried at Mountain View Cemetery in Vancouver, BC, with Lester Patrick, Cyclone Taylor, Si Griffis, Billy "Beaver" Couture, Louis Berlinquette, and Lalonde as pallbearers.

Tributes poured in for the man whom so many had feared.

"Hall was one of the few professional athletes who saved his money. He worked on the railroad during the summer months, and this, with his hockey earnings, enabled him to purchase property in Brandon, which will leave his wife and three children, two sons and a daughter, in comfortable circumstances," reported the *Toronto World*. "Hall played the game for all there was in it, and, although he checked hard and close, he was never known to take a mean advantage of a weaker opponent. He was popular with his clubmates, and had many friends in the cities in which he played hockey."

Hall was inducted into the Hockey Hall of Fame in 1961, perhaps the ultimate approval that his style of play was more the norm than the exception during his era.

SPRAGUE CLEGHORN With a stick to the head of
Newsy Lalonde, blood on the ice, and a handful of stitches, Sprague Cleghorn of the Wanderers officially opened Toronto's new Mutual Street Arena on December 19, 1912, with a pre-season exhibition game, introducing the city to six-on-six professional hockey. Shortly thereafter, Toronto's police force opened a file on Cleghorn.

But what if it was all part of the show? An attempt to market the expanding National Hockey Association, which was about to admit a Toronto franchise. On the passing of Cleghorn on July 12, 1956, *Hockey News* columnist Baz O'Meara wrote that Lalonde and Cleghorn conspired to make a memorable moment. Odie Cleghorn,

Sprague's younger brother by a year (who died in his sleep on the day of his brother's funeral), was also in on it. According to O'Meara, Lalonde had cross-checked Odie, and Sprague "rushed up at full speed and swung his stick at Lalonde's head from behind. Fortunately for the integrity of the famous lacrosse-hockeyist's top-not, Cleghorn changed his mind as he swung, checked the blow, and turned the blade. At that the flat of the blade struck Lalonde a resounding smack on the side of the head and sent him back to the ice with a gashed scalp, which took ten stitches to sew up."

The affair itself went unpenalized but resulted in $75 in fines immediately for Cleghorn and a month's suspension. Police entered the dressing room, determined to drag the heralded defenceman off, but were convinced to wait before pressing an assault charge.

According to O'Meara, "The story goes that they had agreed to put a little pepper into the proceedings, as they were both good friends. Newsy rasped Odie Cleghorn. Sprague proceeded to rap him over the head. A police case ensued, but both were acquitted. Sprague's straight faced explanation was that the episode was all the result of a spirit of good clean fun."

On the morning of Friday, December 27th, Cleghorn was before Magistrate Denison, charged with committing aggravated assault on Lalonde. Both players appeared in court. Cleghorn, electing to be tried by a jury, pleaded not guilty. Detective George Guthrie, who was present at the game and swore out the information, was the only witness called. "I saw Lalonde check Odie Cleghorn, brother of the defendant," said Guthrie, "both men went down on the ice. While Lalonde was down, Sprague Cleghorn skated over and struck him on the head with his stick."

"Struck him on the head!" exclaimed Magistrate Denison. "Did he want to kill him?"

"I don't think so. He was just taking the law in his own hands," replied Guthrie.

The following day, Lalonde made a strong plea for leniency for

Cleghorn through his counsel, and the magistrate slapped Cleghorn with a mere $50 fine and the charge was reduced from aggravated to common assault.

It was hardly the only blotch on Sprague Cleghorn's rap sheet during his remarkable Hall of Fame career—one during which he was traded for train fare. "He was truly one of the great hockey players of all time. Sprague was a tremendous competitor and few players would run the risk of taking liberties with him," said Frank Selke when Sprague died. "He typified the old time, driving player."

Sprague Horace Cleghorn was born on March 11, 1890, in Montreal, and Odie (short for Ogilvie) followed in September 1891. The brothers both broke into pro hockey with the Renfrew Millionaires in 1910, where coach Al Smith converted Sprague from left wing to defence. For the next 16 years, with a season off with injury, Sprague banged out a reputation with the Montreal Wanderers, Ottawa Senators, Toronto St. Pats, Montreal Canadiens, and Boston Bruins. He won Stanley Cups with Ottawa in 1920 and with the Canadiens in 1924.

The story of how he ended up in Ottawa bears repeating. Cleghorn, a member of the Wanderers, had broken his ankle following the 1918 season, and, while walking down a Montreal street during his recuperation, fell and broke his other one. With no one expecting him to return, Sprague rang his old friend T.P. (Tommy) Gorman, who was running the Senators and part-owner. "He called me up and said he would be in good shape by the fall. We took a chance on him," Gorman once said. "Do you know what he cost us? The price of a railway ticket from Montreal." He'd play nine more top-level seasons after healing (and he sued the City of Montreal for not clearing the ice).

Cleghorn was durable as well as double tough. He once played 75 straight games, which was a record at the time. "He was my brother, and I don't like to boast, but I never saw a tougher or better man," said Odie upon Sprague's death.

There is a story that was oft-told by Irvin "Ace" Bailey, who played with the Maple Leafs against Sprague in his rookie year. Toronto was winning against the Bruins, and Cleghorn was arguing with the referee. "I butted in, making some wise-guy remark and, not even looking at me, bang! his fist came from nowhere, caught me right on the nose, and knocked me down," Bailey recounted. "I started to scramble up but our defenceman, Bill Brydge, pushed me back. 'Don't get up,' Bill said matter-of-factly. 'He'll kill you.'"

Yet that story, from 1926, is relatively tame for "Peg" Cleghorn stories, a man Jack Adams once labelled an "unwashed surgeon" for his stick work and to whom Trent Frayne devotes an entire chapter in his 1974 book, *The Mad Men of Hockey*.

Playing for the Canadiens in the 1923 playoffs, Sprague assaulted Lionel Hitchman of Ottawa with a vicious cross-check that got him tossed from the game, suspended for the following game, and a $200 fine—from his own manager.

"Jesus, he was mean," said Red Dutton once. "If you fell in front of Cleg he'd kick your balls in."

The lives of the Cleghorn brothers—the first brothers to both be NHL captains—were so intertwined, it perhaps was not a surprise that Odie died just hours before his brother's funeral. Elmer Ferguson of the *Montreal Herald* wrote that the brothers "were vastly different in personality."

"Odie was serious about hockey, about business," wrote Ferguson. "There was nothing of the playboy about Odie. In his playing days, he was known as the Beau Brummell of hockey. He was always impeccably garbed, debonair to a degree. As a player, he was a great stick-handler and superior goal scorer."

Oddly, both ended up coaching. Odie was manager and coach of the Pittsburgh Pirates and Pittsburgh Yellow Jackets in 1924 and 1925, and he is credited with introducing the three-line system of forward combinations. He later became an NHL referee.

Sprague's greatest pupil may have been Eddie Shore. The

36-year-old Cleghorn skated with the Bruins and took Shore under his wing. "I broke Shore into the big time and I claim some credit for making him the standout defenceman he became," Cleghorn is quoted in *Eddie Shore and That Old Time Hockey*. "He had a lot of stuff when he joined us, but there were still things he needed to learn and I taught him those things."

As a coach, Cleghorn's first assignment was the Newark Bulldogs in the Canadian-American league in 1928–29, and the following two seasons he was with the Providence Reds. In 1932, with the Montreal Maroons, he was a playing coach—"That was his forte, polishing up his defence players," wrote O'Meara. Up next were stints with the Quebec Senior League's Verdun Maple Leafs and the Edmundston Eskimos squad in New Brunswick in 1935. His 1936 job with the International Hockey League (IHL)'s Pittsburgh Shamrocks ended prematurely and in controversy, with Cleghorn suing successfully to receive his full salary, including bonuses, after being dismissed. In 1947, he put on hockey clinics in Cornwall, Ontario, and ran the Cougars in the Quebec Senior League.

Even when employed as a coach, Sprague never lost his well-known sense of humour. "One he got the greatest kick out of was to get behind a guy on the pullman steps and pull his derby down over his ears," said Harry Meeking. "Derbies were the big thing then. Cost about $12 apiece." Another practical joke, which made his obituary, was catching a teammate asleep and applying a can of black shoe polish to the unfortunate soul. As a coach, he would call up rookies on the hotel phone and, pretending to be a woman, invite them out.

Post-hockey, he worked various jobs, including as a receiving inspector at Canadair in Montreal. His toughness never left him. In 1943, Sprague was working in a Montreal defence plant when a steel bar weighing 1,200 pounds fell on his leg. "The steel bar was badly bent," wrote Charles Edwards of the Canadian Press. "Sprague suffered a few torn muscles and tendons."

JEAN PUSIE: THE GREAT ENTERTAINER

Jean Pusie's on-ice skills never came close to matching his talent for putting on a great show. Though the defenceman lasted only parts of five seasons for the Montreal Canadiens, Boston Bruins, and New York Rangers, he did manage 17 years in various minor leagues, which are the source of many of the rich stories about him—"He's had a fight in about every town in Canada," Tommy Gorman once said.

With an expressive face, natural stage presence, and unique sense of timing, Jean Baptiste Pusie was only a few steps away from a Vaudevillian actor.

Alone on the blue line with four foes rushing in, Pusie once dropped to his knees, looked pleadingly at the crowd, and lifted his arms in surrender.

During a game with the Rangers, he took the time to stack his gloves and stick neatly in the corner before responding to a challenge.

When given the opportunity to take a shootout, Pusie would make the most of it. He'd stand at centre ice and fix his thick, dark hair before skating off toward the goal in long, loopy strides, waving to the crowd or shrieking out a war cry; stopping in front of the goalie, he'd offer his hand as if apologizing for even considering scoring on him. Upon the actual shot, Pusie, more often than not, would put one past the flustered keeper. Without pressure around him and enough space, he was armed with a powerful shot that could, on occasion, knock the goalie's glove off his hand, prompting Pusie to leap into the net to retrieve and return the mitt.

The Canadiens had high hopes for Pusie. Born on October 15, 1910, in Montreal, the 19-year-old, 5-foot-11¾ and 131-pound Pusie was assigned to the London Tecumsehs of the International League for his pro debut, having done his time in the Railway-Telephone League and on Canadiens amateur teams. His subsequent road map took him across the continent, from the Vancouver Lions to the Providence Reds to the Cleveland Barons to the St. Louis Flyers.

Pusie's love for show business went beyond the rink. During the off-seasons, he had a couple of bouts as a professional boxer and moonlighted as a professional wrestler in Toronto and Montreal.

Unpredictable on the ice, Pusie was known to hurl himself into the crowd to confront his detractors. In St. Louis, one of his teammates was being ridiculed in the penalty box by the fans, and when he started fighting back, chairs started to rain down on the ice. Pusie leapt into the stands. "It was a merry scramble with everybody swinging at everybody else and nobody knowing who hit him. But out of the whole bunch, Pusie was the only one who was jailed," said Bill Grant, the president of the American Association.

After leading the Western League in scoring in 1932–33 with Vancouver, Pusie was signed by Lester Patrick of the Rangers, but he did little more than entertain in 19 games, tallying just two assists. "[Patrick] had a keen appreciation of Pusie's showmanship, even though he realized his shortcomings as a big-leaguer," wrote Milt Dunnell after Pusie's death of a heart attack in Montreal on April 23, 1956. Dunnel continued, "One of Pusie's failings was that he loved to hog the puck. Patrick blistered him for it. After one of these lectures, Pusie grabbed the puck, rushed down the ice, drew the defence, and passed to an open wing— only there was no teammate to receive it. When he returned to the bench, Patrick asked: 'Why in the world did you pass the puck when there was no one there to take it?' Pusie looked hurt as he asked Patrick: 'How should I knew we have men in penailtee box?'"

RED HORNER Leading the league in fighting for eight straight seasons doesn't usually get you into the Hall of Fame. Yet after being overlooked for a number of years, Conn Smythe, the man behind the Toronto Maple Leafs, pleaded to the Selection Committee on behalf of his "policeman," Red Horner, in a letter dated May 5, 1965.

Most clubs had two or three policemen on their team. Red was our policeman and I would venture to state his penalties never hurt us

REGINALD HORNER

at any time, as he took on at least three or four of the toughest on the other club and although he would get ten or twenty minutes penalties a game, the other team would have the same number of penalties spread around amongst three or four players . . . Of all the great bodycheckers there have been in the National Hockey League, no one hit a man fairer or harder than Red Horner."

Frank Selke seconded the motion, understanding the appeal of Horner, both at the home rink and abroad: "It could be said that Horner was somewhat of a sacrificial lamb and a good man for selling tickets because many of the fans in outside cities attended the games in the fervent hope that somebody would present Horner with a brick house, letting him have the bricks one by one."

Bobby Hewitson of the *Toronto Telegram* wrote that "Horner oozed colour. Was in fact a veritable rainbow. Who was it the fans in Chicago, in Detroit, in Montreal, in New York and in Boston went to see when Leafs performed? It was Horner. They wanted to see some home town player crown the Leaf bad man. That alone would be worth the price of admission. Yes—he dragged many a fan to the ticket window in those rinks. They hated him and they loved to see him smacked down."

In August 1965, Horner was indeed enshrined in hockey's hallowed hall, proving that there is much more to a man than just his goals (42) and assists (110). In his 12 seasons, accounting for 490 regular-season games, Horner sat out for 1,264 penalty minutes. Doing the math, that would seem to be a modest 2.5 PIM/game—but consider Horner once collected 17 penalty minutes in the first period.

George Reginald Horner was born in Lynden, Ontario, on May 28, 1909, and began life as the son of a farmer. The Horner family moved to the town of Ancaster, then to the cities of Hamilton and Toronto. By his early teens, Horner was playing bantam hockey with North Toronto, staying with his half-brother, who was a grocer. Frank Selke, who ran the Marlboro juniors team, was one of Red's clients on his grocery delivery route, and he would become a benefactor. "I knew Mrs. Selke better than her husband and she sure gave me good cookies on the deliveries," Horner once quipped.

The 18-year-old Horner's NHL debut came on a busy weekend in 1928. He played for the Marlies on Friday night, in an industrial league game on Saturday afternoon, and then suited up for the Leafs later that night.

The Leafs of the '30s were a powerhouse, and Horner—"two hundred pounds of human dynamite" according to a Toronto game program—was the one opponents had to deal with if they took liberties with the likes of Joe Primeau, Charlie Conacher, and Busher Jackson. "No one, not even the toughest guys in the NHL, took liberties with the Leafs," King Clancy once said. "Do one of us dirty and you had to deal with Red. That was absolutely no fun at all. He was as tough as any man who played the game, an excellent bodychecker who fought only when necessary."

Horner's most famous right hand came in response to one of the game's most ugly, vengeful fouls. On December 12, 1933, in the second period, Bruins defenceman Eddie Shore tripped Irvin "Ace" Bailey, toppling him into the Boston Garden ice, fracturing Bailey's skull and ending his playing career. "I skated over to Shore, who had gone down to the middle zone, stood in front of him and told him in no unmistakable terms just what I thought of his dirty playing. He never spoke a word, just stood there with a vacant expression on his face," said Horner in C. Michael Hiam's *Eddie Shore and That*

Old Time Hockey. "So I repeated my statement and with that let him have it smack on the button. Sticks never entered the argument. My fist shows how hard he was hit." Shore went down with one punch, and, like Bailey, he was stretchered off the ice, X-rayed for damage to the skull, and sewn up with seven stitches; Shore would return to hockey, and the whole incident resulted in the first All-Star Game, as a benefit for Ace Bailey.

Arthur Siegel of the *Boston Herald* laid the blame on Horner: "There have been occasions when the frightfulness was bloodier," wrote Siegel. "Two players were the chief bad actors, Shore of the Bruins and Red Horner of the Leafs. Horner is colourful and capable, but has a habit of getting into trouble. In this case he was the starter of the whole trouble, and Bailey was the innocent bystander. The first period of the game, as had been so many other meetings between the two great rivals of hockey, was fast and short tempered, with Referees [Odie] Cleghorn and [Eusebe] Daigneault failing to crack down on the players who were doing things to each other."

Horner was so well thought of by his teammates that he served as captain of the Maple Leafs from 1938 until his retirement in 1940. He wore the jersey of an NHL linesman for two seasons, but that didn't mean he was living clean. On January 11, 1943, Horner officiated the Leafs versus Red Wings at Maple Leaf Gardens. Taking issue with an icing call, Detroit manager Jack Adams berated Horner and later gave him a push when lined up for a faceoff near the Detroit bench. Horner swung an elbow at Adams, and Detroit's Syd Abel took a swing at Horner before referee Bill Chadwick calmed things down.

Despite his reputation, Horner was no slouch away from the rink. He was president of Toronto's Rosedale Golf Course and used his notoriety to seamlessly move into business.

"The experience of being in major league sports certainly prepares a man to withstand the rigorous ups and downs that confront most businessmen from time to time," Horner said in 1969, when he was president and major shareholder of the Toronto-based Canada Coal Corporation. Horner actually got into the coal business in 1936, five years before he quit the NHL, as the manager of the industrial coal division of Elias-Rogers Co., then the largest domestic coal supplier in Canada. He moved to Canada Coal in 1950 as VP in charge of sales.

Famed sportswriter Trent Frayne sought out Horner for the "My Biggest Night in Hockey" feature in the Maple Leaf Gardens program in 1948. "I was a misunderstood hockey player. I run into people nowadays who remember me as a bad man and I don't understand that," Horner confided.

As a high-profile retired name from the past, Horner made many appearances. When the Chicago Blackhawks faced Toronto in the final game at Maple Leaf Gardens on February 13, 1999, Horner and Mush March, a former Hawk who had played against Horner in the arena's opening game in 1931, did the ceremonial faceoff. Horner then passed a banner to Leafs captain Mats Sundin to be moved to the Air Canada Centre.

Confined to Toronto's Clairmont retirement home in his final years, Horner stayed proud, with a set of exercise grips nearby to keep up his hand strength. Horner's death on April 27, 2005, after a two-week battle with pneumonia, closed the door on a major part of hockey history.

COUTU WAS KING OF SUSPENSIONS

Incidents of hockey violence have a way of making it into mainstream media in a way that a Savardian Spin-o-Rama or an upside-down toe save don't. That is the unfortunate reality of the news cycle, which is more voracious today than it has ever been before.

The assault is news, while the redemption often goes unreported.

Take Billy Coutu.

His name is often thrown out when NHL suspensions are discussed, and with good reason—he was suspended for *life* in 1927. Coutu was a tough, cagey defenceman from North Bay, Ontario, who ended up with a rap sheet as long as his arm by the end of his career—a decade with the Montreal Canadiens and seasons in Hamilton (on loan from Montreal) and Boston. There were fines and suspensions for rough play, misconducts, and for tripping referee Jerry Laflamme (remember that name) during a game in January 1926.

But it is Game 4 of the 1927 Stanley Cup Final with which he is most associated. About to be swept away by the Ottawa Senators, the Bruins prompted a bench-clearing brawl. When it ended, the Sens had the Cup and Bruins coach Art Ross was furious with the referee—Laflamme. "After it was over, Ross got us together in the dressing room and said, 'Okay, the first man who gets that referee gets a $500 bonus,'" said Bruins centre Frank Fredrickson in *Eddie Shore and that Old Time Hockey*.

Coutu punched Laflamme, knocking him down, and apparently a fan and Bruins owner Charles Adams got their licks in as well. President Frank Calder suspended Coutu for life and fined him $100 to boot (taken from the player's share of the playoff monies and donated to charities in Boston and Ottawa).

The irony is that, once reinstated by the NHL in 1932 (he had already been playing, and suspended, in the minors), Coutu would take up coaching and *refereeing*, in the minor leagues at least.

So, with that in mind, here is a list of the longest suspensions in NHL history and the date of the infraction.

30 GAMES Chris Simon, New York Islanders, December 15, 2007: Simon slammed his skate into the foot of Jarkko Ruutu of the Penguins. It was Simon's seventh suspension, and he agreed to seek counselling. "I have enjoyed a long career achieving my dream of being a player in the National Hockey League and I'm proud of my accomplishments. But I acknowledge that time and assistance is needed before I return to the game."

25 GAMES Jesse Boulerice, Philadelphia, October 10, 2007: Boulerice delivered a cross-check to the face of Ryan Kesler of the Canucks away from the play. "I reacted in a bad way—the wrong way," Boulerice said following the game. "I wanted to give him a hit back."

Chris Simon, New York Islanders, March 8, 2007: Simon two-handed the face of Rangers forward Ryan Hollweg; his suspension ran for 15 games that season, five playoff games, and five more in 2007–08. "I just finished my check on the half wall," recounted Hollweg at the time. "I think he was a little fazed by it. I turned around, and the next thing I knew he's winding up and hitting me in the face."

23 GAMES Marty McSorley, Boston, February 21, 2000: McSorley's two-handed chop to Canuck Donald Brashear's head got him suspended for the final 23 games of the season, and the suspension was extended by NHL commissioner Gary Bettman to February 20, 2001. McSorley never played another NHL game. In October 2000, British Columbia Provincial Court found McSorley guilty of assault, and Judge William Kitchen imposed an 18-month conditional discharge.

Gordie Dwyer, Tampa Bay, September 19, 2000: Having already fought with Capitals Joe Murphy and Joe Reekie in an exhibition game, Dwyer left the penalty box to go after Reekie again. He bumped linesman David Brisebois, and referee Mark Faucette was pulled to the ice. "The penalty box door never shut," Dwyer explained. "I just touched two feet into the box and then came back out onto the ice. I didn't think it was such a big deal."

21 GAMES Dale Hunter, Washington, April 28, 1993: After Pierre Turgeon of the New York Islanders scored in a playoff game, Hunter blindsided him. Hunter said he was "just trying to finish my check . . . I'm sorry he got hurt. I'd take it back if I could."

20 GAMES Steve Downie, Philadelphia, September 25, 2007: During a pre-season game, Downie left his feet to deliver a deliberate hit to the head of Ottawa's Dean McAmmond. "My game is hitting and finishing checks," Downie said. "I'm just trying to earn a spot on a roster. It's part of my game and I apologize for him getting hurt. I thought I got him clean. Unfortunately he hit the boards after."

Todd Bertuzzi, Vancouver, March 8, 2004: Bertuzzi sucker-punched and bulldogged Colorado forward Steve Moore to the ice, allegedly in response to Moore injuring Markus Näslund earlier in the season. Bertuzzi's suspension was for 13 regular-season games plus the playoffs, but he was prevented from playing anywhere else during the year-long lockout as well. A criminal charge against Bertuzzi resulted in a guilty plea and a sentence of one year's probation plus 80 hours of community service. A civil case in the Ontario Superior Court of Justice is still pending, with the Canucks and the Orca Bay ownership also named in the suit.

Brad May, Phoenix, November 11, 2000: While back-checking, May slashed Columbus' Steve Heinze on the nose. "I feel terrible," May told the *Arizona Republic*. "Honestly I just wanted to tap him on the arm."

Tom Lysiak, Chicago, October 30, 1983: Lysiak was sent home for tripping linesman Ron Foyt. Lysiak was frustrated after being waved out of the faceoff circle during a game against Hartford. "Not only doesn't the punishment fit the crime, I don't have the right to give my side. There's no appeal. That's unconstitutional," said Lysiak.

16 GAMES Eddie Shore, Boston, December 12, 1933: Enraged by being felled by a heavy hit by Red Horner, Shore blindsided Toronto's Ace Bailey to the ice. Bailey fell, hit his head, and never played a game again. Horner subsequently knocked out Shore. The first NHL All-Star Game was a fundraiser for Bailey—and Shore was allowed to play, shaking hands with Bailey before it started.

15 GAMES Tony Granato, Los Angeles, February 16, 1994: Granato delivered a two-handed slash to Pittsburgh defenceman Neil Wilkinson. "I got hit on the head and woke up a right wing," cracked Wilkinson afterwards.

Dave Brown, Philadelphia, October 26, 1987: Brown cross-checked Tomas Sandstrom of the Rangers across the face and broke his jaw.

"If he did the same thing on the street tonight, he'd get 10 years in jail," said New York coach Michel Bergeron. "He didn't just try to hurt him—he tried to kill him." In March 1987, Brown got five games for a cross-check across the visor of Sandstrom's helmet.

Wilf Paiement, Colorado, October 25, 1978: Paiement swung his stick and hit Detroit's Dennis Polonich in the face. Criminal charges were considered, but ultimately not laid. "We have a lot of murderers and rapists running around [Detroit] and we determined that we would only be wasting valuable time and money charging and prosecuting hockey players," said John Thompson, the assistant Wayne County prosecutor who considered the case. "Numerous fans interviewed said the same thing: [Polonich] got what he deserved. In fairness, these same people invariably said that Paiement over-reacted, was vicious in his retaliation. In the end we had to decide that charging the player was not worthwhile."

Maurice Richard, Montreal, March 13, 1955: The Rocket's suspension for levelling linesman Cliff Thompson came in a game against Boston with playoff implications. Incensed by Hal Laycoe, who had cut him with his stick, Richard attacked the Bruins defenceman repeatedly with his own stick, prompting the referees to intercede. Thompson was struck twice in the face during Richard's rage. Three days later, NHL president Clarence Campbell ruled Richard out of the last three games of the season and the playoffs. At the Red Wings–Canadiens game in Montreal the following night, with Campbell in attendance, the fans rioted.

CHAPTER 2

THE ORIGINAL SIX

FOR 25 YEARS, from 1942–43 until the start of the 1967–68 season, the NHL had just six teams: Toronto, Montreal, Boston, Chicago, Detroit, and the New York Rangers. The stability of the league bred familiarity—and hatred—in the players. There was a fierce competitiveness for roster spots, and you didn't make the NHL unless you were able to handle yourself physically.

Over time, the teams began to recognize the need for specialists in the rough stuff, leaving some of the more skilled players more room for their on-ice magic.

GUS MORTSON
Right from the start, Gus Mortson made his presence known. In 1946–47, his rookie season with Toronto, "The Nugget" led the NHL with 133 penalty minutes.

The Hockey News (THN), also in its first year, said it was Mortson's style of play more than his fists that resulted in the hefty accumulation of PIM. "Since he'd step into a fast moving train if he thought it would stop a goal being scored against his team, Mortson naturally is on the receiving end of a large number of penalties," wrote Les Russell, adding that Mortson "never misses an opportunity to paste a stiff bodycheck on an incoming forward, should that worthy fellow fail to look where he's going."

A decade later, in 1956–57, Mortson again led the league, as captain of the Black Hawks, with 147 PIM. "Mortson serves as a good example, for few Hawks have displayed their fighting desire so consistently," praised THN at the season's conclusion.

At 6-foot, 185 pounds, James Angus "Gus" Mortson, born out of granite in New Liskeard, Ontario, on January 24, 1925, became a rock on defence for the Leafs and a part of the 1947, 1948, 1949, and 1951 Stanley Cup–winning squads. With his family in mining in Kirkland Lake, Mortson used to work weekends in a mine. "There were two shifts, and we got a big pay for it, $4.95 for the shift," he recalled.

"Old Hardrock" grew up and began playing hockey in Kirkland Lake. Winning seemed to follow him. Mortson won the Northern Ontario and All-Ontario juvenile championships with Kirkland Lake in 1942–43. Not having gotten the attention he thought he deserved in the northern Ontario mining outpost, Mortson hit the road. In two seasons of hockey in the Ontario Hockey League (OHL), he won two Memorial Cups, one with the Oshawa Generals in 1944 and the other with the Toronto St. Michaels Majors in 1945.

"I figured if they weren't going to come to me, I'd have to go to them. I'd have to get myself in an advantageous spot," Mortson told the CBC in 2000. "I went down to Oshawa and I tried out with the Generals but I didn't click. Then I went home and spoke to the priest who was running our juvenile team and he made arrangements for me to enroll at St. Mike's."

As the story goes, the Leafs scouts had him on the team's watch list after just a period of action at Maple Leaf Gardens and beat two other teams to signing him by only minutes. Following the season with the St. Michael's College Majors, Mortson was picked up by Oshawa as a military replacement.

With both St. Mike's and Oshawa, Mortson was paired on defence with Jim Thomson, a partnership that would last in Toronto as well. "The Gold Dust Twins" had differing styles, with Thomson a stay-at-home defender and Mortson willing to mix it up or join the rush. "We played well together. He had his own system, and I had mine. We got along very, very good," said Mortson.

His one-year apprenticeship with the Tulsa Oilers of the United States League, in 1945–46, was the first place he tangled with Gordie Howe, who, 60 years later, Mortson would say was the toughest he ever fought.

On one occasion, Mortson hit already-injured Bill Quacken-bush's knee. Howe came over to Mortson. "There was so much adrenalin flowing that I didn't say anything, I just stood up and I drove him as hard as I could. He went down to the ice alright, but he was up in about two seconds flat and we were both at it," Mortson said in 2000, adding: "I had a little advantage, as I was at least on the boards by the bench and he was on the ice. When that happened, the whole Detroit team came off the bench and on the ice and they came over. When that happened, the Toronto team came out. So there was a whole fight, everybody was fighting, everyone had someone. Even the fans were throwing chairs down. It was quite a time."

"Gusty" Gus had a reputation around the league, said Lynn Patrick, who once attacked Mortson in the hallway of Maple Leaf Gardens and had his hand sliced open on Mortson's front teeth. "I'll admit that I might have had it in for Mortson ever since I came into this league," said Patrick in 1950. "I've seen him a lot of times taking a man from behind during a fight. That's what I thought might happen. I had gone over to try to break up the fight between Jim Thomson and Chuck Rayner. All of a sudden I look over my shoulder and there's Mortson's face just about a foot away. I just punched it—mostly because it was Mortson's."

From his home in Timmins, Ontario, where he has good days and bad days struggling with dementia in early 2012, Mortson defended himself: "I never hurt anybody. If I took them into the boards, I made sure he was standing when I left him. I didn't want him to be hurt at all."

His son James Mortson, one of seven kids, said his father's fights were unlike the staged fights often a part of the modern game. "I think it's taken out of context a little. In fact, I thought about that a number of times over the years. He didn't always fight. It's not like you're on the ice and you're fighting."

Mortson also had to fight to get back into the game: a broken leg in the first game of the 1947–48 Stanley Cup Final with Detroit resulted in anemia, and the blood disorder would affect him for the rest of his life. To strengthen his leg, Mortson took to water-skiing, and he got so good he performed with a professional troupe at the Canadian National Exhibition on Toronto's waterfront that off-season. Then in the Leafs' 1948 training camp, he fractured a bone in the same leg. "I was out for six weeks so I decided, what the heck, I might as well get married," he quipped.

Mortson played in eight All-Star Games. Outside of the rink, he was recognized for endorsing cereal and Beehive corn syrup—though he was quick to point out that any money went to Conn Smythe and the Leafs while he got 4 quarts (about 4 L) of corn syrup. Mortson said that in his best year in professional hockey, he made $12,000.

Though he is not in the Hockey Hall of Fame, there is a letter on file there pitching Mortson's worth: "Excellent bodychecker . . . Undenied defensive abilities . . . Team leader . . . Great shooting abilities . . . Team morale booster in dressing room . . . Fierce competitive desire."

When he decided to step away from the NHL following the 1958–59 season, *The Hockey News*' Chicago beat writer praised the defender. "Hockey players that are both good and colourful are rare discoveries," wrote Bud Booth. "One of Mortson's strong points has always been his competitive spirit and willingness to do all he can for the team. His brand of hockey, naturally, is the strongest point of evidence to this fact, but there have been countless incidents in point too."

While he was done in the NHL, Mortson wasn't done with hockey. He played in the American Hockey League (AHL) for the Buffalo Bisons ("It was then that I found out that I was making more money down there," he joked) and was player-coach on Senior A teams in the Ontario cities of Chatham and Oakville. At the end of the '60s, he moved his family back north, where he was president of Pelangio-Larder mines and had investments in Alberta's Loki mines.

LOU FONTINATO

Lou Fontinato's infamous end—falling head-long into the end boards at the Montreal Forum on March 9, 1963, and carted off the ice on a stretcher, his neck fractured—will never be forgotten.

Fontinato prefers to look at it as a turning point in his life, a chance for a new beginning and doing something he'd always planned on—farming.

The year recuperating was just a delay.

"I was only going to play one more year. I was telling my wife, at that time . . . 'One more year of this and I'm quitting, because the injuries are starting to crop up,'" said Fontinato. "I knew I could buy a farm and a little bit of machinery, and to hell with hockey. Now your kids are growing up, changing schools—that's not my style of living. My style was having a farm—you've got to play a little hockey to get enough money—but I liked farming every bit as much as I liked playing hockey."

He's still out there today, a one-man operation on land outside of Guelph, Ontario, which he bought with the farm plan in mind in 1960 for $36,000.

The rugged Louis Fontinato was born on January 20, 1932, in Guelph. He was fighting almost from the start, though that was in the schoolyard. "Hey Louie, why don't you hit so-and-so? We'll give you a dime," was the taunt, rarely turned down. He never

Lou Fontinato, shown here in the penalty box during the 1955–56 season, had his career cut short by a horrible accident, but he was a memorable player during his nine years in the NHL, mostly with the New York Rangers. (IHA/Icon SMI)

lacked courage, bravely knocking on doors around Guelph, peddling his father's carrots and cauliflowers.

On the ice, Fontinato developed into the man he became under the auspices of Howard "Swat" Mason, who had played senior hockey around Ontario and was the long-time coach of the Guelph Junior B squad.

Fontinato can still hear Mason telling him before a playoff series,

"Louie, if we stop Ray Ross we'll stop the whole team." Message received. As Fontinato recalled, "At that time they had a screen instead of glass, and I put his head right through there. I didn't aim for his head, I just hit him, because I was following orders."

Mason encouraged Fontinato to man up in his game: "The thing is if you're an enforcer, some guys just don't want to drop their gloves or act a certain way. So he saw in me, he was one of the guys that really started me taking the man out, hard too, and the odd fight," said Fontinato.

Those Guelph Biltmore Mad Hatters teams featured a couple of future Hall of Famers too, Harry Howell—Fontinato's defensive partner—and Andy Bathgate, and another future NHLer, Dean Prentice. The 1952 squad claimed the Memorial Cup, destroying the Regina Pats in the process. Howell, Bathgate, and Fontinato remain close friends.

For his first three seasons as a professional, Fontinato played in the Western Hockey League (WHL), for the Vancouver Canucks and Saskatoon Quakers. He saw his first action for the New York Rangers in 1954–55, getting into 27 games. The following season, he made the team for good.

"Leapin' Louie" became a huge favourite of the throngs at Madison Square Garden, and he led the league in penalty minutes in his first full season, with 202, breaking Red Horner's 20-year-old record. "It seems on certain nights, Louie gets a bug in his system and just itches for trouble even before the opening faceoff," wrote Stan Fischler early in Fontinato's career.

Gordie Howe put it more succinctly: "Every once in awhile he'll go ape."

Howe and Fontinato battled often, both when Fontinato was with the Rangers and the Canadiens. "Gordie Howe was a son-of-a-bitch to play against. I got cauliflower ears from him," said Fontinato. "We fought. He broke my nose, and I broke his ribs. We went at it pretty good."

Their most famed battle came on February 1, 1959, at MSG. Fontinato admits he was looking for trouble—why else would a Rangers defenceman be behind the Red Wings net? "I gave Howe three of my best shots to the head and I peeked up to see why he hadn't gone down," Fontinato told the *Toronto Star* in 1983. "He planted one right on my nose and not only broke the nose which had been broken lots before, but he broke the blood vessels in my face as well. We were separated then and I had to go to the hospital to have my nose fixed and [Ranger coach] Phil Watson sent *Life Magazine* over to take my picture. He told me it would be good publicity for hockey."

To this day, Fontinato denies he really lost the fight and claims he gave as good as he got. *The Hockey News* had a page and a half of coverage of the fight: "Howe Retains 'Fist' Title At Louie's Expense" was the headline splashed across the fifth page.

Beyond the Howe fight, Fontinato's rap sheet is still pretty incredible, from cutting Guy Talbot's jersey to ribbons to catching Dave Balon's face with his blade and waving his stick as a baton to further his old admirers at MSG into a greater "Get Louie" chant.

Fontinato knew how to hold a grudge. During a January 18, 1961, Leafs-Rangers tilt, he suffered a 24-stitch cut on his knee and believed Bert Olsmstead was responsible. He kept his anger in check when the teams met a month later. On March 19th, it was time. Fischler was there to see it unfold:

Then it happened, with the suddenness and surprise of a detonated land mine. Fontinato leaped at Olmstead like a mad bull, cross-checking the Leaf across the left cheek with the shaft of his stick and following through with an inhuman check into the boards as the stick broke in two. Olmstead collapsed to the ice while Louie dramatically went into a crouch awaiting an onslaught from the entire Leaf team. It could have been 'Fontinato's Last Stand,' except that the Leafs never attacked. Fontinato was lustily cheered until

Referee Dalton MacArthur congratulated him with a five-minute major penalty for cross-checking, a sentence which provoked a ten-minute delay of paper tossing and ice cleaning.

His June 1961 trade to Montreal—in exchange for the incomparable Doug Harvey—showed that Fontinato's style of play was valued:

> When I went to Montreal, Toe Blake called me in halfway through the season, because I had a little argument about my contract before that season started. He called me into his office, and he said, 'Louie, what do you think of the All-Star team?' I said, 'Well, if I was listening to my wife, I'd probably be on the first or second All-Star team.' He said, 'Louie, you're doing what you're here to do. I'm going to see to it that you get a real good bonus at the end of the year.' I got the equivalent of winning the Stanley Cup, my bonus was the equivalent of winning the Stanley Cup. Toe Blake was a good man. He gave me a lot of pats on the back.

"His hitting is wearing off on the rest of our players and the other teams are no longer chasing us out of the rink," said Canadiens managing director Frank Selke during Fontinato's second season with the Habs. "The Canadiens wanted me because I could play it rough so I'm not going to kid myself that I can be a fancy-dan," Fontinato said at the time. "As a matter of fact, the coach took me aside after one of the games to tell me about rushing—he told me that I was better as a defensive man."

The injury that ended his hockey career, which happened in the second period with Vic Hadfield in pursuit of the puck, was an accident. He was fitted with a Minerva jacket, a plaster of Paris cast from his waist to the top of his head, for four months, which allowed him to sit up in his hospital bed. Fontinato accepted his fate, saying that "the risk is too great" to ever play again.

REGGIE FLEMING
In death, on July 11, 2009, Reggie Fleming made his greatest contribution to hockey. His health had declined over a five-year period, and Fleming's son, Chris, got a call out of the blue from Chris Nowinski of the Sports Legacy Institute. Nowinski wanted Reggie's brain to study the effects of concussions during his 13 seasons in the NHL with six teams.

The findings were conclusive—Fleming's brain tissue proved that his brain had degenerated over time. In medical terms, it was chronic traumatic encephalopathy.

It opened doors for Nowinski's organization. "Certainly players in sports only take notice when they find one of their own with the disorder. Reggie Fleming proved that this existed in hockey and I'm sure was responsible for accelerating the timeline of changes that have been made," said Nowinski, referring to the extra vigilance put on shots to the head from youth leagues right up to the NHL.

For Fleming's family, it answered a lot of questions. Chris Fleming had studied psychology in university in part to understand his father's behaviour, including his problems with drinking and gambling, but it didn't all come together for him until he was at a banquet honouring the Black Hawks enforcer with his mother, who had been divorced from Reggie.

Nowinski showed photographs of Reggie's brain and the damage to the tissue, and he explained, based on the evidence gathered through many other studies, how an aged adult with the disease would behave. "When [Nowinski] said certain aspects of my dad's aggression, the certain way he acted, I looked at my mom, and we're both, 'Oh my God. That's our dad to a T,'" said Chris Fleming.

"I'd tell my dad one thing and five minutes later he would then tell me the same thing, and then get mad and yell at me," said Chris. His father had a short fuse and would break down emotionally at unpredictable times.

"It made sense," Chris said of the study, adding, "It healed my mom, because it made my mom realize it wasn't really her fault that led to the divorce, that my dad had no control because of what was going on. So it healed her to a degree and it helped me understand my father a lot more."

Understanding Reg Fleming on the ice is no less complex.

As an only child born in the east end of Montreal on April 21, 1936, Fleming was shuttled between his parents, grandparents, and aunts and uncles growing up. An anglophone in a mostly franco-phone neighbourhood, he learned to skate on local homemade rinks, and occasionally he could skate *down* the street to the local rink. As a youngster, he got the chance to practise on occasion at the Montreal Forum, and his team would then be privileged to watch the Canadiens work out. The local squad inked him to a develop-ment deal, and while with the Montreal Junior Canadiens he started to use his fists a little more.

His high-water mark in the minors came in 1957–58 with Shawinigan Falls, where Fleming scrapped to 227 minutes. From there, he learned to control his boundless enthusiasm a little more, totalling 112 PIM with Rochester of the American League the next season and 91 with Kingston's Eastern League squad after that. "I think I learned my lesson about not hurting the team by getting a lot of cheap penalties that year at Shawinigan Falls," Fleming said upon being called up to the Chicago Black Hawks as a rookie in 1960, Montreal and Chicago having consummated a seven-player trade before the season began.

"Fleming has a background for getting a lot of penalties. That's because of his aggressiveness and his spirited makeup. We like this type of player," said Chicago coach Rudy Pilous at the time, adding, "Somewhere along the line it has to be tempered to a certain degree. But we're building a scrapping outfit here and Fleming suits our style."

A notorious breakout moment came on October 19, 1960, when Fleming amassed 37 PIM at New York's Madison Square Garden, setting a new single-game record. The three majors for fighting, two minutes for high-sticking, plus a misconduct and a game misconduct, resulted in a $175 fine by NHL president Clarence Campbell.

Pilous took some of the blame, and his dressing room orders to No. 6 became part of Fleming lore: "I was annoyed in the first period when [Andy] Bathgate [of New York] was getting the better of Stan Mikita and Reg didn't do much to help. I told the players this is a team effort and if there is any trouble we are to help each other out and be on the winning side. I used Fleming as an example— he was filling in at left wing for Ab McDonald who was injured. I told him if he wasn't going to help out, to take the sweater off. What I said went for the whole team," Pilous said. "Maybe that was the green light Fleming needed to assert himself in the fights with [Dean] Prentice and [Eddie] Shack and the rhubarb with [goalie Don] McCartan which followed."

Despite the notoriety, the 5-foot-8, 170-pound Fleming would always point back to his rookie season as proof that he could play too. In the deciding game of the Stanley Cup Final between the Hawks and the Red Wings, Fleming scored the tying goal while killing a penalty, inspiring his team to a 5–1 win and the first Chicago Cup in 23 years.

In the subsequent years, Fleming would continue to contribute to team after team, his value as a penalty-killer and his versatility— he was able to play the wing or defence—were only outweighed by his muscle. In short, as his coach Emile Francis once said, "He keeps the opposition honest and helps out his centre in the corners."

Harry Howell, a teammate with the Rangers, is okay with the "agitator" label for Fleming: "But he served a purpose and he could play too. He could probably play as well as most of the guys on our team."

Fleming was, at various times, known as "Mr. Clean"—"Because I used to clean up on fights, beat up on people"—and the less com-plimentary "Cement Head."

"I've been called a lot worse than that," Fleming told Brian McFarlane. "I guess they knew they couldn't hurt me by hitting me in the head. In fact, when opposing players and the fans *stop* calling me names, I'll know my image is fading and I'm becoming a softie."

During his tour of the league, Fleming claimed that he became smarter. "I'm not a lover, so I have to be a fighter. That's the style that got me to the top; I might as well stick with it," he told Stan Fischler in 1968. "I've gotten smarter. I pick my spots. I know who to instigate and who not to. I stay away from tough guys like Ted Green and Johnny Ferguson. No sense fighting just for fighting; that's too easy. The trick is to take a big scorer like Bobby Hull off the ice with you."

After dropping out of the league following the 1970–71 season and bouncing around the minors and the Chicago Cougars of the Western Hockey Association for two seasons, Fleming was an afterthought for many until Earl McRae's highly praised piece for *The Canadian* magazine in 1975. The plaudits for "Requiem for Reggie" included Fischler saying it was "the greatest hockey story ever written." In the lengthy tale, McRae catches up with a 39-year-old Fleming selling trinkets in Chicago and still being goaded into fights in a local beer league.

After Fleming's death, McRae revisited his classic, summing it up: "Fleming anguished about how when his ageing, hurting fists weren't so effective anymore, he was kissed off by the potentates who once embraced him, refusing to even take his phone calls or answer his letters pleading for another chance, pleading for work of some kind. When his fists and the attitude that drove them were diminished, Reggie Fleming was nothing more to them than useless, decaying meat."

The feature didn't change Fleming's life—he always said that he hated it and would get McRae one day—and it wasn't until new technology came along that his family truly understood what his impact on hockey had been.

Confined to the Claremont Rehab and Living Center in Chicago's suburbs following a stroke, three heart attacks, and the removal of his gallbladder, Reggie's son, Chris Fleming, took to videotaping his father in bed, inspired by Mitch Albom's *Tuesdays with Morrie*. He would later edit eight different videos, filmed over three years, and post them on YouTube. The clips are heartwarming and heartbreaking, showing a declining fighter hanging on, his mind often muddled, yet willing to challenge his son's assertions of the way things had happened.

During his visits, Chris would bring in emails and letters to read to his dad, which numbered in the thousands over the years. Not understanding the technology, Reggie would insist that Chris thank each person.

"There were a couple of things that came out of it. One thing, it brought my father and I closer together in ways, we got to share things both on-camera and off-camera. Sometimes he'd say, 'That's enough, Chris. Turn it off.' I'd turn it off and we'd have these big, long conversations," said Chris, one of two children of Reggie and Patricia Farrell. "But the most remarkable thing was that the people that saw this, it touched them in a couple of different ways. Those that weren't that familiar with hockey or my father would see the film and say, 'Oh my God, my parents are sick, and they're in a hospital. I don't talk to them too much.' It got people to open up and start communicating with their loved ones, because they weren't taking the time to do that, and weren't realizing what was really important."

There's far more on tape than was ever presented online, said Chris, who hopes to do a book on his father one day. One of the segments has a grandfather saying hi to future grandchildren.

In the final online video, Chris Fleming laid it out: "I felt it is necessary to videotape him and share his finest memories, to see past the tough guy he was known for, and instead the kind soul he really is. I pray you look into your own heart and soul and spend whatever moments you can with your own family, putting aside any differences and allow only one thing to truly matter . . . love."

Hockey Movie Mayhem

Forget *Slap Shot* and *Goon*, the most violent hockey movie ever made was *Hockey Homicide*.

Never heard of it? Probably because its star wasn't quite as big a name as Paul Newman or Seann William Scott, but his film career has lasted longer than either and is still going strong, at least on TV.

The star?

Goofy.

Hockey Homicide, which came out in September 1945 from Walt Disney Productions and runs just under eight minutes, is a frantic, slap-dash look at hockey. The nuances of the game are explained by narrator Doodles Weaver in a world populated by Goofys. Referee "Clean Game" Kinney, who likes to keep extra pucks in his pants, can't keep the game under control and is continually physically abused. Most notable are the frequent offenders: "Here come Bertino and Ferguson out of the penalty box . . . and there go Bertino and Ferguson back in the penalty box." Naturally, the on-ice hijinx get the fans into it as well.

Violence is part of hockey, but it is not necessarily prevalent on the big screen, said hockey historian Jean-Patrice Martel. "Hockey-themed comedies love the on-ice violence for reasons that anyone who has ever enjoyed a Road Runner cartoon will immediately understand," he said. "At the other end of the spectrum, dramas have used hockey violence for the opportunity it gives them to portray one of the most basic— and camera-friendly—of emotions: fear. Yet, it may come as a surprise, but if you take out your calculator and start counting, you're forced to acknowledge that the violence is absent, or limited to the off-ice action, in a majority of hockey-centreed feature films."

For every quotable line from 1977's *Slap Shot* ("I am personally placing a hundred-dollar bounty on the head of Tim McCracken. He's the head coach and chief punk on that Syracuse team") or *Goon* from 2011 ("You have my respect. Whatever that means to you, you got it. But, know this shit's hard. If ever there comes a time when it gets down

to the morrow, and it's you and me. Kid, I will lay you the fuck out")
there is a hockey flick that isn't centred on swinging sticks or flying fists.

Early hockey movies from the late 1930s—like *King of Hockey*, *The
Game That Kills* (where a player gets killed on the ice—by his own
teammates), and *Idol of the Crowds* (starring John Wayne!)—are more
about gambling than the game on the ice.

There have been interesting studies of superstars, like *The Rocket*,
and behind-the-scenes stories, like *Net Worth* and *Gross Misconduct*.
Real-life accomplishments and oddities get the treatment in *Miracle*
and *Mystery, Alaska*.

There is *The Mighty Ducks*, which spawned a franchise (three
movies and an actual team), and a genuine *MVP—Most Valuable
Primate*, for those uninitiated (which offers two homages to *Slap Shot*,
albeit with a chimpanzee).

And when they are bad, they are really, really bad. Mike Myers's
stinker *The Love Guru* should be suspended indefinitely, and 1971's
Face-Off is a mishmash of Canadian content rules with speaking parts
for George Armstrong, Derek Sanderson, and Paul Henderson ("You're
a real swinger!").

ORLAND KURTENBACH
Orland Kurtenbach has
never liked to talk about fighting. Back in 1966, when he was the
reigning heavyweight champion of Maple Leaf Gardens, he rejected
the whole concept. "I hate it," he told the *Toronto Telegram*. "I'd
rather be known for my ability to score goals and kill penalties. Kids
see it on television and they don't understand that sometimes, men
have to fight. It's part of the game. Most of us are content to mind
our own business, but there are a few who go out of their way to
make things, shall we say, difficult. You can only take so much, and
then you have to straighten them out."

During the 1960s, there were few better at straightening them out
than "Kurt." But come 1970, he transformed into something quite

ORLAND KURTENBACH   CENTER

VANCOUVER CANUCKS

exceptional and different. Taken in the expansion draft by the Vancouver Canucks from the New York Rangers, Kurtenbach found himself thrust into the unlikely role of team leader, both as captain and as one of the top scorers.

Punch Imlach was the coach and general manager in Toronto when the team acquired Kurtenbach, along with Pat Stapleton and Andy Hebenton, from Boston for Ron Stewart, prior to the 1965–66 season. "He gave me a policeman for my bench, which we lacked last season," Imlach explained. "I was right, too. I don't think he's lost a fight all season. Any time anybody starts trouble with us, he's got to look out for Kurtenbach." Canucks coach Hal Laycoe was charged with putting the various loose parts into a cohesive unit. "Kurt's values are far in excess of his ability to score. He can thump a guy with a bodycheck; he's a good checker; he controls the puck tremendously; he's a good positional player; he's good in the faceoffs," raved Laycoe. "He just doesn't have any weaknesses and, along with a real dominant, strong personality, he makes any group he's in a better group."

It is hard to believe the two coaches are talking about the same player.

The strengths Laycoe discussed continued to benefit Kurtenbach after his playing career was done, whether it was behind the bench of the Canucks or the British Columbia Junior Hockey League's Richmond Sockeyes or as the figurehead for the Canucks alumni association.

A native of Cudworth, Saskatchewan, born on September 7, 1936, Kurtenbach first gained notice with the Saskatchewan Junior Hockey League's Prince Albert Mintos, and he won a Memorial Cup with the Flin Flon Bombers in 1957. Moving west to the WHL's Vancouver Canucks for the 1957–58 season, Kurtenbach notched 54 points in 52 games and was the Coast Division Rookie of the Year. He was heralded as another Béliveau, given his 6-foot-2, 195-pound size, centre position, and ability.

But the NHL was a tough nut to crack at the time, with just six teams. Playing in Buffalo as a Rangers prospect, Kurtenbach was dubbed a "million-dollar prospect." After just 10 games with the Blueshirts in 1960–61, he was claimed by Boston in the intra-league draft in June 1961. It was the same story—a few NHL games then off to the minors, toiling from one coast (Providence) to the other (San Francisco). "It was hard to make the National Hockey League when there were only six clubs," Kurtenbach said, referring to his days with the minor-league Seals. "I was ready to quit, find a job and stay there. But we won the championship and the following year I went back to Boston." After two successful seasons with the Bruins, centring Dean Prentice and Andy Hebenton and with a respectable 37 and 26 points, the Leafs got him in a trade.

Though he played just a season in Toronto, Kurtenbach was easy copy for the sportswriters. "To put it bluntly, Kurtenbach is the type who doesn't know the word impossible. He has always believed he can play in the National Hockey League, even if he is half a step behind," reads a *Globe and Mail* profile. "To make up for a lack of speed, Kurtenbach starts early and doesn't stop, which is why he sometimes can be found as the last line of defence, backing up his own men."

His skills having improved along with his reputation, Kurtenbach was claimed by the Rangers in the 1966 intra-league draft, and he spent four seasons on Broadway. "He was one of the best tough guys," said perennial Ranger Harry Howell. "He was another guy that looked after his teammates. Everybody liked him."

Spinal fusion surgery derailed him in early 1969, his back having bothered him since his Boston days. Predictably, the tough guy started walking 11 days after surgery. "It was real tough to handle," he said in 1972. "I had a 12-inch brace in front and a 16-inch brace in back supporting my back after the operation. For months, I couldn't even tie my own shoes."

Left unprotected when the NHL expanded to 14 teams, the Canucks took him as their second pick (after Gary Doak), and Kurtenbach's career was extended another four seasons. If not for the torn ligaments in his left knee from a Bobby Baun bodycheck, Kurtenbach might have taken a fourth Cyclone Taylor Trophy as the Canucks most valuable player. Loyal to a fault, Kurtenbach turned down a reported tripling of his salary offered by the WHA's Los Angeles Sharks after the 1971–72 season.

Montreal journalist Red Fisher has written repeatedly that Kurtenbach was the best fighter he ever saw, comparing him to the better-known John Ferguson of the Canadiens. "He earned 628 penalty minutes, roughly one-half of John Ferguson's total, even though the latter played in 139 fewer games," wrote Fisher. "Kurtenbach, unlike Ferguson, was a standup fighter. Jab. Hook. Uppercut. He had size . . . Most of his bouts were over quickly. Opponents rarely asked for return matches."

Broadcaster Jiggs McDonald saw Kurtenbach often: "I don't think he was ever knocked off his skates. I don't recall ever seeing him get knocked down. He had a wide stance when he got into a fight, and not a guy who fought every game by any means, and not in the category of coming off the bench to start things, but he would certainly clean it up for you if you had a problem."

Kurtenbach was less successful as the Canucks coach, however. He took over for Phil Maloney during the 1976–77 season and compiled a 36-62-27 record before Harry Neale came in for the 1977–78 campaign. He would later coach in the BCJHL, winning the Centennial Cup in 1986–87, and serve as the league's director of community relations. Away from the rink, Kurtenbach was a broker with Westland Insurance and raised six children with his wife, Laurel.

He is still sought out for Canucks events, and he was front and centre as the team celebrated its 40th anniversary in 2010. Kurtenbach was the first member of the Vancouver Canucks' Ring of Honour, eight years after his induction into the British Columbia Hockey Hall of Fame.

"It's a culmination of time and place and a nice acknowledgment that it was all worthwhile," Kurtenbach told the *Vancouver Sun* before the ceremony. "Vancouver's been very good to me. I'm very proud of my time here, dating as far back as my two years here when the team played in the Western Hockey League."

JOHN FERGUSON John Ferguson will be remembered as

the original enforcer, the first player whose primary function was to keep overzealous checkers and other assorted ruffians in line. He broke the mould—personally and with bad intentions.

After winning an unprecedented five straight Stanley Cups in the 1950s, the Montreal Canadiens of the early '60s became vulnerable to bigger, more physical clubs, like the Toronto Maple Leafs and Chicago Black Hawks.

"Imlach's Maple Leafs didn't win Stanley Cups in 1962 and 1963 on skating and stick handling skill alone. They had big players like Frank Mahovlich, and tough ones like Tim Horton, Bobby Baun and Eddie Shack," Bernie Geoffrion said in *Boom Boom: The Life and Times of Bernard Geoffrion*, adding "players like Shack and Chicago's Reggie Fleming ran all over the place hitting people and if they weren't neutralized, they could make life miserable for the opposition."

Coach Toe Blake was one of the few Habs throwing punches in the early '60s. Montreal's Stanley Cup streak ended in 1961, when the Hawks took out the Canadiens in the semifinals, and Blake directed his rage at the referees. In one game, he disputed a tripping call by rushing across the ice to throw a punch at referee Dalton MacArthur. In another contest, he went after Vern Buffey.

It was all too clear to Blake and management that the Habs were getting manhandled. Their first attempt at adding a physical element came with their acquisition of New York Ranger Lou Fontinato. They even took a look at a young minor-leaguer by the name of Don Cherry. But it was Ferguson who would eventually be brought in to protect the club's less pugilistic scoring aces.

"*That* is how the enforcer was born in the NHL. As Casey Stengel used to say, 'You could look it up!' It was September 1963 and the cop on the beat was John Bowie Ferguson," Ferguson wrote in his memoir, *Thunder and Lightning*.

Before then, NHL teams employed few specialists. Penalty-killers and power-play workers took regular shifts. Even in the case of Gordie Howe—a heavy hitter and excellent fighter—his physicality was an adjunct to his main purpose, which was to play hockey, Ferguson said.

Ferguson rose through the ranks in the minor leagues, playing a season with the IHL's Fort Wayne Komets and three more for the Cleveland Barons of the AHL. Not a noted skater or shooter by any means when he arrived in Cleveland, Ferguson worked hard and became a solid player in his final season with the Barons, racking up 38 goals and 40 assists in 72 games and earning a spot on the All-Star Team.

"He's a bad skater with no finesse. But he seems to overcome this by sheer determination," Emile Francis said about scouting Ferguson in the AHL. "I've seen him in quite a few fights and he's never lost one. He always seems to come up with the puck and he hits everything he gets close to. I know he had the respect of the whole American League."

By 1963, Ferguson was ready for the big time. He ran everyone he met in Montreal's training camp scrimmages, and Coach Blake liked what he saw—so much so that he not only kept him on the team, but he put him on the top line with Jean Béliveau and Geoffrion. Blake told Ferguson before the season opener at Boston Garden that he wanted him to look after his linemates.

"Let me tell you, John Ferguson was something else. First of all he had hands the size of Virginia hams and he knew how to use them," said Geoffrion.

Ferguson made a statement on October 8, 1963. In front of Beantown's faithful, he challenged the league's reigning terror, former Hab "Terrible" Teddy Green, whom the Bruins had claimed off waivers. Green had fought every chance he got in his rookie year and rarely lost.

Only 12 seconds into the game, the rams charged each other to decide who was the dominant male. Both Geoffrion and Béliveau watched the action in awe, knowing the fight could have far-reaching significance for their hockey club.

"And it did. Fergie destroyed Green in record time. Bam! Bam! Bam! Three straight right crosses and the fight was over. Ted Green was dead meat, and for the first time since I became a Canadien, I could say that we had a full-time enforcer," said Geoffrion.

"That's the way I wanted it and the message would soon get around the league: John Ferguson is prepared to defend his team," said Ferguson, who further punctuated his importance to the team by also counting two goals and an assist in a 4-4 draw.

The 5-foot-11, 190-pound baby bull finished his first season as runner-up for the Rookie of the Year, and for the next seven seasons he maintained his playing philosophy of being the biggest son of a bitch on the ice.

"I considered everyone on the opposition to be a mortal enemy. Every game was a blood war, and there was absolutely no way that I could view the enemy in any but the meanest terms," Ferguson said.

"He was a very important person to that team, because he never let anybody beat up on any of his teammates at all," said Rangers All-Star defenceman Harry Howell.

Even the referees were intimidated. Retired ref Bruce Hood

admitted in his memoir, *Calling the Shots*, that Ferguson plain and simple scared the wits out of him. "The ferocity and intensity he brought to the game was intimidating, even to the officials," he said, adding, "Every time Fergie stepped on the ice, it was like a do-or-die situation for him. He looked and acted like he was always one step away from exploding, and that's what scared me. I always figured if he ever snapped, he'd go right through the end boards and take someone with him."

So the last person you'd expect to take it easy on the opposition would have been John Ferguson. And yet, he *did* have a soft spot for one of the most-hated pros in the bigs, Bryan "Bugsy" Watson. The two had struck up a friendship as members of the Canadiens, and Ferguson found himself hesitating against his old pal, who was now wearing Detroit colours.

One night, Watson charged Ferguson in the corner, and Ferguson responded by punching Watson in the back of the head. Watson responded by swinging his stick with both hands. It barely missed Ferguson's head and hit him on the shoulder. But rather than erupting as he would have under normal circumstances, Ferguson skated over to referee Art Skov and told him to take it easy on the kid. He was more concerned about Watson getting tagged with a $250 fine.

"When I reached the penalty box, Watson said, 'Hell, why'd it hafta be you?' I told him he was lucky. If it had been anybody else, he'd probably be dead," Ferguson said.

Canada's *Weekend Magazine* would call Ferguson the "Heavyweight Champ of Hockey," and at one point he considered taking on Canadian boxing legend George Chuvalo. *Toronto Sun* columnist Paul Rimstead wanted to promote a three-round bout between the two heavyweights, and both participants would have been ready to rumble had it not been for the intervention of Habs GM Sam Pollock.

"When I broached the subject to Sam, he said '*Absolutely not!*' Too bad. It would have been very interesting, and I wouldn't have been the least bit worried about slugging with him," Ferguson said.

Just as well he didn't, as his services were very much in demand on the ice, where he helped the Habs win five Stanley Cups in his eight years with the club.

Béliveau credited Ferguson as a role-player who, besides allowing the Canadiens to play their freewheeling offensive style, also got them going when they were in a slump. Opponents saw another side to Fergie as well. "He could play hockey too. He wasn't just a fighter," said Howell.

Ferguson, too, believed he offered more than just punching power and never considered himself a goon, resenting any suggestions that he was.

"By scoring 29 goals in 71 games during the 1968–69 season— including, by the way, the one that clinched first place for us—I demonstrated that my game was multi-dimensional. Nevertheless, it was the fighting that got me the biggest headlines, and it never stopped," he said.

As someone who could knock you down with a bodycheck, punch your lights out, and score goals to boot, Ferguson became the measuring stick for tough guys to come. Many that followed in his wake attempted to pattern themselves after him, by balancing their fighting abilities with goal scoring and leadership contributions. Tiger Williams even donned the same No. 22 and wore it throughout his career.

"Back in the day, for guys like myself, we looked up to John; you had to get 20 goals a year and take care of business," said Dan Maloney. A noted heavy during the 1970s with the Chicago Black Hawks, Los Angeles Kings, Detroit Red Wings, and Toronto Maple Leafs, Maloney was hired by Ferguson to coach the Winnipeg Jets two days after being fired by the Leafs, and he was absolutely thrilled to get the job.

"It was a great honour for me to work for John Ferguson because he was the man who set the bar for guys like myself as we were coming through the National Hockey League; he was a very classy guy and a very respectable guy," said Maloney.

For Ferguson, there always seemed to be a job waiting for him. With the New York Rangers, he was the head coach (1976–1977) and general manager, relieved of duties in 1978. He was in charge in Winnipeg from 1979 to 1988, and briefly took over as coach in 1986 for the last 14 games of the season and the playoffs (three games and out to Calgary). After managing the Windsor Raceway for four years—his middle name of "Bowie" referred to Bowie Race Track in Maryland—Ferguson was director of player personnel for the Ottawa Senators from 1992 to 1995. His last hockey job was as a senior scout for the San Jose Sharks.

Ferguson struggled in the last years of his life, fighting cancer. He won the first round against the prostate cancer doctors discovered in 2005, but he couldn't overcome it when it returned. The legendary battler died on July 14, 2007, at the age of 68.

Hundreds packed All Saints Anglican Church in Windsor, Ontario, for the funeral. Ferguson's son, John Jr., then the general manager of the Toronto Maple Leafs, delivered the eulogy. "I strive to imitate my father's traits," said John Jr., "his passion, his unfailingly positive disposition, his exceptional loyalty, determination, class, and last but certainly not least, his compassion."

CHAPTER 3

EXPANSION

ST. LOUIS BLUES

MONTREAL'S SUCCESSFUL EXPERIMENT with John Ferguson and the end of the six-team era would contribute greatly to both the number of enforcers in the NHL and their importance.

"When the expansion came, that opened the door up for everybody," said Dennis Hextall, who, like scores of others buried in the minors, benefited when the NHL doubled from six to 12 teams in 1967–68.

During the Original Six days, rosters were basically set before training camp even started. But in the resized NHL, those who previously couldn't make the grade were now able to secure positions.

"A lot more players had the opportunity to make it who maybe weren't as skilled, but were tough or strong," said Terry Harper. "There were tough guys when there were just six teams, but they couldn't get by just on toughness alone. I think after, there was a while there they could."

"It was the wild west back then," said journeyman minor-league tough-guy Kurt Walker, best remembered for his stint with the Toronto Maple Leafs. "It was wide open; anything went, the fans were crazy, and you had a lot of bench-emptying brawls."

The St. Louis Blues, in addition to stocking up on veteran stars, also specifically targeted some of the more pugilistic career minor-leaguers around.

"An example of this would be the Plager brothers, Bob, Barclay and Bill, who became known as 'The Royal Family of Mayhem,'" said Ferguson. "Before expansion, none of them could have made it to the NHL."

Although the Philadelphia Flyers are popularly remembered as the first expansion team that made intimidation part of their game plan, it was St. Louis that started the trend. "Bob was the only Plager fighter I considered to be a legitimate tough guy, but they got into their share of scraps and, between the two of them, Barclay and Bob turned the Blues into the first fighting expansion club," Ferguson added.

"Bobby would dance with anybody who wanted to go—even off the bench. Those were the days of the bench-emptying brawls," remembered broadcaster Jiggs McDonald, who received the Foster Hewitt Memorial Award from the Hockey Hall of Fame in 1990.

The brothers' notoriety went all the way back to their teens. "I remember signing Barclay when he was 16 and I was working for the Canadiens," Lou Passador, who later became chief scout for the New York Rangers, told George Csolak, former hockey writer for the St. Louis *Globe Democrat*. "Everybody laughed at us. He wasn't just a bad kid, he was terrible. They said we'd never be able to handle him."

Barclay went on to break the Junior A record for penalties, which stood until brother Bob shattered it two years later with Guelph.

The brothers also found themselves in a few scraps against each other. The most memorable was probably their junior encounter, which started when Barclay clipped Bob with his stick and split his

Bench-clearing brawls, like this one between Boston and Montreal during the 1975–76 season, were common in the 1970s. (IHA/Icon SMI)

lip open after the whistle. Making things worse, Barclay didn't apologize. Bob dropped his gloves and landed a couple before Barclay started throwing back. Finally, too tired to go on, they were broken up and led to the penalty box. But it erupted again, and finally ended with Bob in his team's dressing room and Barclay being restrained in the hallway. Their father's reaction? "Did either of them go down?" The brothers weren't overly upset about the brouhaha either. Later that night Barclay approached Bob in a restaurant to put in $15 toward a Christmas present he'd be buying their mother, the latter recalled in *Bob Plager's Tales from the Blues Bench*.

It wasn't the first time the brothers exchanged punches (although it was the first in uniform), and it wouldn't be the last, as Barclay and Bob battled some more in the Central Hockey League (CHL). Bob also fought youngest brother Bill in a playoff game when the latter was playing for the Minnesota North Stars.

Both Barclay and Bob arrived in St. Louis for the Blues' inaugural season and would help the club reach the Stanley Cup Finals three years in a row.

"I never saw anyone who hated to lose more than Barc," said Scotty Bowman, who coached the golden-era Blues.

"If anyone ever did more for a franchise, I haven't seen him," said Emile Francis, who, as St. Louis general manager, later hired Barclay to coach the team. "Barc gave his blood for the Blues."

Another Hall of Famer, Al Arbour, watched Barclay from the ice as a player and behind the bench as coach. While with St. Louis, where the sun was setting on his playing career but dawning on his coaching one, Arbour gave Barclay the ultimate compliment, calling him "the greatest competitor I've ever been associated with."

Fan favourite "Barc the Spark" captained the team, played in four All-Star Games, and accumulated over 1,000 penalty minutes in 614 games. The club retired his No. 8 in 1981, and he died on February 6, 1988, of a brain hemorrhage.

Brother Bob made his living hip-checking the opposition upside down and throwing right hands. He recorded the club's first assist, penalty, and game misconduct. His No. 5 was honoured by the club, and he drew rave reviews from Arbour, who played alongside him as well as coached him. "Bob was very good at blocking shots, but he was also one of the best bodycheckers. It's a lost art, the way he used to hit guys. He'd throw his hip into someone and they'd go flying," said Arbour.

The three Kirkland Lake, Ontario, brothers—Barclay, Bob and Bill—played for St. Louis from 1968–69 to 1971–72, and Bill would prove he was a Plager all the way.

At first, Bill's older brothers would do his fighting for him. That is, until Bill took on the much larger veteran heavyweight, Orland Kurtenbach.

"Billy had Orland's sweater and they started throwing punches," Bob wrote in his memoir. "Orland landed a few, but Bob did very good. *Very* good. Barc and I looked at each other and we said, '*We've* been going out fighting for *him*?'"

"They come to play," said Bowman. "I don't have to worry about them being up for a game."

Added Lynn Patrick, then-Blues general manager: "I've never seen guys like them. All they talk about is hitting!"

Also terrorizing opponents was defenceman Noel Picard.

Picard played in the minors with Barclay, who'd warn his younger brother to keep his distance: "He's the toughest guy I ever saw," Bob remembered Barclay saying.

"He was the big goon for St. Louis," said Curt Bennett, who tried making the Blues before becoming a regular with Atlanta. "He was a big, tough French guy, and he tried to start playing like a regular man, finesse and stuff. And as soon as he did, he didn't belong on the team any more, he wasn't going to make the team. That was not his role. He had a certain way he had to play, and if he did that, he was very valuable."

Early into the '70s, the Blues decided to take toughness to a greater extreme. At their 1973 training camp, they invited the likes of John Wensink, Battleship Kelly, Bob Gassoff, Ray Schultz, Gary Gresdal, and, maybe the wildest of all, Steve Durbano, a.k.a. "Demolition Durby" or "Mental Case Durbano."

"He was one of the craziest that ever played. He was just nuts," Bennett said.

Durbano exploded out of the Ontario Hockey Association as its most penalized junior player ever. Although he only managed 90 games in his first go round with the Blues (he'd cap his whirl-wind career there in 1978–79 with another 13 games), the 6-foot-2, 220-pounder certainly managed to make an impression there and elsewhere, compiling a massive 1,127 penalty minutes in a mere 220 contests.

"He was the most raucous player I've ever seen," Mike Murphy, who played with Durbano on the junior Toronto Marlies and the Blues, told the *Toronto Sun*. "He was an elite character right out of the movie *Slap Shot*. You think those guys are invented? You don't know Steve Durbano.

"He scared me when he played with me and when he played against me. He was very likable, funny, friendly and genuine. But he used his stick in a vile way."

Wilf Paiement played with Durbano in Kansas City and Colorado and can easily recall being glad the tough guy was on his team. "When I first came into the league he played in Pittsburgh and I sure didn't like to play against Pittsburgh. He was a very aggressive player and a big boy too."

Steve Vickers, Durbano's Marlie teammate and roommate when the two started out as professionals in Omaha, said in an interview with the *Globe and Mail* that Durbano represented the beginning of a breed, establishing a trend in hockey that teams like the Philadelphia Flyers picked up on. "In time, guys like Steve weren't that uncommon in the NHL."

THE BROAD STREET BULLIES

The lesson Conn Smythe had drummed into the Leafs for years—"If you can't beat 'em in the alley, you won't beat 'em on the ice"—was a lesson the Philadelphia Flyers took to heart.

But it was the St. Louis Blues who ultimately convinced the Flyers to become the Broad Street Bullies. For Philadelphia, it wasn't simply a matter of emulating the menacing Blues, it was *survival*.

The Flyers led all expansion teams in 1967–68, the first year of the 12-team league, but they fell in the playoffs to the Plager brothers, Noel Picard, and the rest of the Blues.

"The Plagers ganged up on Ed Van Impe and broke his thumb," complained Flyers owner Ed Snider at the time. "And then their big Frenchman, Picard, cold-cocked our Claude LaForge from the blindside. They beat us in seven games. And they beat us up, too."

The Blues swept the Flyers in a playoff rematch the next year, and in the spring of 1969, management began building a team that wouldn't be intimidated by anyone anymore, taking Bobby Clarke, Dave Schultz, Don Saleski, and Bob Kelly in the draft. They also traded for the Blues' André Dupont in 1972.

"Up to then, they'd always intimidated us, because we had a lot of small guys on the team. And they had guys like the Plager brothers, Noel Picard, Bob Gassoff and Bob ['Battleship'] Kelly," retired Flyers defenceman Joe Watson told the *Montreal Gazette* in 1985. The Flyers, however, went from the bullied to the bullies in a '72 exhibition game against the Blues. "This time we had a big guy named Dave Schultz. And as soon as Battleship Kelly hit him a shot, Dave dropped his gloves and beat him. Before the game was over, Dave beat him twice more . . . Schultz was a major factor in our success. He gave us courage, especially on the road."

Although team captain Clarke and goalie Bernie Parent have received the greatest accolades, John Ferguson believed no one should underestimate Schultz's contributions. "You can give Schultz all the credit in the world for helping that team take two championships. They played mean, and that's why they were successful. Schultz helped send the Flyers on their way to the top," he said in *Thunder and Lightning*.

Schultz's teammates held his contributions in high regard as well.

"Next to Bernie [Parent], Davey might be the most important acquisition the Flyers had in the last few years," said Clarke during the team's heyday. "He gave us a personality. We went from an ordinary team to a battling team."

"Some follow, others show the way," added Watson. "Davey showed the way. He was a leader, a force in the dressing room."

"Whether we were fighting or just throwing our weight around along the boards, we thrived on intimidation," explained Schultz in the summer 1999 edition of *Hockey Digest*. "Just ask the rest of the league; it stood by and watched us win two Stanley Cups."

No expansion team would come to specialize in acts of intimidation quite like the Philadelphia Flyers. Their gang tactics terrorized many other clubs. It did not sit well with traditionalists.

"The NHL did that goofy thing of letting that stupid Philadelphia team play, encouraging them—as if they needed it," complained Terry Harper, who'd watched great, skilful hockey as a defenceman for the great Montreal Canadiens teams of the 1960s. He thought the Flyers style of play took hockey backwards. "They wanted to make expansion work and they kind of turned a blind eye to that. Whatever Philadelphia wanted to do, they could do. That Shero, he'd just send guys out there to get guys all the time."

"Intimidation is a big part of the game," justified Flyers coach and ringmaster Freddie "The Fog" Shero.

When Shero sent out combinations like Schultz, Kelly, and Saleski along with Dupont on defence, he was sending a message that even other Flyers could clearly read.

"It was scary sometimes," said Flyers centre Terry Crisp. "You just knew that before the puck was even dropped, all hell was gonna break loose. And if I was out there, I knew guys from the other team were gonna be looking for me because they wanted no part of the 'Hammer' and the 'Hound.'"

Many a player who arrived in Philadelphia to play the Flyers would claim to be under the weather before game time.

"The Philly Flu, no question about it, you'd go in there and all of a sudden guys weren't feeling well or if they were feeling well, they didn't want to touch the puck," said journeyman Blair Stewart.

The Flyers established a league record of 1,742 penalty minutes in 1974 and broke it the next season with 1,980. (Incredibly, a post–Bully Flyers squad shattered the team record with 2,621 penalty minutes in 1980–81.)

"Guys didn't like going into Philly—I didn't give a shit, but there were a lot of guys on my team who were throwing up before the game; they were nervous," said Kurt Walker, who played for the Toronto Maple Leafs. "It was no place for a nervous person."

"They had eight to 10 guys that could fight anybody in the league," said Wilf Paiement.

And anyone who got an upper hand on one of the Flyers would soon find himself attacked on all sides.

"Philly, if you fought one guy, you had three or four others coming after you. And that was more their style than any other team. It was a bully thing," said Stewart.

In retirement, Moose Dupont recalled defenceman Ed Van Impe lending his form of assistance to fellow Flyers.

"During brawls he would come over to see how you were making out and then would give the guy you were fighting a little jab in the ribs with his stick. And then he'd say, 'Are you doing better now?' And we always were because the guy we were fighting could barely breathe," Dupont reminisced in *Oldtimers* by Gary Mason.

If opponents were scared of the Flyers, officials were just down-right frustrated. "Coach Fred Shero's system was to create as much havoc as possible. He knew his team would be penalized for many but not all infractions," said Bruce Hood in *Calling the Shots: Memoirs of an NHL Referee*, adding, "They had good goaltending and good penalty killing so they did almost anything they wanted. And they used their intimidating tactics before and especially after the whistle. . . . Once one Flyer got involved in an altercation, the others weren't far behind to lend a hand."

Dennis Hextall opined that the Flyers were far tougher as a group than individually.

"If you take the teams where they won the Cups, they weren't individually that tough," Hextall said. "When you played for Fred Shero, he had a way of getting everyone to stick together as a team. And when you went into Philly, you were going to get gang attacked. If your team wasn't willing to stand up, then you saw part of the Philadelphia Flu, and they knew that, and they used that to their advantage."

The Soviet Red Army would discover that first-hand in an infamous exhibition match in 1976, when the entire squad walked out in the first period, only returning after promoters threatened to withhold their pay if they didn't get back on the ice.

Schultz explained Shero's game plan that night as laying back in the neutral zone and daring the Soviet players to try to skate through the Flyers: "When they came forward, he wanted us to greet them with ill will. And when one of the officials came into the locker room before the game to tell us that Lloyd Gilmour was refereeing that night and wanted us to play our game, I knew it was going to be fun."

The big moment came when Van Impe burst out of the penalty box and made a beeline to Valeri Kharlamov, knocking him to the ice and leaving him lying there. Irate Russian coach Konstantin Loktev waved officials over to his bench, and delayed putting his next line on the ice when he didn't get the call he was looking for. After referee Gilmour assessed a delay of game minor, the coach ordered his players into the dressing room.

Soviet goaltender Vladislav Tretiak claimed that because the Red Army was scheduled to play in the Olympic tournament in less than a month, his coaches wanted to avoid injuries.

"No Red Army player wanted to play against the Flyers. Each of us could have been hit from behind, cross-checked, kicked—what kind of sport was this? It had nothing at all in common with the game of hockey," said Tretiak in his book *Tretiak: The Legend*. "We didn't know before that a pack of barbarians could put on skates and get away with hunting hockey players in front of thousands of spectators."

When the Soviet players finally did return, the Flyers quickly pounced. Seventeen seconds into it, Reggie Leach scored a power-play goal. Rick MacLeish made it 2-0 late in the first, and the Flyers went up 3-0 early in the second. The Soviets got on the board midway through the second, but the Flyers put it away with another early goal in the third period.

"They went out and hit the hell out of them the first period, and Russia wouldn't come back on the ice. And that was just part of them—that's the way Philly was," Hextall said, adding that the league implemented the third-man rule with the Flyers in mind.

Russia had previous experience with one Flyer in particular, Bobby Clarke, who had deliberately broken Kharlamov's ankle with a slash in the 1972 Canada-Soviet Summit Series.

"Bobby Clarke, what a competitor. He'd kill to do whatever he had to do to win. He did things that were maybe on the edge sometimes, but he had players to back him up, believed in him," said Paiement. "They were like a pack of wolves playing together. And they had a goalie who was very, very hot. Bernie Parent was awesome."

Shockingly, it would be one of the practitioners of fire-wagon hockey, the Montreal Canadiens, who would first crack and then shatter the mystique around the Bullies.

"The Canadiens broke our system with their skating, always in motion," said Watson. "You'd beat one guy, and you'd look up and there were two more there."

Some have speculated that the Habs made their statement that they wouldn't be intimidated by the Flyers during the 1976 play-offs, pointing to a particular play in game two of the Stanley Cup Final where Larry Robinson smashed Gary Dornhoefer into the boards so violently that the boards actually broke. But according to Robinson, the game in which the Habs showed the Flyers they wouldn't back down actually occurred in the Spectrum during the 1975 pre-season.

The two teams met in a home-and-home series, and at the Forum in Montreal, the Flyers iced their full lineup and tried to send a message to the Canadiens. The only message Montreal seemed to receive, though, was to fight back. Montreal arrived in Philly with added muscle in the forms of Sean Shanahan, Glenn Goldup, Pierre Bouchard, and Rick Chartraw.

"Apparently Scotty Bowman was upset that the Flyers had

pushed his team around so much. He wanted the Canadiens to play it tougher and it wasn't long after the opening faceoff that he got his wish and the fights began," said Bruce Hood, who refereed the second game.

The result was that the Canadiens beat the Flyers not only on the ice but in the alley as well. Robinson remembered Chartraw besting Schultz in both of their fights, Bouchard mopping up the boards with Jack McIlhargey, and Doug Risebrough "whaling the tar" out of Clarke.

"Everywhere you looked, red shirts were hammering orange and white," Robinson recalled in *Robinson for the Defense*. "When it was over, the Spectrum was strangely quiet."

Hood called the match early and sent both teams to their dressing rooms "since nobody seemed to care about the game anymore." He ended up assessing 334 minutes in penalties. For Robinson, Montreal had "ended the Broad Street Bullies. Never again would they dictate their system or style of game to us, and eventually the rest of the league."

When the two teams met in the 1976 final, the Habs swept the Flyers in four straight, albeit closely contested, games.

It was the beginning of the disbanding of the Bullies, and some of the players who thrived under the Philadelphia's gang mentality were left exposed to retribution from opponents with long memories.

"I remember when other guys from that team got traded to other teams . . . they weren't as tough!" said Curt Bennett. "They seemed tougher when they played for Fred's team than they did when they got traded to other teams."

"As I saw it, there were quite a few mythical hard men on that Philadelphia team. It was kind of pathetic to see how some of those hard men fared when they were cut from the pack at the Spectrum," Tiger Williams said in *Tiger: A Hockey Story*. "I'm thinking particularly of people like Orest Kindrachuck and Don Saleski. When Saleski went to Colorado, he took some beatings because in

Philadelphia, with the wolf pack around him, he was a big street guy. On his own, it was a different story. We were looking for guys like that when Philadelphia broke up and we got them."

THE BIG BAD BRUINS AND DON CHERRY'S LUNCH PAIL GANG

Even before expansion, the Boston Bruins were experimenting with adding numerous bruisers to their lineup, with Orland Kurtenbach, Forbes Kennedy, Gary Dornhoefer, Ted Green, Reggie Fleming, and Ace Bailey taking their turns on the ice for Boston around the mid-'60s.

But it wasn't until after expansion that Boston became the "Big Bad Bruins." John Ferguson remembered the Bruins talking intimidation tactics before the Montreal's 1967–68 playoff series against Boston.

"This was one of the first times in memory that the expression 'intimidation' began to get much use around the league. It started with Boston," Ferguson said in his book.

"The Boston Bruins, or the Big Bad Bruins as they were called, set the early standard for goon hockey in the late sixties and early seventies," said Hood.

Hood added that the Bruins didn't have "goons" as such, since players like Green, John "Pie" McKenzie, Wayne Cashman, Bobby Orr, Phil Esposito, and Gerry Cheevers could all play hockey, "which gave the Bruins the right combination of toughness and skill—the best form of intimidation a team can have."

"They didn't come any tougher than Cashman," recalled announcer Jiggs McDonald, who called NHL games for nearly 40 years, starting in 1967 for the expansion Los Angeles Kings. "He had a lot of skill, a lot of talent, great hands, but he could drop them and go with the best."

But Hood didn't especially respect Cashman. "He made sure

everyone knew that if you messed with him, you messed with all the Bruins. He liked that power and took advantage of it. When a guy was down, Cashman always looked ready to kick him."

Tiger Williams remembered Terry O'Reilly protecting him from one of those kicks. With Williams wrestling on the ice with O'Reilly, Cashman came over and apparently got a skate through the melee, leaving a cut on Williams's head that required six stitches.

"But it was obvious he wasn't going to leave it at that. It was then that O'Reilly said, low enough to escape Cashman's hearing, 'Put your head under my body; I'll shield you.' I guess he believed that Cashman was capable of kicking my eyes out," Williams said in his book.

Hood remembered "Pie" McKenzie as a reckless player. "Some nights he reminded me of a fox going into a chicken house. He'd fly into those corners at full speed, arms and elbows flying, and come out with the puck on his stick and a grin on his face. He loved it!"

"Terrible" Teddy Green came to Boston from Montreal, where he had made a name for himself at the age of 18 when he flattened all three Richard brothers (Maurice, Henri, and Claude) in succession during training camp.

After being sold to the Bruins, he fought anyone he could get his hands on and soon became the best fighter in the league.

"He had narrow slitted eyes and he had a way of staring at the opposition to intimidate them. It was a long, cold, hard, deep stare. It didn't take long to figure that he was a tough SOB," Ferguson said.

Ferguson saw a bit of himself in Derek "Turk" Sanderson, a player with an ornery streak and someone who loved to fight. Sanderson also "wouldn't hesitate to play you dirty, given the chance."

"The Bruins had become the ultimate intimidators in the league," said Ferguson. "Turn your back on Derek Sanderson, Johnny McKenzie or Wayne Cashman, and you'd be in trouble. Lay a hand on Orr and you could bet that Ted Green, Ken Hodge, Don Awrey or even Eddie Shack would be coming to his rescue. Not that he needed it, because Orr could be one of the most ornery characters this side of John Ferguson, if you rubbed him the wrong way."

Joe Watson, best known for his years with the Flyers, actually started his NHL career in Boston. As tough as the Flyers became, they were never as tough as the Bruins of the mid- to late '60s and early '70s, according to Watson. "We had two guys who could fight, Schultz and ['Hound Dog'] Kelly; and two guys who were swordsmen, Clarkie and Ed Van Impe."

A new generation of tough guys would join the Bruins once Don Cherry assumed the coaching helm, but Boston remained as tough as ever. Boston reporter Fran Rosa dubbed them "The Lunch Pail Gang," explaining that they "punch the time clock at 7:30 p.m. and never stop working."

"Boston was different [than Philadelphia], trickier," said Williams. "They had Cashman and O'Reilly and Kenny Hodge, Bobby Schmautz and Stan Jonathan. Schmautz could fight, but he would sooner spear you. Sometimes you wondered whether he was going to pick your eyes out. Hodge was a big, tough guy who did a lot for a couple years and then went quiet but you were never sure whether he was going to produce something. You couldn't really relax with him. By comparison, Philadelphia was straightforward."

"I think, man-for-man, Boston was the tougher team," added Kurt Walker.

"The toughest team I ever played against was definitely the Boston Bruins," said Dan Maloney, who added that besides being physically tough, Boston's enforcers could score 20 to 30 goals too. "You go into that little building, the old Garden, when they got playing their game, there wasn't a hell of a lot of room in there."

"It seemed you had no room to move there," agreed Wilf Paiement. "And they had three of the toughest left wingers in the league when I played against them. I was a right winger and I had to play every shift against Stan Jonathan, John Wensink or Al Secord. For myself, what a battle it was going there."

Not even the fans were safe from the ire of Boston's bruisers. At Madison Square Garden on December 23, 1979, the Bruins scaled the glass to take on a group of rowdy Ranger patrons.

"It was right towards the end of the game and the puck was in our end," reminisced Wensink. "The puck came up along the boards, as the siren went, to Stanley [Stan Jonathan]. . . . A fan had rolled a program up, reached over the glass, and took a swipe at Stanley with it and caught him in the face. When that happened, Stanley brought his stick up, not knowing what was coming his way. So he brings his stick up and one of the other kids grabs his stick."

Wensink and his fellow Bruins, seeing the fans messing with their teammate, sped over to help and before they knew it, "one thing led to another."

"Guys were going over trying to help one another—[Mike] Milbury, [Peter] McNab, Terry [O'Reilly] and myself, we were over," said Wensink. "It's funny, I grabbed a guy and he turns around and says he's security. So I let him go and grab another guy and *he* says he's security! Finally, I just kinda stood there to make sure everything is okay and that's exactly what I ended up doing."

Most notable and memorable was Milbury hitting one of the fans with his own shoe. A lawsuit would later be announced, but nothing came of it. Wensink said the boys still joke and reminisce about the wild scene when they're on the bus heading to an old-timers game.

Of all the Lunch Pail Bruins, the one who gets the greatest raves from opponents is O'Reilly. "When you focus on the post-Orr and post-Espo Bruins, the face you put on the uniform is that of Terry O'Reilly. He was their heart and soul as long as he played," Larry Robinson said in his book. "Nobody ever gave more to his team than Terry did. . . . And he did it with class, even though he was a player who had to get into a lot of fights.

"The thing I remember most about Terry is the night I got knocked out in the Garden, the only one who came in to find out how I was was Terry. That's the type of guy he was. He'd play tough, as tough as it took, but nothing dirty."

"Terry and I used to go at it just about every game," said Maloney. "You always knew you were in the game when you got to play against Terry. He was a damn good hockey player and a hell of a Bruin."

"He wasn't a goon; he was just a real hard, hard-nosed player that gave 120% every time he stepped on the ice, which you had to respect," added Blair Stewart.

Hammer Schultz believed he must have fought O'Reilly 10 times.

"I'd be checking the schedule and think to myself, 'Oh, shit! We're in Boston in two weeks,'" Schultz said in an interview with the *Calgary Herald*. "I remember squaring off against one of their players one night at the Garden in the corner, can't even remember who the guy was, and out of the corner of my eye all I see is O'Reilly. He's weaving his way around players, between players, running through players, and then there he is, all of a sudden, right in front of me, his gloves are off, and again I'm thinking 'Oh, shit!'"

Schultz admitted feeling anxiety playing the Bruins, particularly in Boston Garden.

"I will never forget sitting [in] the penalty box and having Bobby Orr and Phil Esposito skate by and say, 'Hey, asshole, the boys are going to get you tonight.' You don't think that was intimidating? There were times I had the 'Boston Flu,' too, trust me," he revealed in the book, *The Code*.

Wensink didn't lose much sleep before games between the Bruins and the Flyers but wasn't surprised Schultz did.

"He may not have been able to sleep before Bruins games because he stirred up a lot of crap, and when you [do], you're bound to spill a little bit on you," Wensink said.

The Lunch Pail Gang would be broken up not long after Cherry was ousted as Bruins coach.

"When Grapes was there, we went to the finals twice and semis once. A lot of the players that were in the line-up, we were his team— he had moulded the Bruins [in]to what he wanted," Wensink said.

It was a close team, and Wensink said that he still keeps in touch with O'Reilly and Cherry.

"He's one of my best friends. He's our oldest daughter's godfather and believe me, if I were to go into battle, he'd be one to be on my side—I'd pick him. Just a good guy," Wensink said of O'Reilly. "The amazing thing is, I get to Boston, we ended up driving in and out together, he has hobbies, he likes doing things with his hands and collecting antiques. He was more into the antique stuff, I was more into building it from scratch. We both like woodworking, we had some interests away from the game that we both enjoyed and so we shared that."

And even though Wensink, O'Reilly, and Cherry can go long periods without communicating, when they do have a chance to chat, it's like hardly any time has passed at all.

"I don't see Don as much as everybody thinks I see him. I don't necessarily talk to him a whole lot on the phone. But I'm sure if I called him today it would be like we never missed a beat," said Wensink.

CHAPTER 4

HEAVIES

THE NAMES THAT follow are a sampling of the best fighters from the recent decades and should in no way be taken as a definitive who's who of toughs throughout the ages, which would fill volumes. Some of them were pretty one-dimensional players, while others were key factors on championship teams.

All of them could hold their own—and spin a good tale.

THE DUOS

Many sleepless nights preceded games against teams that could ice intimidating one-two enforcer combinations. The following section profiles the twosomes who caused not unjustified panic in opposition policemen.

The rivalry between Bob Probert and Tie Domi spanned many years and many teams. Here, Probert of the Red Wings battles Domi of the Rangers less than one minute into a game at Madison Square Garden in December 1992. (AP Photo/Ron Frehm)

BOB PROBERT & JOEY KOCUR, DETROIT RED WINGS

Bob Probert The Muhammad Ali of hockey enforcers, Bob Probert combined size, strength, punching combinations and accuracy, and an ability to give and take punishment better and for a longer stretch of time than any other player. However, his reputation did little to scare away other toughs. Rather, it made him something of a marked man, as Young Turks tried to make a name for themselves by challenging him.

Dennis Bonvie made no bones about it. In his first exhibition game for the Edmonton Oilers, the then–American Hockey League penalty-minute record-holder told Probert, "You're either going to make me or break me."

"And it's true, if you think about it. If he beat me up, I was probably not going to play again; if I did okay, I'd hang around a little longer," Bonvie said. "There was really no in-between. You either do good and you get another game, or go back to the minors." Given that he took on all comers, it should come as no surprise that Probert ended his 16 years in the NHL with 3,574 regular season and playoff penalty minutes.

"The guy that everyone looked up to and wanted to be was Bob Probert," said Florida Panthers original Paul Laus. "He was the guy that everyone wanted to test. If you can put a bar against someone, that would be the guy you wanted to fight and see how you stacked up against him."

Besides tangling with all the best and up-and-comers, Probert also took a regular shift on the ice, filling the role John Ferguson had previously occupied, that of the standard bearer for enforcers.

Born in Windsor, Ontario, Probert got many of his attributes from his father, Al, a big, tough, city cop. At 16, he caught the eye of junior scouts at a tournament in Vancouver in which he was named the left winger on the All-Tournament First Team. He was drafted by the Brantford Alexanders in 1982. He demonstrated a flair for fighting and, after his first season in the OHL, the Detroit Red Wings drafted him in the third round, 46th overall. The following year, he was picked to be an OHL All-Star, but he didn't play after getting sent home for partying too hard and missing the photo session. The next season, he was playing for the Sault Ste. Marie Greyhounds. Once in the NHL, he saw lots of ice time while still taking on the toughest guys around.

"What I admired about Bob was he played 15 to 18 minutes a game," said St. Louis Blues heavyweight Tony Twist. "A guy like me, I played three. So he had to go play the game and then at some point, he had to deal with me. And I'm on the bench resting and all I'm thinking about is beating the hell out of him. I admired the fact he never turned anybody down, he went out there and did it and he was very good at it."

While generally rated the best overall fighter, Probert saved his absolute best for when he was genuinely angry.

Tie Domi found that out the hard way. Domi had a decent showing after their first fight in February 1992, and he let everyone in Madison Square Garden know it as he hot-dogged his way to the penalty box, gesturing he'd just taken the heavyweight title away from Probert.

"I didn't care for that, or for the way Domi acted after. I didn't like the way he was building himself up," Probert wrote in *Tough Guy*, his posthumously released autobiography. "And when people start going to the press and mouthing off, well, that's not cool."

The rematch had to wait until the next season. It was as highly anticipated as an Ali-Frazier main event, and New York newspapers plastered the tale of the tape with Probert's and Domi's pictures on their front pages. Less than 40 seconds into the December 1992 contest, Probert went right after Domi at the faceoff and ended up throwing 47 punches to take the unanimous decision.

Getting the best of Probert was a guaranteed way of facing him again. After getting knocked out by Todd Ewen in their first ever tilt, Probert came right back the same night to win their second go-to. And more famously, when super heavyweight Troy Crowder edged him in their first fight, Probert evened the series as soon as their two teams met again.

"There are a lot of tough guys in the league, but with his size and strength, I'd have to say he's the toughest," Wendel Clark, who had a number of run-ins with the 6-foot-3, 225-pounder throughout his Toronto career, said to the *Waterloo Region Record*, adding,

"You have to really watch him when his sweater comes off. Once his sweater comes off, you have nothing to hold on to, and he can swing at will. It's all part of his strategy."

Clark's days as a Leaf are often remembered for his battles with Probert. "In the old Chuck Norris days we had a lot of run-ins," Clark told the *Toronto Star*. "We played a lot of games against each other, Friday-Saturday home and home. It was very heated in the old days. There were a lot of good battles and a great rivalry."

"The toughest guy was Bobby Probert . . . the more you hit him the more he got pissed," recalled Jimmy Mann.

Bob McGill, who played for Detroit's divisional rivals Toronto and Chicago, was happy to still be around to tell the tales about his run-ins with Probert. Their first fight started after a line brawl had broken out, and officials were too busy quelling the donnybrook to come look in on how McGill was faring. He and Probert ended up tussling for about five minutes before being separated. "That was pretty scary . . . I probably fought him six different times, but I'm still talking about it today so that's a good thing, I guess."

It seemed as though the longer the fight went, the better Probert became.

"During a fight, instead of getting tired, something inside me would take over," Probert said in *Tough Guy*. "I wanted to win so badly that I overcame the fatigue."

No one fought Probert more than Stu Grimson—13 times by Probert's estimates. "Bob Probert was probably as all-round tough as anybody I ever fought and I fought him a lot of times," said Grimson. "You always knew you had your hands full when you fought Bob because he was so good with both hands and he could take a punch. You really needed to get a good piece of Bob before you were going to knock him down or get him to back pedal."

Probert could even put the fear of God into toughs on his own team. Basil McCrae, during his brief stay with the Red Wings, told author Ross Bernstein that before a game against Chicago, Probert ordered him to stay *away* from Al Secord, with whom Probert had a score to settle. Probert was far from satisfied when McCrae told him he'd try to abide but wouldn't shy away from answering the bell if Secord insisted on starting something with him.

"Probert just looked at me and said, 'If you fight Secord tonight, you are fighting me tomorrow in practice,' and he just walked away. I was like, holy shit, this guy is seriously crazy," McCrae said in *The Code.*

Aside from his prowess as a fighter, Probert demonstrated a flair around the net, and before his substance abuse issues set back his career, he was on his way to becoming a premier power forward. He was an NHL All-Star in 1987–88, when he scored 29 goals and 62 points to go along with his personal and team high penalty mark of 398 minutes. During the playoffs, with star Steve Yzerman injured and out of the lineup, Probert eclipsed Gordie Howe's 1955 club playoff-points record of 20 by a single point.

"He was actually a very good hockey player," said long-time voice of the original NHL Winnipeg Jets, Curt Keilback. "People looked at him as a fighter but he would have been in the National Hockey league as a big, physical, talented winger even if he couldn't have fought."

"Probert was a guy respected throughout the league. It was how he played," Clark told the *Star.* "He became more than just a fighter. He scored. He played a regular shift. He did a lot of things . . . He was a tough guy who played smart hockey."

In the foreword to Probert's memoir, Red Wings captain Steve Yzerman said players revered him not only for his toughness, but because he was a great player.

"Bob knew how to play the game. He was an intelligent player with great hockey sense. For a player with fists of stone, he had incredibly soft hands," Yzerman wrote. "His passing, playmaking and scoring touch made him a rare commodity."

Alcohol and drug abuse, however, caused Probert to fall short of his billing as the next Clark Gillies. He tried cocaine for the first time the night he won a Calder Cup with the AHL's Adirondack Red Wings in 1986, and his substance abuse spiralled from there.

The Red Wings issued him Antabuse, a drug for alcoholics that caused one to throw up if one drank. But Probert would replace the pills with aspirin and continue partying. He started buying cocaine, and his abuse escalated to several times a week, according to his autobiography.

While two DUIs and several trips to rehab didn't stall his career, Probert's playing days seemed over after he was arrested on the U.S. side of the Canada–U.S. border when Customs agents found over 14 grams (1/2 ounce) of cocaine on him. Probert would return to hockey a year after his arrest, but he was prevented from playing in Canada, fearing he would not be allowed back into the U.S. if he crossed the border. (In December 1992, he was cleared to cross again freely.)

Even a motorcycle accident while impaired didn't keep him down, and he signed as a free agent with the Chicago Blackhawks shortly afterwards.

Probert missed the entire 1994–95 season as the NHL forced him into drug rehab, but he'd return to the ice and stay clean for the next six years with the Blackhawks. But in his last season, when the club was looking to get out of its contract, he started drinking again. He even found a way to cheat the urine tests the team demanded from him. The cocaine habit returned as well.

Although Probert spent the summer of 2002 training hard, coach Brian Sutter wouldn't play him, and the Hawks let him go. In time, pain pills became his drug of choice and he began snorting OxyContin, at one point going through 20 pills a day.

Probert was working on his memoir when he died of a heart attack on July 5, 2010. He was 45.

Joey Kocur
Lacking the stature of the typical super heavyweight, Joey Kocur was nonetheless a solidly built Saskatchewan farm boy at 6-foot, 220 pounds, who threw every ounce of himself into his punches.

"When he swung, he swung for the back of your head," said

St. Louis Blue Kelly Chase. "He hit like a truck and had hands like phonebooks."

Chase's friend and teammate Tony Twist, a feared fighter himself, said many players feared Kocur because of his great right hand. New York Islander Brad Delgarno suffered more than any other opponent, missing a season-and-a-half of hockey after his face was smashed by that right.

With all due deference to his pal Twist, Chase believed Kocur was far and away the toughest enforcer in the league and the only one who could end someone's career by hitting them.

"Tony hit hard, Tony broke guys' cheekbones and beat guys, but I think everybody that played will tell you that nobody ever wanted to get hit by Joe Kocur—because if he hit you, the damage could be far worse than missing a day or two with a broken nose," Chase said, adding, "All the guys that played then will tell you if there's a choice between who you're going to get hit by, it was a pretty easy choice."

Lyndon Byers of the Bruins said both Twist and Kocur threw bombs: "They're a couple of scary people. I would vote Joey Kocur probably the toughest guy ever."

Super-pest Dennis Polonich, best known for skating with the Red Wings in the 1970s, played with Kocur while winding down his career with the AHL's Adirondack Red Wings. He too was awed by the youngster. "Guys you were afraid of were [like] Joe Kocur. Maybe they didn't throw many punches but, my God, when they threw, it was a haymaker," Polonich said.

"Kocur may be the best puncher around," confirmed Wendel Clark in an interview with the *Toronto Star*. "He doesn't care where he punches you, on the helmet, pads. He's broken helmets with his fists. . . . He's hurt some guys by punching them on the helmet."

"I was fortunate that I never took it full brunt. If you did, he might have fricken broken your face," added Clark's one-time teammate, Bob McGill.

Former Edmonton Oiler Kevin McClelland said Kocur might have been the "scariest" enforcer out there because "if he hit you,

you were probably going to have a little nap for a while." He saw that for himself one night when Kocur broke Edmonton teammate Don Jackson's jaw. "I fought him a little different: I was a left-hander, he was a right-hander, but I knew I wasn't going to stand there and go toe-to-toe with him. Every guy you had a different way of fighting. [With Kocur], try to keep him off-balance, not let him load up."

Winnipeg Jets defenceman Jim Kyte failed to do so one night in Detroit and had to be carried off the ice. Winnipeg play-by-play man Curt Keilback recalled Kyte had gotten into fewer and fewer scrapes that year and ended up getting knocked out by Kocur in a very one-sided tilt. "[Winnipeg General Manager] John Ferguson had the best line about that: 'If you're going to go into [a] heavyweight championship battle, you've got to spar a little first.' And he hadn't sparred in a long time." Many, including Keilback, believed that loss finished Kyte as a big-time heavyweight.

Ken Daneyko, who'd get to see Kocur more often after the Red Wings traded him to New Jersey's divisional rival the New York Rangers, said everyone respected Kocur: "He could hurt you. With a lot of guys, you get cuts, bruises, stitches, black eyes. But Joey could really damage you." According to Kocur, whose primary purpose was to "keep the flies off Stevie [Yzerman]," he was getting paid to never lose a tilt: "I won't fight dirty. I won't jump someone from behind. But when I go to hit someone, I want to hit him in the face," he was quoted as telling *The National Sports Daily*. "I'm trying to hit as hard as I can. And a few times it has happened that someone got hurt." Kocur made up one half of Detroit's famed Bruise Brothers alongside Bob Probert. Kocur was drafted from the WHL's Saskatoon Blades in 1983, and, along with Yzerman and Probert, instantly took the league by the throat and forced the opposition to give Detroit greater respect on the ice at a time when the team was struggling to shake off its "Dead Things" tag.

"Those two guys reaped fear and intimidation through the entire league for a good three years," said Twist.

Jay Miller, who battled fellow heavyweights on behalf of the

Boston Bruins and Los Angeles Kings, always knew his hands would be full in a game against Detroit: "I'd say Joey Kocur is the hardest hitter. Bob Probert, it's a question mark, and that's in a good way. You never knew what he was gonna do," Miller said.

"You looked at what Joey Kocur and Bob Probert did for the Detroit Red Wings' resurgence—they were a big part of it," said Dave Manson, who had his share of run-ins with both as a Chicago Blackhawk. "They were two of the best. It was tough for opposing teams knowing that you had to line up against those guys. But you still had to do it."

If anything, the two of them might have made the opposition think twice about routing the Red Wings after getting up by a couple goals. "The Red Wings weren't a very good team when Kocur and Probert first got there. . . . But I'm sure there might have been a few tough guys on other teams that would say to the good players on their teams, 'Hey, we're up by a couple, let's not rub it in,'" explained Bob McGill, laughing.

"They were two tough boys, I'll tell you—exceptionally tough," said Dan Maloney, chuckling as he recalled watching Kocur and Probert from the Toronto bench as Leafs coach. "Probie was a pretty good hockey player and got to play with Yzerman. Joey was a good player too in his own right and he probably had the hardest punch I've ever seen in hockey. He could really hit. He destroyed his own hands hitting people."

Kocur demonstrated another side to his game by stymieing the scoring efforts of Clark with masterly shadowing during the 1987 playoff showdown between the Red Wings and the Maple Leafs. He was an asset to the Rangers in their 1994 Stanley Cup run, and he showed off his checking skills again when his career was resurrected by Red Wings bench boss Scotty Bowman during Detroit's back-to-back championship years. Kocur played alongside Kris Draper and Kirk Maltby to form the elite shutdown Grind Line.

"I knew he was as tough as they come, and the rumour was that he had one of the hardest punches in the league. But to play with him, I never knew he was as good a hockey player as he is. So tough down low on the puck, and so strong along the boards. He's a great linemate to play with," said Draper in *The Ultimate Bad Boys*.

Kocur listed Detroit's Cup victory in 1997 as his proudest moment, even though it represented the second time he'd lift the prized trophy over his head. "This one was special because Maltby, Draper and I were members of the Grind Line. Scotty [Bowman] didn't consider us a fourth line; we were important members of the team. The best part was, in the final game, we were on the ice for the start of the third period and we were on the ice for the final minute of the game," Kocur told the *Holland Sentinel*.

In a roundabout way, it was his old partner in crime Probert who got him his return to Detroit. In 1996, Kocur was playing in a beer league and looking for a comeback. Aware of Detroit's need for toughness, Kocur asked Probert for a favour when Chicago arrived for a road tilt against the Wings.

"I was between teams at the time and I couldn't get a job. I was talking with Probie when he was in Chicago and I knew when they went to Detroit for their next game that he was going to play dirty. Well, he kind of ran roughshod over some of the Wings players and the next day the press was calling for the Red Wings to get me back," Kocur said to the *Sentinel*.

"That night, I speared [Jamie] Pushor and fought [Brendan] Shanahan, and the next day, Joe got a call from the Red Wings. He still thanks me for that," Probert told the *Windsor Star* in 2007.

That, of course, didn't prevent the two from getting into a couple scraps. But they'd fought before, when Probert was in Detroit and Kocur in New York, so it wasn't anything personal. Both reunited and reminisced the night other former Red Wings gathered to celebrate the retirement of Yzerman's sweater at Joe Louis Arena.

"At one point in the game, Joe pointed to this spot on the ice and said, 'Remember? That's where we had our fight,'" Probert told the *Windsor Star*'s Bob Duff.

Kocur maintained his close ties to the club in retirement as president of the Detroit Red Wings Alumni Association. He also runs Kocur Enterprises, a manufacturing representative firm in South East Michigan, and in 2012 he created the Joe Kocur Foundation for Children.

TONY TWIST & KELLY CHASE, ST. LOUIS BLUES

Tony Twist If not for a motorcycle injury that cut his career short, Tony Twist might have become *the* undisputed hockey heavyweight champion of all time.

Already the alpha dog before the accident, Twist was about to enter a period of total domination.

"I was 272 pounds, probably 7.5% body fat, and I trained specifically to hurt somebody. There was no doubt in my mind that that was the year I was going to make somebody an example," said Twist. "And then I got in the motorcycle accident and thank God I was in the shape that I was in because it saved my life."

He had spent the previous five seasons as the chief peacemaker for the St. Louis Blues and believed he had a good chance of signing with the Philadelphia Flyers as an unrestricted free agent in the summer of 1999. But Twist, who annually raised money for the Head First Foundation with his Iron Horse Tour, was thrown off his motorcycle when a car cut him off. He suffered a broken and dislocated pelvis, ligament and cartilage damage to his left knee, and internal bleeding. Although he vowed to return to action, the 31-year-old was ultimately forced to retire. A huge collective sigh of relief likely emanated from enforcers around the league.

Twist may have been genetically predisposed to earning a living forcefully keeping the peace. His paternal grandmother, Ethel Twist, was a Hall of Fame lacrosse player nicknamed "Dirty Andy"; her husband, Harry, reigned as Western Canada's welterweight champion; and Stan Twist, Ethel and Harry's son and Tony's father, became an RCMP officer. Even his mom, Carole, could put unruly types in their place. Sitting in the Vancouver stands watching her son's Quebec Nordiques take on the Canucks, a fan seated in front of her made the mistake of shouting, "Twist, you goon, get off the ice!" after he dropped the gloves with Gino Odjick. Her response? She smacked him in the back of the head.

"I told him if he ever repeated those words, he would have to deal with me," she told *Sports Illustrated*. "In the second and third periods he and his friend were cheering for Tony."

Kelly Chase and Tony Twist grew up together, and both played with the WHL's Saskatoon Blades. Chase said that while Twist worked at his hockey ability as best he could, he knew his chance at the NHL hinged on toughness. "Tony always knew what his role was and he worked on the smaller parts of his game, but he made sure that the fighting part . . . was the best . . . because he knew that was the way he was going to have an opportunity," Chase said.

Twist relished his role and made it his mission to become the best in the business. He studied hours of fight tapes, toughened his knuckles punching concrete, and built himself into a goliath. "I was a student of what I did because I did it every game. If you're going to fight every day, and that's going to be your job, you damn well better be prepared, just like a goal scorer and goaltender," he said.

He's accumulated at least 500 VHS tapes of fights over the years, not only for study but recreation as well. "I really enjoyed watching them, back from the Bobby Orr days, as far back as I can get 'em. I've got some real classics there. Most of the old stuff I've got is the old Bruins and Broad Street Bullies."

With a background in boxing and kickboxing, he also worked to condition his hands for everyday wear and tear. "Every fighter watches what another fighter does. So if he watches another guy scrap the night before and realizes his hand's hurting, of course he's going to take advantage of him and the team if the guy's not on his game."

Adapting a martial arts technique, at the end of the season, Twist would start pounding his knuckles into sand. He graduated to lead beads and then to his basement floor. It would be a controlled punch that would condition the ligaments and tendons in his hands so that the swelling that would occur after a fight wouldn't last long.

But perhaps his greatest advantage was his power—his strength allowed him to string out opponents, keeping them away from him while he landed bombs at will. "I started lifting weights when I was 12 or 13 and really enjoyed working the body and the transformation and what you're able to accomplish over the course of time if you dedicate yourself to what you want to do," he said.

Whereas a goal scorer would practise his shot, Twist worked on building his muscles. In his first year with the St. Louis Blues, he weighed in at 207 pounds; by the time he became a regular with the Nordiques, he'd bulked up to around 230.

"I was 20 years old, and at 20, you're not even starting to fill out. Muscle maturation takes some time," he said, noting for a good part of his career, he'd filled out to between 240 and 255 pounds.

He was also very businesslike about his role, wanting to hurt his opponent in order to end the fight as soon as possible. Such a beating would serve as a valuable reminder to his foe: stay away.

"My motto was, 'Fight to win.' A lot of guys out there fight not to lose," Twist explained. "I don't really care if you hit me. Didn't really bother me. But when I hit you, you're going to get it. And the idea is I don't want you coming back. Fear and intimidation saves both wear and tear on the body and it has a more lasting effect than a good beating. Fear and intimidation, you have the guy beat before you even start. I like to leave the mark as heavy as possible."

"He throws hammers," San Jose Sharks right winger Owen Nolan told *Sports Illustrated*. "He throws to kill. I've seen him crack a helmet with a punch. If I hadn't seen it, I wouldn't have believed it."

"You don't want to see him looking at you the wrong way," admitted Los Angeles Kings heavyweight Matt Johnson in the same article. "No one in the league matches his pure punching power. He's an honest player but as tough as they come."

Georges Laraque would go on to become the league's heavyweight champ, but in his second season in the league, he took on the then–reigning titleholder and was put down:

"I remember that like it was yesterday. I'm lucky I came out alive," Laraque said.

Mike Peluso concluded no one was tougher than Tony Twist. Friends off the ice, any ties were put on hold as soon as a game started—as Twist demonstrated as a Nordique when he knocked Peluso out cold. Peluso ended up spending the night in hospital suffering from a concussion.

"I remember afterward showering and putting my suit on in the locker room, and then taking it off and showering again. I guess I did that three or four times. I mean I was really out of it," Peluso said in *The Code*.

Not long before Rob Ray was scheduled to ride with Twist on his charity motorcycle tour, he dropped the gloves against him in a game against St. Louis and ended up with a destroyed orbital bone.

Few could walk away from a fight with Twist unscathed, and most eventually just avoided him altogether.

"And that was a good thing. As Al MacInnis said, 'I'd rather have a cardboard cut-out of Tony Twist on the bench than an extra guy.' I gave him the ability to do what he could do—guys didn't run him," said Twist. "If they did, the guy who did it would pay second. Their best player would pay first. You run my best guy, I'll come after yours. Eventually the two big boys will run up, but after I take it out of their best guy."

The intimidation could start before the puck even dropped.

"I remember once we were playing St. Louis and Tony Twist comes out and he was sitting on the bench and watching our pre-game skate," said Paul Laus. "One of our rookies goes, 'Who's that guy?' And [Twist] had no sleeves on his shirt. And I said, 'Well, that's one guy you don't want to get a hold of or him get a hold of you.'"

"There are guys who want no part of him. There's no one in the league better than he is. When Twister fights, he hurts people," teammate Geoff Courtnall told the *St. Louis Post-Dispatch*.

93

Not only would the opposition avoid taking advantage of the Blues scorers, they wouldn't even talk trash to them. As far as Twist was concerned, teammates like MacInnis, Brett Hull, Wayne Gretzky, Chris Pronger, and Pierre Turgeon all had "diplomatic plates." In other words, he would see to it that they could do as they pleased without bother. "I've been in the league 10 years, and I've never seen so little yapping at the bench," Chase marvelled in an interview with the *Post-Dispatch*.

Twist maintained his connection with the city and his fans, transitioning from hockey cop to proprietor, opening Twister's Iron Bar Saloon and running Twister's Bar & Grill with his wife, April.

Kelly Chase
Discussing the year he led the WHL in penalty minutes, Kelly Chase insists his stats weren't inflated by misconducts.

"None of them were 10-minute misconducts," he stressed of his final WHL season, 1987–88, when he racked up 343 PIM. "They were all majors—fighting. I think I had 48 majors. I never really thought about it much; I still don't think about it much. It was the way that I had to play the game to be effective."

Chase wasn't the lone tough on that Saskatoon Blades team, which also boasted willing combatants like Tony Twist, Kevin Kaminski, and Kerry Clark.

"We had a tough team. We played hard, we cared about one another, and that was all part of it," Chase said, adding, "Sometimes you went out there for different reasons to get into a fight. Sometimes it was maybe to inspire your teammates. Sometimes it was so nobody took advantage of a young kid. Sometimes it was because of a dirty hit on one of your teammates. There were lots of reasons for the way we did it but that's the way the game was played. Different culture, different game now. We just played different then, I guess."

Undrafted, Chase joined the St. Louis Blues as a walk-on in 1988. "I had an American League contract originally," he recalled. "I went there on a tryout and I ended up having a good training camp, and they asked me if I would stay and go to Peoria. I signed an NHL contract from there and eventually had an opportunity in St. Louis."

The resident team enforcer at the time was Todd Ewen, whom Chase called "a tough customer" but added he had no intentions of being so respectful that he wouldn't fight to earn a spot. Chase played some with the Blues, but he spent most of his time with the Peoria Rivermen of the IHL his first three years out of junior before becoming a regular NHLer.

Tony Twist marvelled at his friend, a man who shied away from no one. "He had huge balls: he'd fight anybody, anytime. He wasn't the biggest guy in the league, but he could tie you in a knot and make sure you got what you had comin'," Twist said. "He was a guy who was a very, very good technical fighter. He was 195, 200 pounds, but he fought anybody. And he always did well."

Fighting in the "Chuck" Norris Division was common, and Chase knew that if a score got one-sided, a war could easily break out on the ice.

"You went to bed at night knowing that at the end of the day tomorrow, we're going to have to have a fight here and sometimes it was in your favour and sometimes it wasn't, but there were no misgivings as to whether or not there was going to be one," said Chase. "Sometimes it started early in the hockey game and sometimes it went in throughout the game."

The Blues' chief rival during those years was the Chicago Blackhawks, and no one liked to initiate the rough stuff more than their coach, Mike Keenan.

"Mike was a guy that liked the fighting. I'm sure he'd never been in one before in his life, but he sure liked to see them and initiate guys being in them," said Chase. "He didn't mind sending Stu Grimson, Mike Peluso, Wayne Van Dorp, and Dave Manson. There were a lot of tough customers out there and they weren't afraid to get into it. So, those guys certainly made it hard on you."

In January 1995, the Hartford Whalers picked up Chase on waivers. Twist, who'd been playing with the Quebec Nordiques, was back with St. Louis, and the two friends would soon clash. "[Blues coach] Keenan sent him out there and wanted him to get into it because I was running into their guys," Chase said. "Tony knew his role and said, 'Keenan wants me to come out and say something to you.' And I said don't worry about him, do what you gotta do. And he said he didn't want to fight—because we're buddies. I said, 'Tony, I gotta play the way I gotta play. I don't like Keenan and I gotta do what I gotta do too.' It put him in a bad spot and I understood that. So I said, 'Listen, if you want to go and just get it over with, then you don't have to worry about Mike and the whining that's gonna go on.'"

Twist's version is slightly different, although both stories end in a fight: "He came into St. Louis and it was his first game back. He was going after somebody, and Keenan kicks me in the ass and says get out there and take care of it," said Twist. "So I skated up to him and said, 'What the fuck are you doing?' He goes, 'This is my rink.' I said, 'No, look at your fucking jersey. This is mine.' And we ended up fighting. I was living in his house in St. Louis—I rented his house when he went to Hartford. And afterward he said, 'I guess the rent's going up tonight.'"

In 1996–97 Hartford traded Chase to Toronto, but he only managed two games before hurting his knee and missing the rest of the season. GM Mike Smith traded him back to St. Louis, where he'd close out his career. Fortunately, Keenan's tenure with the Blues had ended. "That was very exciting because I had a real love for the city of St. Louis and I think vice versa, so I was fortunate. I got to go back to a place that I call home now and for me that was exciting."

At the end of his first season back with the Blues, the NHL awarded Chase the King Clancy Memorial Trophy, a humanitarian award for community service, for starting a hockey program for kids with disabilities.

In retirement, everything seemed to be going swimmingly, and Chase worked as a colour commentator for Blues radio broadcasts. On December 15, 2008, Chase received the Jack Buck Award in recognition of his dedication to sports in the city. But during a summer vacation the same year, Chase's fortunes would take a turn. Experiencing numbness in his left hand and the left side of his face, he cut short his vacation in Saskatchewan and returned to St. Louis for a doctor's appointment.

An MRI revealed a 3-centimeter (about 1 inch) lesion on the right side of his brain. Tests ruled out cancer and multiple sclerosis, but doctors had no idea what caused it. "I have an active lesion on my brain . . . it's like a sore on your brain that causes numbness on your body," said Chase. "They're not sure what it is exactly or how it happened but it happens to lots of people, and rather than do a biopsy and cut my head open, we just used a type of steroid and shrunk it."

Following the year-long treatments, Chase suffered from nausea, extremely sensitive joints, and severe fatigue. His weight ballooned as well.

"I put on a lot of weight; I was up to almost 260 pounds," Chase said.

In February 2010, Chase declined an invitation to appear in *Battle of the Blades*, a Canadian TV series that teams ex-NHLers with world-class figure skaters and pits them against each other in a charity competition. But the $100,000 grand prize to a charity of the player's choice was too attractive to pass up, and Chase agreed to appear when asked again, saying:

For that show I had to get down to 200 pounds. I was down as low as 194 at one point. I was lighter than when I played . . . It was hard—I was 43 and to get rid of it, it was hard to do it again. But the advantage that we have is that we know how to train, we've been doing it our whole lives. So when you think you're training hard enough, you have to train harder, and that's how it goes with hockey. People that are just training to get in shape for something, to look good, never really get to—unfortunately—experience how far you can push yourself. And for me, I was lucky enough to know I had to be better by pushing myself and be able to find a zone where I could do that and that's what I did.

Chase called the competition a "great experience." Finishing fourth, he raised $25,000 for the Children's Hospital Foundation of Saskatchewan, a charity he'd worked for before. In the spring of 2011, he raised additional monies by joining 41 former and current NHLers on a bike tour across the province to each WHL city.

"We're one of two provinces in the country that doesn't have a children's hospital, so we were trying to raise some funds and awareness of the importance of the hospital here in Saskatchewan," said Chase. Of his charitable endeavours in general, he explained: "That's how we're brought up; that's what you're supposed to do."

JAY MILLER & LYNDON BYERS, BOSTON BRUINS

Jay Miller More a Bobby Orr guy than a hockey fan per se, it never crossed Jay Miller's mind that he'd make it to the NHL, let alone suit up for his hometown Boston Bruins.

And why would it? He was skating for the University of New Hampshire, where he kept his fists in his gloves because fighting is forbidden in the college game. All the same, Miller was no shrinking violet.

"I was actually a boxer in high school through college. One of my workout routines was at the Natick fire station," said Miller. "If you've seen the old *Rocky* movies, it makes its gym look like Caesar's Palace."

Miller picked up the sport through a Golden Gloves boxer, who's now one of the lieutenants of the Massachusetts State Police, in the basement of the firehouse. There, firemen entered a ring and threw haymakers over who'd buy beer. "We keep laughing about how we all started our careers in that little shitty fire hall with a stink worse than any hockey equipment bag sitting for 10 days in the back of an old station wagon."

Miller was selected by the Quebec Nordiques in the fourth round of the 1980 draft, but he felt like a fish out of water as an

American on a team where Dale Hunter was one of the few other non-Quebecers. He was sent down to Fredericton in the AHL and then ended up in Utica, New York, where Rick Ley was coaching the Mohawk Valley Stars in the Atlantic Coast Hockey League. The next season, he played again under Ley, this time for the Muskegon Lumberjacks of the IHL.

Becoming fed up, Miller quit hockey, but it wasn't for long, as Bruins scout Joe Lyons Sr. urged him to give the game another shot, saying, "Why don't you try out? You're not doing anything."

"They got me to training camp because I was a tough guy," said Miller. "I beat up Brian Curran, Gord Kluzak and John Blum in one practice—they picked on me. And [general manager] Harry Sinden was in the stands and said, 'Sign that kid to a minor contract.'"

Miller earned a spot on the team and showed management they made the right decision when he took on one of the toughest fighters of all time.

"My first game, I was fighting Dave Brown on a Sunday afternoon matinee in Boston Garden. That was something to behold. And I think I took him down pretty good. That was one of my highlights—other than my kids being born, that would have to stand out."

Miller was never the biggest heavyweight of his era—he was about 6-foot-2 and, while listed at 210 pounds, says he played between 222 and 225 pounds with only 12% body fat—but he consistently had strong showings against heavyweights like Brown and Bob Probert.

"They were all bigger than I was . . . They didn't scare me at all. Fear was my biggest ally—I just didn't want to lose! I was making pretty good money back then when I was 25 years old that I didn't want to lose, so I didn't want to lose a fight. That was one way to keep your job."

Miller also developed a not-always-healthy rivalry with the Montreal Canadiens resident tough guys, starting with Chris Nilan. They fought about twice a game eight times a year for three-and-a-half years. A smart-alecky Boston scribe quipped no one would have guessed that a kid from the suburb of Natick could beat up a kid from a badass neighbourhood like Roxbury, where Nilan was from.

"Then John Kordic came to the picture—because the team wanted Chris to play a little more. But Chris was always game, that's for sure," said Miller.

When Terry O'Reilly took over as coach, Miller and the Bruins achieved some of their best success in years, including beating the hated Canadiens in the 1988 playoffs. To put the victory into perspective, the Bruins hadn't defeated the Habs in a playoff series since 1943. Miller and the Bruins would march all the way to the final before bowing out in four straight to the Edmonton Oilers.

"Terry was really the one that got me going," Miller said, adding he first had to get something straight with his coach: "I always told Terry I would never be like him, 'So don't try to make me like you because I'm not gonna be. I do my own thing; I'm not gonna score 20.'"

That '88 team was close then and remains so to this day. "We still manage to see each other quite often. LB [Lyndon Byers] was a great teammate. Bill [O'Dwyer], LB and myself . . . we never left each other's side," said Miller. "It wasn't like today's game, where they all leave and go home. Even at home we hung around together. And summers. LB was quite a team guy—he was one of the smartest team guys we ever had."

However, the next season Miller was traded to the Los Angeles Kings, who were looking for added toughness. L.A. already had muscle with Ken Baumgartner and Marty McSorley, but "Bomber" was still just a rookie, and the coaches needed McSorley on the ice, not the penalty box, according to Miller. "The way Gretz explained it to me, 'I want you to be Semenko and watch my back.' He always had a reason for having players where they were."

Miller was surprised by the trade but explained that it was "a good shock." Not only was he going over to protect "The Great

One," but he'd be paid triple the salary he earned in Boston. Besides, his previous L.A. experiences, as a visiting player, were positive. "I went to L.A. twice before and kind of liked it. When [Gretzky] came in, it was like being in Boston Garden again. It was ridiculous, you couldn't get a ticket. That was a lot of fun; met a lot of good people there."

Coming back to Boston to play the Bruins as a King was a thrill too. "It was exciting as hell. And then parading Gretzky around Boston was fun for my friends 'cause they'd never met him."

Miller didn't harbour any resentment toward his former team, and brawls never threatened to break out with ex-teammates.

"Cam Neely almost knocked me out one day on a check in front of the bench. But he didn't even see me and I didn't see him, he just happened to be standing there when I was going full force. But other than that, we didn't try to hurt each other—there was no reason to," Miller said. "Was it respect? Yeah, but it was more friendship than respect. I mean, we all had respect for each other anyway. Why bother him? Let him play. Unless you're getting killed, then obviously you do something."

Like Montreal against Boston, Edmonton—fittingly, the team that beat his Bruins for the Cup—would become a thorn in his new team's side. Although the Kings managed to beat the Oilers in Miller's first playoffs with L.A. in dramatic fashion—during the spring of '89, the Kings clawed their way back from a three-games-to-one deficit to take the series in seven—Edmonton would win the next three series against Miller and the Kings.

When Barry Melrose took over as L.A. coach, he decided to make changes. Miller, however, had already signed a big contract extension for another three years. "[Owner] Bruce McNall and Wayne Gretzky came into the office, and Gretz stuck up for me and said, 'Pay him.' So they paid me 90% of my contract for three straight years."

Miller said he could have gone to Winnipeg, and he nearly wound up with Boston again, but Sinden didn't believe in double dipping salaries and Miller wouldn't go unless he got a little "extra cheese."

When he retired, Jay Miller said he'd had enough and never looked back. He hardly even plays in old-timer games. The memories seem distant, and one of the few reminders of his playing career is the arthritis in his hands. These days, he's into commercial real estate, and he and his wife own and operate the Courtyard Restaurant and Pub in Cape Cod. When he looks back at his NHL experience, he has no illusions about the role he played: "[Fighting] was my job, plain and simple. I didn't want to score 10 goals a year; I didn't want to have 10 assists. I wanted to be a plus on the plus/minus, and I wanted to make sure when it was my turn to go I was there."

Lyndon Byers

Lyndon Byers was a wide-eyed teenager when he arrived at his first Boston Bruins training camp in 1982.

Dressed in all his gear, he sat quietly in his stall, so excited he felt sick to his stomach while Wayne Cashman smoked a cigarette in his underwear and Stan Jonathan got dressed. A half hour before everyone was supposed to head out on the ice, out comes the coach—retired Bruins ace goalie Gerry Cheevers—casually asking if anyone's been out for a skate. The veterans replied in the negative; the rookies kept their mouths shut.

"He said, 'Well, I don't want anybody pulling a hamstring, so put some sweats on and go for a twirl for half an hour and I think we're good.' And a bunch of us rookies were fully dressed, ready for bear," said Byers. "It was a little weird, a little different, but you were in awe all the same."

Returning to the WHL's Regina Pats, Byers got a chance to grow a little more as a player. Recording consecutive 32-goal seasons and making Team Canada for the 1984 World Junior Championship, he earned a 10-game stint with the Bruins and, not quite as intimidated, he came through with six points and 32 penalty minutes.

Things started well for the rookie in the fall of '84, when he finally made the team. "Geoff Courtnall and Tommy Fergus were having an incredibly great year. I think we were the second line to Barry Pederson and Nifty [Rick] Middleton in '84 and I had eight points in 11 games," Byers said.

Byers had a ball playing for coach Cheevers, who took his young charges under his wing, even lending them money to tide them over on road trips. "It was awesome. Cheesy was the greatest guy ever," Byers gushed. "As a youngster, you never had so much money in your life, so you blow your per diem in two days and have nothing left. And I think Cheesy never had less than ten grand on him, so if you needed to borrow some dough, Cheesy was good for it. But you had to pay it back, otherwise you'd never see the ice."

The highs ended up being too high. After hurting his knee, Byers "proceeded to party myself out of a job. I was a young guy and the city of Boston, it's a great city to be young and a Bruin and I took full advantage of it."

Byers looks back at that time with some regret because Cashman, who'd retired, bestowed his No. 12 upon the young up-and-comer.

"I always respected and loved the fact that he cared about me enough to pass on No. 12, and I've never been more disappointed in myself because I basically partied myself out of the jersey and off the Boston Bruins."

The following season was a wash as the Bruins demoted him after another knee injury. To send him a message, the Bruins shipped Byers first to Moncton in the AHL and then to Milwaukee of the IHL. But a broken wrist would cut short his tour of the minors. His career was on life support until Terry O'Reilly arrived and took over Boston's coaching reins.

"I came back, had a pretty good camp, got sent down and I was gonna quit hockey. But Butch Goring got fired and Terry O'Reilly took over, so I said I'm gonna fight the three toughest guys on the team for the next 10 games and if I don't get called up, I'm gonna quit hockey," Byers remembered. "And the third game into my mission, Terry O'Reilly called me up and I was lucky enough to have a great career with great players and more importantly, lucky enough to be coached by the legend, Terry O'Reilly, who is probably one of the most underrated superstars that ever played the game. No superstar that led a team in scoring took the punishment he took. He's a man among boys."

Under O'Reilly, Byers would enjoy his best professional year, scoring 10 goals and 24 points in 53 games while playing on a fourth line with Jay Miller and Bill O'Dwyer in 1987–88.

"I don't think there were three guys who had more fun in pro hockey than we did, playing under Terry O'Reilly," said Byers. "There wasn't a player that didn't flourish under Terry O'Reilly. The guy's an amazing person and amazing coach, and he expected out of you what he expected out of himself—and that was about 1000%."

The Bruins made it all the way to the Stanley Cup Final that season, and Miller and Byers led the team in regular season penalties. Byers was happy to have a heavyweight on his line. "I was a wet rat at 210 pounds so I'd fight, but I was lucky enough to have a Jay Miller at my side," Byers said. "We'd be on the bench, and Billy O'Dwyer and Jay and I'd be up, and Jay'd always ask, 'Well, who do you want?' 'Well, I'm not stupid,' I'd say, 'I want the lesser tougher guy than you're gonna fight.' And Jay always stepped up to take the heavyweights. So it wasn't very often that I had to fight a Brownie, a Probie, a Knuckles Nilan."

Not that Byers didn't have run-ins with Nilan, who played for Boston's historic rivals in Montreal. In fact, they squared up during Byers's first training camp in an exhibition game at Boston Garden.

"I gave it to him pretty good, but there was nobody better than Nilan. He was 6-foot-1, 200 pounds, and he answered the bell all day long . . . he was as tough as they come. He was the Montreal Canadiens heavyweight and he was potting 20 goals. That's pretty scary if you ask me."

That rivalry with Montreal would stay with Byers to this day: "I'm 47 years old and I could punch P.K. Subban's lights out tomorrow, to put it in perspective. It never goes away; it never goes away for them, and it never goes away for us."

Jay Miller also had a long-running feud with Montreal, in particular John Kordic, which helped take some of the pressure off Byers. "[Kordic] was as tough as they got. He used to pound me pretty good; I didn't play lefties very well," Byers said. "I got better each time I fought him, but he was awesome. I saw him fight Jay Miller many, many times and I don't think there were any better rivals."

But about halfway through the next season, Byers lost his fellow gunslinger as Miller got shipped to Los Angeles. The chances of the two of them clashing, though, were slim. "There was only one guy I would never fight and that would be Jay Miller. He was my roommate for a long, long time. . . . He'd kick my ass anyway, so I didn't want the beating from a buddy."

Miller, however, wasn't so sure that under the right circumstances, something couldn't have happened: "He says to this day that he would have never even tried but I tend to disagree. I mean, I wouldn't have, but if the time and the place warranted, I'm sure."

Byers agreed but with one caveat: With the Stanley Cup on the line, anything could happen. "Hockey players are a different breed, and if it came down to winning a Stanley Cup and you had to fight your brother, I know every hockey player would say they'd beat their brother's ass and let him drink out of the Cup afterwards," Byers said.

Injuries would eventually limit Byers's playing time—the worst one being the broken neck and back he suffered in a freakish mishap.

"I broke my L1, 2, 3, in Quebec when I got hit by Normand Rochefort. . . . We were going on a two-on-one, I gave the puck to Ray Bourque and Rochefort finished his check. I thought I was just at the glass, but it wasn't there and I hit the stanchion and snapped all three vertebrae in my back."

His contract up, Byers and his agent went to see the then-GM,

Mike Milbury. "He said I'd never play another game for the Boston Bruins," Byers recalled. The assignment would be Providence for the whole season or free agency. Milbury gave them five minutes to talk about it and left the room. "We chose to be a free agent and I ended up in San Jose, which was a lot of fun, a great bunch of guys," he said of his 18 games in northern California.

"But now that I look back on it, it was probably one of the worst decisions I made. I probably should have went to Providence, straightened out my attitude, and probably could have played for the Boston Bruins for a few more years."

Byers, however, holds no ill will toward Milbury, comparing him to O'Reilly. "I think the two things that both of those guys share is they were very up front and honest and in your face. They didn't beat around the bush, and I think players respected that. If you were playing like horseshit, they'd have no problem telling you," Byers said. "Coaching is something I don't think I could ever do. It's a 20-person babysitting job, so you gotta rub one guy's back, yell at another guy, leave one guy alone. You've got to be a pretty talented person to be an NHL coach or a head coach in any pro sports."

Byers remains a massive Bruins booster and may have been the most visible alumni during Boston's 2011 championship run. He also still has fun at his day job, which is on the *Hill-Man Morning Show* on Boston's WAAF radio. "I'm lazy and I yap off. I got really lucky. I had a friend named Greg Hill who had his own radio show on WAAF," Byers explained about his transition to the airwaves.

For him, the best part of the job is knowing he's entertaining hard-working Bostonians who commute a couple hours every day and have kids to look after. "If I can make them laugh and they're standing around the water cooler at noon talking about or laughing about something that we talked about or something I did, then I've got them halfway through their day and helped them out and I take pride in that."

Bruins fan Denis Leary also threw Byers a bone, putting him, as well as Cam Neely, on his TV show *Rescue Me*. Byers wryly observed that, suspiciously, every time they appeared, the script called for Leary to beat both men up.

"I'm really, really thankful I've been in Boston for the better part of 30 years and I haven't worked a day in my life. I don't take it for granted and I try to give back as much as I can," Byers said. "My life has been a gift, that's for sure."

TIGER WILLIAMS & DAN MALONEY, TORONTO MAPLE LEAFS

Tiger Williams "Tiger marched to the beat of a different drummer, there is no doubt about it." These are the words of Bruce Hood, one of the countless referees who escorted David James "Tiger" Williams to the penalty box.

It's a safe bet that few would disagree with Hood's assessment of the NHL's most penalized player in history: Tiger earned his nickname, accumulating 3,966 regular season PIM and another 455 in the playoffs over his NHL career.

Williams seemed to be just what the Toronto Maple Leafs needed in the brawl-heavy 1970s. In three years with the WHL's Swift Current Broncos, Williams racked up nearly 900 penalty minutes in 202 games. Scoring 52 goals in his final year of junior was the ultimate bonus, and Williams was scooped up by a Leafs team in need of toughness. He made an immediate impression.

"I first met Tiger when I arrived at training camp in my second season. Walking into the Gardens, I noticed an odd character in front of me with boxing gloves dangling from his shoulders. I next saw him in the dressing room, and he was still carrying the gloves," Borje Salming reminisced in his hockey memoir, *Blood, Sweat and Hockey*.

But after hyping himself up to management, teammates, and the media, Williams seemed more like a paper tiger, as he struggled not only to keep up with the fast pace of the pros but also to match their toughness. After losing a fight to Keith Magnusson in the fall of 1974, he was sent down to Oklahoma of the CHL. Battered but not broken,

Williams did his time in the minors and eventually returned to the Leafs to play 42 games. He never looked back.

"We certainly needed him. During the '70s, successful teams needed one or two good fighters, if only for self-defence. Tiger was a master at his craft," said Salming. "He wasn't the biggest or the strongest fighter in the league, but he had more guts and heart than any fighter I've known. He'd get knocked down and, even if a couple of players tried to pin him, he'd struggle back to his feet, shake himself off, and continue the battle."

Williams could be counted among just a handful of players who actually looked forward to playing the Flyers in Philadelphia.

"There's no doubt a lot of guys suffered on the way to the ice at the Spectrum," Williams wrote in *Tiger: A Hockey Story*. "The Broad Street thing got to them before they even laced up their skates. But it never affected me like that. Before the game, I was ready to fly, even though I probably hadn't slept much the night before. My bed used to be soaked in sweat. I went out wanting everybody to pick a fight with me: Dave Schultz, Moose Dupont, Bobby Clarke. My reasoning was that if you could do it there, you didn't have to do it so much anywhere else."

"Tiger was very competitive, a positive player; he went into any hockey rink and his style of play wouldn't change—he had a lot of desire," said Wilf Paiement. "It didn't matter if he was in Philly, Boston or Montreal, the competition came out of him. He played as hard as he could and did whatever he had to do. . . . These are the players you want to go to battle with. Very, very big part of any team that he played on."

Aside from his physicality, Salming also believed Williams was a good player, taking what limited abilities he had and striving to make the most of them. "When he first joined us in the 1974–75 season, he was a poor skater. But he persevered and stayed after practice for extra skating drills. He took power-skating lessons and even dabbled in figure skating to improve his balance," Salming explained.

Also impressed with Williams was Leafs captain Darryl Sittler, who watched him blossom as a player and achieve more than what his natural hockey abilities should have allowed. Williams practiced full out, and his conditioning and intensity were his greatest strengths, according to Sittler.

"When Tiger broke into the league, he fought all the heavyweights, making his presence felt. Looking back at him then, I would have predicted a career of five or six years," Sittler said in his eponymous memoir, adding "Seeing him play 14 years, and developing his talent the way he did, was quite an inspiration."

With the Leafs, Williams essentially became Toronto's version of John Ferguson, who earned notoriety for straightening out teammates he believed weren't taking the game seriously enough.

"With me, anyone else had to hate to lose. . . . A pro was supposed to do one thing and that was win," said Ferguson.

Ferguson's mindset fit Williams to a tee.

"Teammates knew they couldn't pull anything over on him. If you were dogging it in practice or a game, you could expect to get it from Tiger," Sittler said.

Despite becoming a favourite of fans and owner Harold Ballard, Williams would fall victim to general manager Punch Imlach's housecleaning in the late 1970s. Shipped to the west coast, Williams joined a struggling Canucks franchise that was long on imported talent but short on guts. He helped change that in a hurry and brought a new-found spirit to the team that would eventually culminate in a run all the way to the Stanley Cup Final.

"He's gotta be the league's most valuable player," Ferguson, then–Winnipeg Jets general manager, told the *Winnipeg Free Press* after watching his club get trounced by the Williams-led Canucks.

That was in 1980–81, the year Williams led Vancouver in goals with 35 and penalty minutes with a whopping 343.

Like he had with the Leafs, Williams refused to lie down and lose. During a race for a playoff berth, Williams viciously speared Real Cloutier in a game versus the Quebec Nordiques to ensure a Canucks victory.

"We needed that win very badly," he said in justification in his memoir. "Let's remove the doubt. It isn't pretty, it isn't nice, but I believe it's my function."

Williams seemed to come from another era, like the turn of the twentieth century, when players routinely brawled and exchanged stick blows.

He had a memorable stick fight with Dave Hutchison in Los Angeles while still a Leaf, and he was put on trial by Ontario Attorney General Roy McMurtry in 1977 for hitting Pittsburgh Penguin Dennis Owchar on the head with his stick. His foul on Owchar opened a wound that required 46 stitches to close, but as far as Williams was concerned, it was accidental and far less serious than other encounters he'd been involved in. And in Vancouver, when he'd heard enough of Scotty Bowman's taunts to another Canuck, Williams raised his stick once more and silenced the Sabres coach with a blow to the side of his head.

"I don't recognize the term *policeman* as it is applied to those players who have to inject some toughness into their teams. A policeman should be a peacemaker. I've never wanted to be a peace-maker," Williams said, rejecting the notion of a fair fight. "Someone should have the advantage and he should be using it. The guy who wants it to be fair should look at himself in the mirror and ask himself if he's in the right business."

"He hated losing, really despised what that represented," Canucks teammate Darcy Rota said in the commemorative book *Canucks at 40*. "He changed the complexion of our team. Winning was every-thing to Tiger. He would battle or fight anybody. There were no shortcuts. He wanted to win so badly."

Williams believed everyone on his team should be willing to die to win and expected no less. Given his roots, it's not surprising. Tiger and his brothers followed in the footsteps of their father, Taffy, a Welsh immigrant who settled in Weyburn, Saskatchewan. An ex-army man and willing scrapper, Taffy set the pattern and reputation of his family. Taffy occasionally drove the bus for Tiger's team to small towns in the chill of the blasting cold of Saskatchewan winters. If they dared lose, he refused to turn on the heater for the trip home. As a pro assessing his performance, Williams needed only to think of what his father would say to know how he'd done.

While certainly among the most driven and ruthless NHLers of all time, there was another side to Williams too.

After spilling blood against Bob Gassoff for years, Williams went out of his way to comfort Gassoff's family following Bob's untimely and tragic death. Before the Leafs were scheduled to take on the Blues in St. Louis, Williams skated over to Gassoff's widow and son. After chatting a while, he took the child in his arms and skated around the rink his father had played on.

Tough guys probably lead the way in giving back to their communities, and Williams was among those at the forefront, with an especially big place in his heart for disadvantaged kids. In Toronto, he often visited the Hospital for Sick Children.

"I never turned down a request to do something for those kids. And when I went down there, I wouldn't just walk down a few wards with some dingy nurse. It would irritate the hell out of me when some other guys did that: just whisk through the place, say 'Hi,' and then piss off in their flash cars," Williams said.

Referee Bruce Hood, who vehemently disliked the "goons" of the '70s, worked with Williams at the Special Olympics in Calgary in 1987 and was highly impressed with what he saw. "He was coaching a team in the floor hockey division and his enthusiasm rubbed off on the players. He had them bouncing all the time, and it was great to see," Hood said in his memoir.

Even while down on his luck, Williams would take time out to help the helpless. One March morning in 1985, Williams was headed out of Detroit, on his way to an uncertain hockey future with the Red Wings' farm team in upstate New York. Driving in the other direction was teammate Colin Campbell, who heard the squeal of brakes. He looked over the median and saw Williams rescue a wandering dog from oncoming traffic.

"I thought, 'There's Tiger being a hero again, rescuing another dog; but he's gone now, and who's going to rescue Tiger?'"

Of course, Williams managed just fine, revitalizing his career with the Los Angeles Kings—he gave the Kings' announcer Bob Miller a copy of his autobiography inscribed "Dear Bob, now you have to like me"—before finishing his NHL days in Hartford. In retirement, Williams wrote a cookbook before taking his determined attitude into Canada's oil patch. When not engaged in one of his numerous business ventures, Williams continues to give his time to various charitable endeavours and still puts on the skates to the delight of fans.

Dan Maloney
Though he often found himself on solid teams, Dan Maloney missed winning a championship, as dynastic juggernauts barred the path. The native of Barrie, Ontario, played two seasons with the London Knights of the Ontario Hockey Association during the same period the Montreal Junior Canadiens powerhouse teams were blowing away the opposition.

"We were a good team, but the Montreal Junior Canadiens at that time—their starting line up was [Réjean] Houle, [Marc] Tardif, and [Gilbert] Perreault," Maloney said. Those Canadiens teams won 37 out of 54 games in each of the 1968–69 and 1969–70 seasons on their way to back-to-back Memorial Cups.

In Maloney's final junior year, he chipped in with 31 goals and 232 PIM in 54 games while often lining up with future Leafs teammate and Hall of Famer Darryl Sittler. "Getting to play with Darryl was a great honour; he was the captain of our team and he was definitely a blue-chip hockey player," Maloney said. That last year was good enough to get him selected 14th overall by the Chicago Black Hawks in the 1970 NHL draft. His rookie season with the Hawks couldn't have been much better as Chicago earned a club-record 49 wins and reached the Stanley Cup Final. But awaiting them were the Montreal Canadiens. Maloney would come tantalizingly close to grasping hockey's ultimate prize.

"We had them down 2-0 in Game 7, and it was about five minutes to go [in the second period]. I'll never forget it as long as I live," Maloney said. "It was the third week of May and it was terribly, terribly hot, and I remember Jacques Lemaire got over the red line and he just let one go, and the thing kind of went like a Frisbee and skipped over Tony's [Esposito] shoulder, and that was the start. After that, Henri Richard got two."

The Habs won their third Cup in four years. The next season, instead of avenging the loss with his teammates, Maloney was toiling with the minor league Dallas Black Hawks. He returned to Chicago for the 1972–73 season but wouldn't finish the year in the Windy City. Maloney had been playing on a line with Stan Mikita and Cliff Koroll, but when Mikita broke his heel, the Hawks looked for a replacement. They found one in Los Angeles, and Maloney was shipped off to the Kings in exchange for Ralph Backstrom.

In California, Maloney's game blossomed. Besides becoming known as the league's best fighter, the 6-foot-1, 195-pound "Dangerous" Dan also put points on the board, scoring a career high of 27 goals and 66 points in 1974–75.

"We chased the Montreal Canadiens that year. We were, believe it or not, in a division with them. They had 113 points; we had 105. We had Butchie Goring and a bunch of guys that were good solid players and Rogie [Vachon] in net, so we were a pretty good team."

Kings coach Bob Pulford also deserved a good part of the credit for the team's success, Maloney believes. "He definitely was a man's man and a very fair coach. He was one of those guys if you're playing well, you got more ice time. He just expected you to go out there and do what you do best and play as hard as you can," Maloney said. "That little team we had in L.A., we did things that people didn't think we were capable of doing, and you attribute that to hard work, but you've gotta give the coach a hell of a lot of credit too."

Unfortunately for Maloney, his best year with the team would also be his last with them.

When Kings owner Jack Kent Cooke signed free agent Marcel Dionne from Detroit, he paid a high price, losing Maloney and defenceman Terry Harper as compensation. Pulford would call losing Maloney a big blow to the Kings, as he was a valued leader and respected player.

Maloney admitted feeling disappointment about leaving L.A., having bought a home there eight months previously and envisioning success for the club in the years to come.

"But Marcel wanted out of Detroit real bad and L.A. had the opportunity to get one hell of a hockey player, so they jumped on it and Harp [Terry Harper] and I had to leave," he said.

Maloney joined a team in turmoil. The Red Wings at the time were much weaker than the Kings and were ridiculed as "The Dead Things."

"He had problems when he went from Los Angeles to Detroit, problems similar to the ones I experienced on the move from Toronto to Vancouver. He hated floaters," said Tiger Williams in his book, *Tiger: A Hockey Story*.

And yet somehow Maloney managed to repeat his previous season's personal best, scoring the same totals exactly, with another 27 goals and 66 points. His scoring exploits, however, in no way reflected the skating prowess of the man nicknamed "Snowshoes."

Journeyman Blair Stewart credited Maloney's points to stationing himself in front of the net. "He was big and you don't want to piss him off. If you're a defenceman, you kind of let him stand around and have two or three whacks at the puck," said Stewart.

"He had that look about him. Dan had that fire in his eye every shift," said play caller Jiggs McDonald. "It was like, 'Don't come near me. You'll be dead meat.' He was just a tough, tough guy to play against."

Maloney thrived with Walt McKechnie at centre and Dennis Polonich on right wing.

"He was a tough hombre. He had the long arms and the real

intense look. I loved playing with him," said Polonich. "All of us had our most successful seasons when we played together.... The points are one thing, but we were tough to play against.... We had a tough line and McKechnie was the guy with the puck."

Dennis Hextall, also with the Wings, admired Maloney for his hard work and toughness.

"Danny protected anybody on his team," Hextall said, adding Maloney played his game anywhere in the league. "There was no Philadelphia Flu running around with Danny Maloney."

"There's a quiet, quiet unsung hero," Bruin John Wensink said. "He was a player that, if you weren't prepared, he was going to hurt you."

It may have been this reputation that, combined with an on-ice breach, landed Maloney in legal hot water. The night after a November 1975 game in Toronto, Maloney became the first to experience Ontario Attorney General Roy McMurtry's crackdown against hockey violence when he was charged with assault causing bodily harm following a fight against Maple Leaf Brian Glennie. A big hit Glennie had laid on Hextall drew Maloney, and he pounced on the Leaf from behind. After Glennie was down, it appeared as though Maloney repeatedly picked him up and slammed him to the ice. Maloney received a five-minute major and the NHL later said it planned no further disciplinary action. Glennie spent the night in hospital and sustained a mild concussion.

At the time, Maloney claimed he wasn't deliberately trying to hurt Glennie—that Glennie kept falling and that he was trying to pick him up. Tiger Williams offered a scathing indictment, not against Maloney, but his teammate.

"Glennie faked unconsciousness. I know, I was there," Williams said in his book. "There was no doubt that Maloney was very anxious to beat the crap out of Glennie, but whenever he tried to haul him up from the ice, Glennie slipped back down as Maloney kept losing his grip on the sweater. In court they said that Maloney had been banging Glennie's head on the ice, right up to the point of unconsciousness. It wasn't so. I saw everything that happened. There were no marks on Glennie. When he refused to go to court for Maloney's trial, I wasn't surprised."

Maloney was eventually acquitted of the charges and, ironically, Toronto came calling for his services when they felt they needed more toughness. GM Ted Lindsay, a legendary rough, tough leader in his own right during his playing days, named Maloney captain of the Red Wings in the summer of 1977 and in 1977–78, the Red Wings started playing some decent hockey. But when the Leafs came calling and Lindsay was able to exact a stiff price—namely scoring winger Errol Thompson and *three* draft picks, a couple of first-rounders and a second—McMurtry's one-time public enemy number one was on his way over the Detroit River to play for the Blue and White.

The second irony was that the first player who greeted Maloney on his initial foray into the Maple Leaf dressing room was Glennie.

"I sat right beside him and Mike Pelyk. I got along good with Brian," Maloney said.

Williams for one saw the advantages of the acquisition of Maloney, seeing in him someone like himself, a player with an untiring and determined desire to succeed.

"Danny Maloney didn't have great talent, but he had a great will, a great intensity," said Williams. "I don't think I've ever met any-body in the game who wanted to win more than Maloney did. He didn't believe in compromises, on or off the ice. He had his own philosophy, and you couldn't budge him with an elephant gun. He's my kind of guy."

Lanny McDonald too was happy to have Maloney on his side, pointing out he was difficult to play against when he was in Detroit. "As tough a player as has ever played the game, and no one worked harder than he did," McDonald said in his memoir *Lanny*.

His old London linemate Darryl Sittler said the whole team grew a few inches taller thanks to their newly acquired teammate. "As a player, you want to have tough guys on your team," he explained in

Sittler. "The day after the Maloney trade was announced, our guys practically sang and danced their way through practice. Maloney's arrival meant we could do a lot of things in the playoffs, given the right circumstances."

But the media complained—some still to this day—that the Maple Leafs paid way too high a price. The critics must have felt vindicated when the Leafs went on a tailspin immediately after Maloney's arrival. But it was in the playoffs that the deal paid dividends. There, the Leafs advanced all the way to the third round, zipping past the Kings and upsetting the Islanders in seven games—despite the loss of all-world defenceman Borje Salming to injury—before bowing out to the mighty Canadiens.

"People like Maloney, McDonald, Williams and [Jerry] Butler pounded the boards and the Islanders at every opportunity and they proved to be the team that flinched," said Sittler.

"The Islanders were a real up-and-coming young team and we were lucky enough to knock them off," said Maloney. "But the problem we always ran into is we always ended up having to play Montreal before we could advance to the Finals. Back in those days, they were a heck of a team."

Like many Leafs from that period, Maloney believed Toronto was only a couple of key players away from winning it all.

"There was no doubt in my mind because we had one hell of a defence. We had a real good, solid team. We just needed another goal scorer or two; we had to rely pretty heavily on Darryl and Lanny to fill the net for us. One more real good goal scoring forward or two would have gone a hell of a long ways, it really would have."

But Thompson was just such a goal scorer, and he'd been traded away. His friend, Leaf Kurt Walker, wondered if it was the right deal to make. But at the time, owner Harold Ballard wanted Maloney, and it was Maloney the Leafs would get.

"Errol could score goals and he could skate, and Danny was more of the [Terry] O'Reilly type," said Walker. "It's always nice to have an additional tough guy on the team, but at the time, there was Tiger and myself, and we pretty much had things in check, to the best of our ability."

Like Sittler, McDonald, and Williams, Maloney sang the praises of coach Roger Neilson, whom he considered a great asset for the team.

"Roger was definitely an innovator. He was the first guy to use the video replay, and Roger was probably one of the hardest working men in the game I'd ever seen in my life. He lived at the building, he really did," Maloney said. "And we were always in peak shape, which was a tribute to good coaching."

After owner Harold Ballard let Neilson go, he replaced him with '60s Leafs bench boss Punch Imlach, and Toronto took a major step backward.

"When Punch came in, all of a sudden all of the [Alan] Eagleson clients were being traded away, except for Darryl; he had a no-trade [contract clause]. It really was a big change because some of the guys we lost were pretty good hockey players," said Maloney. "It's not to say Punch didn't make a couple good deals because he certainly did, but it was a huge change in a very short period of time."

One of the players traded was McDonald, Sittler's best friend. Wilf Paiement came back in return and said he was pleased to finally be playing with Maloney instead of against him.

"What a competitor Dan Maloney was. He gave me a lot of nightmares when he played in Detroit and Los Angeles. All of a sudden you play with him, that was pretty nice," Paiement said.

Maloney's final season came in 1981–82, during which time the Leafs and most of the league went into a nearly full-scale youth moment and phased out a lot of players that still had some hockey left in them. Maloney often found himself sitting in the press box as a scratch, and when the club asked if he'd be interested in becoming an assistant coach, he went for it. "I joined the coaching ranks there and was an assistant coach with Mike Nykoluk and we started building through the draft and were able to start with [Wendel]

Clark, [Russ] Courtnall, [Gary] Leeman, [Al] Iafrate, [Bob] McGill, [Gary] Nylund and guys like that, so we started to build again."

What sticks out in most fans' memories are the horrendous seasons suffered by the Leafs of the 1980s, and they often overlook the fact that some players drafted by the club turned out to be excellent pros, albeit not always with the Leafs.

Maloney enjoyed only a brief taste of success with Toronto as a coach. Despite a terrible regular season showing of only 57 points in 1985–86, the Leafs somehow managed to come alive in the playoffs, sweeping the favoured Chicago Black Hawks and taking the St. Louis Blues to seven games. But when Leafs general manager Gerry McNamara only offered him a one-year contract extension at the same salary, Maloney walked away.

Just two days out of hockey, the Winnipeg Jets called.

"We had a real good strong young team that was on the upswing;" he said. "I get to Winnipeg and there was a pretty talented group of guys there too—[Dale] Hawerchuk, Thomas Steen and Randy Carlyle, and a bunch of guys who played very, very well for me."

Winnipeg's biggest disadvantage was the division in which it played. The Smythe Division couldn't have contrasted much more from the perennially weak Norris, as it was home to two of the most dominant teams in the league. Over one 10-year period, the Edmonton Oilers and Calgary Flames either won the Stanley Cup or reached the finals eight times. Still, Maloney did lead the original NHL Jets to one of their only two playoff series victories *ever*, with a defeat of heavily favoured Calgary—Cup finalists the year before—in 1987.

"Competition was tough. But it was good. I enjoyed my time there . . . wasn't wild about the weather, but I sure did love the people. They were great."

When the Jets lurched to a horrendous start from which they never recovered in the 1988–89 season, Maloney found himself out of a job four months after GM John Ferguson was sacked.

Dan Maloney stayed out of hockey until 1992–93, when Neilson, his old coach who was then behind the New York Rangers bench, asked if he'd act as his assistant. "Roger gave me a call to come back and give him a hand so I went back," said Maloney, now a real estate agent. "But it was like that old saying, you just can't go back home, you know what I mean? You're on your way and keep moving."

STU GRIMSON & TODD EWEN, MIGHTY DUCKS OF ANAHEIM

Stu Grimson "There's Grimson trying to get loose and now he's gone crazy! This is a man gone mad!"—that was the call from TSN's Jim Hughson at Chicago Stadium on January 16, 1992.

With 3:46 remaining in the third period and Chicago leading in a lopsided 4-0 game against the Toronto Maple Leafs, Blackhawk Steve Larmer blocked a shot in his zone and lay on the puck. In came Wendel Clark, who tried to dislodge the puck from under Larmer but ended up spearing him in the belly instead. Bryan Marchment stopped to intervene, and Clark pushed him off with a cross-check. A full-scale line brawl got underway, with Steve Smith jumping Clark and Grimson trying to get at him as well.

But bigger things were to come.

Referee Dan Marouelli pulled Grimson out of the pile, but he continued to hover to watch over the proceedings. The two struggled until Grimson was free of his shoulder and elbow pads and sweater. Eventually he was pulled to his bench, where coach Mike Keenan held onto him while Marouelli returned to break up the simmering action before it broke out into a riot.

While at the bench, Grimson spotted Bob Halkidis of the Leafs jockeying with Marchment. Ordinarily, Marchment was perfectly capable of handling his own business. But that night, Marchment was wearing a full-face shield to protect a broken cheekbone.

"As I was being escorted off the ice, I motioned over to Halkidis and said, 'Don't get into it with Marchment,' trying to communicate this guy's vulnerable. Well, that was like an invitation to him—he ended up pulling Marchment's helmet off and he started throwing punches," Grimson said.

Grimson broke free of Keenan and charged across the ice to get at Halkidis, swinging at whoever got in his way before diminutive Leafs star centre Doug Gilmour tackled him to the ground.

"I never got there; I was intercepted by the ref and a bunch of Maple Leafs and I think by a couple linesmen in the process. It was really just me looking chaotic and creating a whole lot of mayhem," explained Grimson. "The short answer? The wires touched."

Grimson was automatically suspended after the game for abuse of officials, and he received a 10-game ban. "I think ultimately, league discipline thought I'd probably taken some liberties with the ref, which I think is probably accurate."

Paradoxically, the fierce looking 6-foot-5, 230-pound brute nick-named "The Grim Reaper" is anything but. In civilian life, Grimson is a scholarly born-again Christian. But such are the contradictions of the ice hockey enforcer.

Grimson came by his Reaper handle as a junior with the Pats in Regina, Saskatchewan, thanks to his general manager Bob Strumm.

"I have an easier time with it than my mother does," Grimson said.

The Vancouver native, however, didn't have such an easy time with his enforcer role and had serious doubts about whether he wanted to pursue a career in which he'd have to use his fists to succeed. Originally drafted by Detroit in 1983—the same year they chose Steve Yzerman, Bob Probert, and Joey Kocur—he returned to the draft in 1985 after not receiving a contract offer from the Wings. This time Calgary selected him in the eighth round, but Grimson left the Flames training camp over his lingering doubts, and he ended up skating for the University of Manitoba Bisons.

"It's a tough role, a taxing role physically and mentally; it's a hard one to play," Grimson said. "Oftentimes guys that are in that role play maybe three to five minutes a night and then they're asked to—from a cold start—get involved physically, bang somebody or get in a scrap with somebody. It's a tough thing to do. So I was in a place where I was having a hard time playing that role, wasn't sure I saw myself playing that role at the pro level, so it took me some time to come to grips with that."

Ironically, religion helped alleviate the pressure.

"I was at a stage in my life where I was my own worst enemy; I let some of those pressures and anxieties get the best of me, and then it was around that time my faith began to play a more prominent role in my life and it really was a very important change for me, because it made dealing with those pressures and anxieties much easier. I had more peace about what I was doing and how I was doing it."

Grimson doesn't see any contradiction in being a Christian and a fighter, believing what he did on the ice was actually an extension of his faith.

"I used to look around the locker room and think, 'You know what? If somebody needs to play a role protecting and watching out for these smaller, more skilled guys in our locker room, why can't it be someone like me? Why can't it be a Christian?'"Grimson believed that even though the play on the ice can become violent, it takes place within the context of sport and doesn't carry over onto the street.

In 1987, Grimson arrived in Salt Lake City to play for the Flames IHL affiliate. He racked up 268 penalty minutes in 37 games his first season there.

"That was a real tough league back then, and probably a tough era for hockey too. It wasn't hard to rack up a lot of penalty minutes playing that role because we faced a lot of real tough teams," said Grimson, who played two more full seasons with Salt Lake's Golden Eagles, accumulating another 716 penalty minutes in the process. "It was just a tough, tough league, and a great league for me to cut my teeth in."

Calgary put him on waivers at the start of the 1990–91 season, and the Chicago Blackhawks, who had just lost their heavy Wayne Van Dorp, picked him up.

"It ended up being a great fit for me," Grimson said, adding playing in the old Chicago Stadium was one of the brightest spots of his career.

"It was a real small rink, we had teams that were big and strong and built for that rink. It was just an exciting environment to play in," he said. "The fans in Chicago, especially back then, were very much a lunchbox crowd, and it was just a great, great environment. I can't describe how much I enjoyed those three years of my career."

St. Louis Blues rival Kelly Chase remembered Grimson as a big, tough guy who knew his role.

"He would chirp off the bench . . . but he'd go out and go after you too. You had to respect the way he played. He really did do his role very well and, like a lot of us, understood what his role was and fulfilled his obligations when it came to that," Chase said.

Under coach Mike Keenan, the Hawks became a tough, hard-checking, winning club.

"Mike Keenan was probably one of the toughest coaches I ever played for," said Grimson. "He's a demanding guy, a lot of players have a hard time playing for Mike; I got along with him pretty well. I did my job and I think he respected that. We won when I played for him so I enjoyed my time with Mike."

Keenan helped lead the Hawks to the 1992 Stanley Cup Final, where they fell to Mario Lemieux and the powerhouse Pittsburgh Penguins, who won their second straight Cup.

"I regret that we weren't able to get the best of the Penguins in '92 and ultimately win the Stanley Cup that year," Grimson lamented. "We had a great run getting there, we really did. We had a great team, and I really thought we were capable of going the distance. But I will say this, it was a fun run, it was among the most exciting times in my career without question."

After another season in Chicago, Grimson was claimed in the

June 1993 expansion draft by the Mighty Ducks of Anaheim. It was a major transition, going from an established top team to a club just starting out and stocked with a collection of third- and fourth-line cast-offs from around the league.

"That was an interesting start; '93 was the first year of the Mighty Ducks, and it was kind of cool to be a part of that," said Grimson. "For a lot of us, and certainly this is true for me, it was a great opportunity because I got a lot more playing time and leadership responsibilities. . . . It was a great move for me [and] I really did enjoy my time in Anaheim."

Coach Ron Wilson clearly appreciated tough players, naming Grimson and Todd Ewen assistant captains and former Penguins tough-guy Troy Loney captain. In a TV interview, he called Grimson and Ewen the team's "nuclear deterrents."

"It doesn't mean you have to push the button and fire them off, but when other teams are considering damaging action against you, they get to look over and see the two missile silos," he added in the interview.

"The one thing the organization really made part of its focus was they weren't going to get pushed around; they may not win every game, but if they were going to be competitive, they needed to be physical, and that's the kind of team they built there pretty early on. You don't often see a couple of heavyweights like Grimson and Ewen on the same roster," said Grimson.

The approach worked, as the Ducks tied the Florida Panthers for most wins by an expansion team in its first year, with 33. (Although the Panthers, who started the same season, ended up with 83 points to Anaheim's 71.)

While happy with the team and coach, Grimson pushed for a trade the following season when it looked like he'd have difficulty coming to terms on a new contract. Days before the spring deadline, Grimson got his wish and found himself back in the Red Wings fold.

Detroit won the President's Trophy in that lockout-shortened season for the best regular-season record, and the team marched all the way to the final for the first time since 1966. But they fell short, getting swept by the New Jersey Devils. Nevertheless, Grimson enjoyed the ride and the fact that coach Scotty Bowman played him regularly and relied on him for leadership.

"I think he is probably the best bench boss I've ever played for. He runs a great bench and I've heard many other coaches say he's hard to coach against because he does a lot of things that are very unconventional, and it's hard to predict what Scotty's going to do next," Grimson said.

Grimson would return to Anaheim after spending a couple of seasons with the Hartford/Carolina organization. The Ducks missed a full-time enforcer in 1997–98 after Ken Baumgartner signed with Boston as a free agent. When Paul Kariya was lost for most of that season to a concussion suffered from a cross-check he received to the face, it became obvious the club's stars needed the protection a Grimson could provide.

"Just having him in the line up, the other team knows they can't do any dirty things. Opponents can play hard, they can play tough, but they have to play clean," Anaheim's other scoring ace, Teemu Selanne, told *The Hockey News*.

After a couple more years in Anaheim and another with L.A., Grimson closed out his career as a Nashville Predator, retiring as a result of lingering concussion symptoms. The damage occurred in the second-to-last game of the season against Edmonton during a fight against Georges Laraque.

Still nursing the head injury, Grimson got into it again the following game with another very hard hitter, Sandy McCarthy of the Rangers. "I guess discretion was not the better part of valor on that occasion," Grimson admitted.

That proved to be his last game. Unable to shake the after-effects, he officially called it a career in 2003. It took about a year and a half before Grimson felt like himself and was able to work out and get above a resting heart rate without experiencing symptoms like pressure in his head and nausea.

After dressing for 729 regular-season NHL games, Grimson returned to school, finishing the economics degree he'd started at the U of M.

"I kept up my undergraduate studies early in my pro career; I had whittled down my undergraduate to the point where I had about a year left. So I finished that off, and went to law school at the University of Memphis."

Grimson said he picked law because a number of former players had pursued that path and had gone on to exciting jobs, like Ken Dryden, who became general manager and president of the Leafs before turning to politics, and Mike Liut, who became an agent. Ultimately, Grimson worked for the NHL Players' Association as in-house counsel before moving back to Tennessee, where he practised civil litigation and family law.

He has also served as a colour analyst on the Predators Radio Network, and 2012–13 marked his first full-time season with the Predators broadcast team.

Looking back and weighing his hockey career, Grimson stresses the positives.

"I always felt like I had the appreciation of my teammates and, whether it was a tap on the pads or just a quick phrase they uttered during the course of the game as they were dropping off my gloves at the penalty box, they always affirmed me for playing that role, because I think they recognized how challenging a role it is to play. Somehow, that made it worthwhile."

Todd Ewen If anyone knows there's little glamour and a lot of sacrifice in becoming an enforcer, it's Todd Ewen. While competing for a WHL job in Kamloops, British Columbia, Ewen's jersey got soaked in his best friend's blood after he beat him up.

"It's tough when you have to punch a friend in the head; it takes a different mindset," said Ewen. "But if there's that honour code involved . . . at the end, whatever happens, happens. I've always been confident in the fact that I was doing it for the right reasons. I wasn't out there just to jump on and pound people."

Saskatoon's Ewen would make his bones further west with the New Westminster Bruins, a tough team on which he assumed a fighting role alongside Craig Berube, Darwin McPherson, Mike MacWilliam and a host of others. "The game at that time [was] very rough and aggressive," Ewen noted.

But the Edmonton Oilers, who'd drafted Ewen, wanted to see Ewen's role expand beyond mayhem and told coach Ernie "Punch" McLean the same.

"[Oilers chief scout] Barry Fraser saw that I had over 200 minutes in penalties and six points by Christmas, and then he had a talk with Ernie and said, 'If the kid doesn't start playing with the puck, get rid of him.'"

Ewen ended his last junior season with over 50 points and was named most improved player in WHL, saying "It was a great end to my junior career."

No matter what anyone said, fighting was always expected of him. When Ewen was loaned to the Maine Mariners of the AHL for the playoffs during his final year of junior, he ended up centring a line with notorious brawlers Archie Henderson and Mitch Wilson. Ewen compared it to the movie *Slap Shot*.

"The puck dropped and so did the gloves. It was interesting. Archie is quite the character—tough as nails, big guy. And Mitch is just an all-around tough kid, not very big but he can throw with the best of them," Ewen said. "I don't think we even got a shot on goal or went into the [offensive] zone. Pretty much just dropped the puck and started swinging."

The Oilers traded Ewen to the St. Louis Blues, which would spark a long-running series of fights between Ewen and Bob

Probert. Their first tilt occurred on January 24, 1987. It was memorable not only for Ewen's knockout of Probert but for the fact that he had no idea he'd dropped the league's top heavyweight.

"I was never one of those guys who had 5,000 tapes to study the fighters," Ewen said, explaining he only found out whom he'd gone up against when his brother told him. "I said, 'Hey, I fought this guy,' and he asks, 'What's his name?' and I said 'Bob Probert or something like that,' and he goes 'Oh my God!' and tells me who he is."

After the knockout, Probert came back the same game looking for revenge, and the two engaged in a long, classic tilt.

"It was a great introduction to the NHL, because to just know how long these guys can fight, how tough they are, to be able to have two fights in the same night with Bob was just a tribute," Ewen said.

Ewen remained a Blue until 1989–90, when the team brought in a handful of gladiators to compete for his position. The 6-foot-2, 220-pound Ewen saw the writing on the wall.

In training camp, we had me on one team and on the other team, they had Kelly Chase, Tony Twist, Darwin McPherson, Craig Coxe and Herb Raglan. And [GM] Ron Caron had gone in the room and said, 'Anybody that beats up Todd gets their job.' Well, I had 12 fights in training camp. My hands were hamburger; it was awful. I couldn't believe that after having the great fights with Probert and coming through for them, that that's the way they wanted to treat my position.

Ewen was traded to the Montreal Canadiens in 1990, which he had no problem with: "It was fine with me, because I got a Stanley Cup out of it."

The difference in the pressure to win between St. Louis and Montreal was unmistakable: "We won the Stanley Cup and as we're carrying it back, the reporters are asking, 'So will you win next year?' We hadn't even had a chance to celebrate yet and they want to know if we're going to do it again."

As a Hab, Ewen would also run into Twist, one of his Blues training camp rivals who was by then skating for Montreal's top rival, the Quebec Nordiques.

Twist revealed that before one game, Nords owner Marcel Aubut pulled him aside and point blank told him he hated scrappy Canadiens winger Shayne Corson. It didn't take Twist long to decipher what Aubut was hinting at.

"I get skating out after Shayne. He looks at me and says, 'You big goof, I'm not fighting you,'" Twist said. "So I went after Todd. Todd wouldn't fight me but I was playing defence. He came out from behind and tried to sucker me. Well, he hit me on the helmet and I got the best of him in that game for sure. And we always had a running rivalry."

Since then, Twist and Ewen have gone on to coach their sons together: "He was one of the toughest that played, a gentleman through and through and just a great guy," Twist said.

Heading into the 1993 expansion draft, Ewen heard Montreal planned to leave him unprotected. While vacationing in the Bahamas, Ewen called his agent to tell him he'd go anywhere except the Mighty Ducks of Anaheim. The Ducks did not in fact end up drafting Ewen—they traded for him instead.

Upon arriving in Anaheim, coach Ron Wilson reminded Ewen of the time he laid him out while Wilson was still an NHL defenceman. But Wilson didn't hold it against Ewen, naming him an assistant captain. "Ron's a great coach, really knows what he wants; he's very creative in the way he coaches," Ewen said.

The Ducks were fairly successful by expansion standards, which Ewen attributed to the character of the franchise. Many on the roster had become expendable to their previous teams, and it gave them something to prove.

"I think it was just the character, the hunger and the drive of everybody that thought this was their last shot, and it came through in us being very successful."

Ewen appreciated having Stu Grimson, another heavyweight, on his side.

"It was the first time in my [NHL] career I got to share the fighting with somebody. So that was just great to have and understand how it is to work with a teammate in that whole physical aspect. They were a class organization from beginning to end. Other than winning the Stanley Cup, the highlight was playing for them."

Unfortunately for Ewen, his time with Grimson would be short. Grimson was traded to the Detroit Red Wings, and although he lamented the loss of his friend, it didn't stop Ewen from going out and fighting him the next time he faced him.

"When you're traded as much as we are, you always run into a best friend. But you have to do your job," Ewen said.

Going out and getting into a fight was a possibility before every game, and Ewen made sure to prepare himself.

"I'm never really scared of anything that's going to happen. I'm never worried about fighting somebody. I just went out there and did the best I could. I'd know if I gave 100%, I'd do okay. Sometimes you did well; sometimes you did poorly."

The brawls, however, did punish his body, and he recounted the heavy wear and tear he endured: "I have broken every finger in both hands at least twice and stopped counting. I've had sixteen operations. I've got wires in my face, hands, and I've got plates and screws in my knees," said Ewen, adding he endured multiple knee surgeries. Injuries were unavoidable, and one simply had to play through them. "But it was fun," Ewen admitted.

In his final season in the NHL, Ewen was signed by the San Jose Sharks. He tried out for the Phoenix Coyotes the following year, but another knee surgery forced his retirement.

Ewen, like many tough guys, is a study in contrasts. Nicknamed "The Animal," Ewen claimed he's really just "a mean nerd."

"Everybody expects a tough guy to kick open the door, order

raw meat and slap somebody in the head, and that's probably the opposite of who I am," Ewen said.

He always relished his creative side and amazed his Ducks teammates with his hockey-tape sculptures, including one of goalie Guy Hebert's mask: "I think I spent too much time in the penalty box by myself with a roll of tape," he joked.

Ewen also taught himself to play the bass, piano, drums and guitar, and he even authored and illustrated a children's book, titled *A Frog Named Hop*.

"That came around because I wanted to do something for the D.A.R.E. [Drug Abuse Resistance Education] program . . . I was a contradiction of stereotypes and that's kind of the theme of the story, that just because you're different, doesn't mean that you can't make something of yourself. So the kids that we see that fall in the wrong direction don't understand that some of their talents are actually attributes that they should focus on."

Ewen may be busier in retirement than he was as an active player. "I wasn't the big money-maker, so I'll have to work for the rest of my life." He's produced coaching videos after having coached at the university, midget and mini-mites levels and has earned his stockbroker, life insurance, health insurance and real estate licences, as well as an IT degree.

"On top of that, I have three patents to my name and my wife and I are in real estate together. Life's about taking advantage of opportunities and I'll never stop learning."

THE SCORERS

Enforcers who followed John Ferguson aspired to contribute to the scoresheet while still protecting their teammates, just as he did. Some managed to accomplish this feat in the NHL, while others demonstrated a scoring prowess in junior before being converted to specialists once they became pro.

CLARK GILLIES

Clark Gillies might have been the most dominant fighter ever if he'd had the inclination. Instead, he was a sleeping giant who was voted Islander Good Guy in 1981–82 by hockey writers.

"He's a giant teddy bear on the street," said Wilf Paiement, who was drafted the same year as Gillies. "He's the father of three girls. He watched soap operas! But you get him all pissed off . . . he wakes up and plays a lot better. He's not one of those guys who would agitate anybody. Leave me alone, make sure you don't touch [Mike] Bossy and [Bryan] Trottier, and everything's going to be fine."

"If someone went after Mike Bossy, I think we tried to establish that they couldn't do that. But that's why they had Clark Gillies on his line," teammate Bob Nystrom pointed out.

"[Dave] Semenko and maybe Clark Gillies would be the two toughest guys I ever saw. Gillies didn't even like fighting; he used to throw up before every Boston game and then he'd go out and beat up on Terry O'Reilly," said play-by-play man Curt Keilback, who called WHL action while Gillies was with the Regina Pats. "We'd go up to Flin Flon, and Flin Flon had that tough, tough team; Gillies hated fighting even then, but to my knowledge, he never lost."

A dominant power forward in the juniors, Gillies made his point early and often, and thereafter he found himself with more space. After getting into a number of fights his first year and accumulating nearly 200 penalty minutes, his third year was both quieter and more productive, as he scored 46 goals and 112 points and won the Memorial Cup.

The New York Islanders took notice of the big man nick-named after the lovable powerhouse bumpkin from *The Beverley Hillbillies*, taking "Jethro" fourth overall in the 1974 amateur draft. Gillies never played a game in the minors, immediately cracking the pro lineup. Besides scoring 25 goals in his rookie campaign, he would serve notice that he wasn't a guy that should be tested.

"Gillies and I had a couple that people remember," said Dave

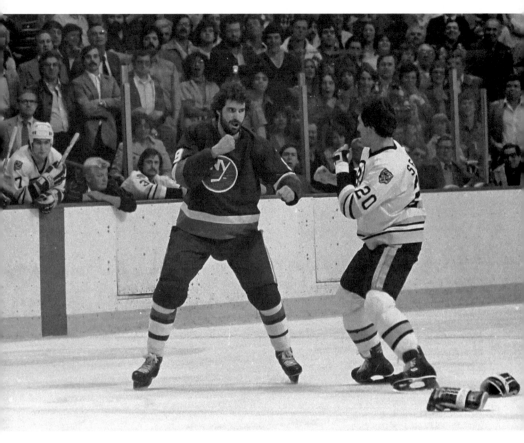

Both Clark Gillies of the New York Islanders and Al Secord of the Boston Bruins could score as well as fight — a rare combination. (IHA/Icon SMI)

"The Hammer" Schultz in an interview with the *Calgary Herald*. "The first fight was pretty close. The second . . . not so close. In fact, I saw Gillies at a banquet somewhere and I said to him, 'Remember that second fight? Lucky thing for you, Moose Dupont pulled me out from underneath you, wasn't it?'"

Nevertheless, Gillies was still young and not completely immune to being physically punished, as he discovered in his third season when he and the up-and-coming Islanders took on the dynastic Canadiens for the second straight playoff year.

"Rick Chartraw caught Clark Gillies with his head down and knocked him clean over the boards and into the penalty box," Larry

Robinson said in *Robinson for the Defense* about Game 4, which the Habs took 4-0 at Nassau Coliseum. "A couple of years later, when Jethro stopped growing, there wasn't a player in the league who could do that anymore."

In fact, it was the Gillies Railroad that players were looking out for.

"I cut toward centre, and all of a sudden, train No. 9, Clark Gillies, hit me so hard that my helmet popped off," Lanny McDonald said in *Lanny*. "I landed on my right shoulder, slamming my ear into the ice. I remember lying there and Borje Salming being the first guy to reach me. I couldn't see him, but I could hear him. 'Mackie, Mackie, talk to me.' I tried to talk, but nothing was working. Borje turned to the rest of the team and said, 'I think he's dead!'"

Both of McDonald's shoulders were separated, he suffered a concussion, and it took 26 stitches to sew his ear back on.

Although few players would come looking for Gillies, some couldn't help themselves. One was Terry O'Reilly.

Before Game 1 of the 1980 Islanders-Bruins semifinal series, a Boston television report concluded the Bruins would intimidate and quickly bounce the Isles out of the playoffs. The Islanders would prove otherwise. "I remember two games between the Islanders and the Bruins—I wasn't coachin' the Bruins at the time—when O'Reilly had two fights with Clark Gillies," Don Cherry told the *Toronto Star*. "In one of those fights, Gillies beat up O'Reilly so bad, he needed 25 stitches. When the third period started, who's out there but O'Reilly, saying 'Let's go again. Send out Gillies.' Al Arbour didn't send out Gillies. I've been told Gillies said he never wanted to beat up another guy like that again."

Ed Hospodar of the New York Rangers didn't seem to have a better sense of self-preservation. In an October 1981 game against the Islanders, Hospodar raked his stick across Gillies's face, which earned him an elbow later on. In a following contest, Hospodar again liberally applied his hockey stick to Islanders players. Having tried but failed to correct Hospodar's transgressions with verbal warnings, Gillies ended up drilling him, breaking his jaw, knocking out three of his teeth, and cutting him for eight stitches.

"One night at the Garden, there was a skirmish . . . and I got a little close to the pile, and all of a sudden somebody grabbed me by the shoulder, and I turned around and it was Eddie. And I just . . . I really lost it. I don't remember a whole lot about it," Gillies told the *Daily News*.

"It was just one punch, and goodnight, Eddie. Oh, he just creamed him, one shot, boom," remembered Islanders announcer Jiggs McDonald. "You just didn't wake him up. Don't make him angry. If you got Clark irritated, he would tear you apart. I don't think the man knew his own strength."

"He would talk to guys: 'Hey, listen, lay off.' Things like that," Bob Nystrom said. "He had a long fuse. . . . But he still felt there were times when he had to establish things."

The 6-foot-3, 225-pound Gillies's reputation was cemented by incidents such as the Hospodar fight, but he never cracked the 100 penalty minute mark once in any of his pro seasons. "People want me to run around the ice hitting everything that moves. But that's not me," Gillies told *The New York Times*. "If a teammate needs me, I'm there and the guys know it, and the opposition knows it. When it counts, I'm there, but I don't run all over looking to show how big or tough I am. The other teams know I can fight if I have to, but I would rather just play hockey."

"Clark Gillies was a player who didn't have to fight too often, because he was simply one of the best and toughest ever," Al Secord told Finnish reporter Jukka Suutari. Secord knew this first-hand: "When he dropped his gloves and I saw his fists, I got nervous. His fists were so unbelievably big, and he was a big guy, too. All I saw were his hands. He punched me twice and I went down."

"If Gillies really had the desire to hurt people, I would put him alongside Semenko, but he doesn't. He only rearranges your face if you insist," Tiger Williams said in *Tiger: A Hockey Story*.

Semenko thought highly of his rival Gillies.

"I always thought Gillies was the ultimate. He was big and strong. When he fought, he got the job done, and he didn't have to do it very often. He'd play on the All-Star team, get his 30 goals a year, and nobody pushed him around. You can't get a better combination than that in a hockey player," Semenko said in *Looking Out for Number One*.

Gillies scored over 30 goals six times, was named to the First All-Star Team in 1978 and again in '79, and won MVP in the 1979 Challenge Cup series against the Soviets. But sometimes the bear's gentle nature could put him in hibernation, and he never looked more sleepy than during the 1983–84 regular season leading up to the Islanders last appearance in the finals, as he scored a measly 12 goals in 76 games. But with everything on the line, Gillies came alive again, equalling that goal total in only 21 postseason contests.

It turned out to be the final high-water mark for Gillies, as he never achieved anywhere near that kind of production again. In the summer of 1986, the Islanders exposed him in the annual waiver draft, and he was picked up by the Buffalo Sabres.

Gillies struggled to acclimatize himself to a new city and team as his family stayed in Long Island. He only scored 10 goals his first year, and in his second, he was limited to 25 games.

"I came in that season, my fourteenth, in probably the best shape I had ever been in. After a good start, I was feeling like a kid again," Gillies said in an article for the Hockey Hall of Fame website.

But a heavy hit by Craig Muni of the Edmonton Oilers hyperextended and tore ligaments in his knee. When he returned, a knee brace hampered his effectiveness. After coach Ted Sator benched him in the final game of the year, Gillies decided it was time to call it a career.

While playing out the string in Buffalo, Gillies never stopped being a dangerous presence: "Gillies is still capable of tearing a guy's head off," said Edmonton's Marty McSorley.

If his days as a Sabre weren't career highlights for Gillies, they *were* for some of the new toughs entering the league—many looked up to the big man and seemed honoured to be able to drop the gloves against him.

"Massive," Lyndon Byers said of his respect for Gillies, adding, "He was my favourite player growing up because he was a Regina Pat and a right wing, and we all watched the great Islanders from '80–84. He was a legend. It was one of those things when he came to Buffalo, we fought a bunch of times in the playoffs. But he's a beast, he was a big old bastard from Saskatchewan. That's the surreal part about being an athlete: you can have an idol and then the next thing you know, you're playing against him. And even better, you get to punch his lights out. But don't tell him that cause he'll come try to find me."

Todd Ewen said his hardest ever fight came against Gillies, who was playing in his final year.

"That was the toughest because I always looked up to him—he was a tough guy that could play. I didn't even want to fight. In my mind he was the greatest fighter ever so I think I was going into that one losing just because I didn't want to win," Ewen said, laughing.

Gillies's No. 9 was retired by the Islanders in 1996, and he was elected into the Hockey Hall of Fame in 2002. He remained an Islander good guy, establishing the Clark Gillies Foundation; its aim is to raise funds for physically, mentally, and financially handicapped children to improve their quality of life and encourage their participation in sports.

WILF PAIEMENT The media have always been notoriously fickle in how they judge the sins of pro athletes. They will willingly forgive certain stars for their transgressions yet refuse to absolve others. Mark Messier and Chris Pronger were darlings whose infractions were often whitewashed, even though some would say their cheap-shot exploits could fill volumes.

And then there's someone like Claude Lemieux.

One of the all-time finest clutch forwards in history, Claude

Lemieux's name will always be tied to Kris Draper's. Pancaking the Detroit Red Wings winger into the boards from behind will always be mentioned next to the fact that he won a Conn Smythe Trophy as playoff MVP and four Stanley Cups with three different franchises.

Todd Bertuzzi is similarly labelled; no matter what he does, his write-ups will always include the fact that he ended the career of Steve Moore.

But any time a major stick infraction occurs, people think of Wilf Paiement. His 1978 attack on Dennis Polonich has always overshadowed his other accomplishments. His offensive prowess is rarely, if ever, mentioned, even though Paiement was one of the premier power forwards of his day. The Earlton, Ontario, product was a First Team All-Star and reached the magic 50-goal mark for the St. Catharines Black Hawks in his last year of junior. His touch around the net combined with his physical intensity got him drafted second overall in 1974. Unfortunately for him, it was by the horrendous Kansas City Scouts, a weak and unstable franchise that moved to Colorado before finally finding a home in New Jersey.

Meanwhile, two spots later in the draft, another recent expansion team, the New York Islanders, chose Clark Gillies.

While Paiement would toil away with some truly awful teams like the Scouts, Colorado Rockies and Toronto Maple Leafs, Gillies skated with a powerhouse club that reached the Stanley Cup Finals five years in a row, winning the first four.

"If you want me to compare teams, Clark played for 12 years with a guy called Mike Bossy, as well as Bryan Trottier, Denis Potvin and others. I didn't have the luxury of playing with superstars like that," said Paiement.

Nevertheless, Paiement retired with better production totals than Gillies, with 356 goals and 458 assists in 946 games, versus Gillies's 319 goals and 378 assists in 958 games. That's a 117 point difference in 12 fewer games.

Like Gillies, Paiement was a big, physical forward for his day—at 6-foot-1, 205-pounds, he could dish out punishment.

"My dad was French Canadian and my mother was Irish, and I guess I inherited the size of my dad and I inherited my mother's attitude," said Paiement.

Paiement chipped in a very respectable 26 goals his rookie season, a feat made all the more remarkable given the Scouts finished with a miserable 15 wins that year. The club found new ways to fail the following season, winning only 12 times. Paiement, however, still somehow netted 21 goals in 57 games.

Moving with the Scouts to Colorado for 1976–77, Paiement continued to improve. In spite of the club winning only 20 games, he rose above "Rocky Hockey" by scoring 41 goals. With the Rockies missing the playoffs, Paiement was selected to join Team Canada at the World Championships. But he didn't get kudos for his sacrifice. Instead, his rough, at times overzealous, play earned him the ire of the press, which castigated him with epithets like "hooligan" and "barbarian."

"There were moments when the animals ran the zoo," Red Fisher of the *Montreal Star* wrote of Canada's 11-1 loss to the Soviet Union. "If anybody associated with hockey can persuade me that this spoiled, overpaid brat deserves to continue playing with Team Canada, he's quite a salesman."

Not unlike Bobby Clarke and many others of the 1972 edition of Team Canada, Paiement aggressively engaged his overseas competition. But his chippy (and at times dirty) play, which included high-sticking Sweden's Lars Erik Ericsson, clipping Soviet Sergei Babinov upside the head, and chopping Vladimir Shadrin's ankle, drove reporters to their soapboxes.

According to *Vancouver Sun* columnist Jim Kearney, "His stick-swinging temper tantrums in the last two games have been such an embarrassment to the team, even [Team Canada coach Johnny] Wilson, who coaches him at Denver, declined to defend him."

A second strong showing with Colorado—87 points—led Team Canada officials to ask Paiement back for the '78 tournament. Still stinging from the previous year's biting criticism, it took some convincing from his agent and Team Canada chairman Alan Eagleson to persuade Paiement to again don the red-and-white maple leaf sweater. This time reporters applauded his strong play.

"Kids like Don Lever, Wilf Paiement and Glen Sharpley stood in there toe-to-toe with one of the finest hockey machines in the world and nearly won it. And dammit, they deserved to win on the basis of the night's play," wrote *Winnipeg Free Press* sports editor Hal Sigurdson of a game against the Soviets.

Paiement scored the tying goal in that match, beating Vladislav Tretiak to get Canada on the board, but it was in a losing cause as Canada dropped a 2-1 lead with four minutes left. The Soviets rallied to win 4-2.

His newfound media love affair was short-lived. After a stick swing on Polonich several months after the tournament, reporters were again calling to banish Paiement. What actually happened was never captured on film, but eyewitnesses described Paiement swinging his stick like a baseball bat and striking Polonich in the face. It cost Paiement 15 games, but it perhaps cost Polonich his career. A concussion, along with facial lacerations and a broken nose that required reconstructive surgery, kept Polonich out for 18 games. His production plummeted when he returned, and not long after he found himself riding the minor league buses before retiring prematurely at 29.

"Wilf could get you a few goals. Wilf had ability, but he earned the space. He earned the space because you didn't want to challenge him," said broadcaster Jiggs McDonald. "You knew you'd better be ready if you were going to get into his face or do anything that irritated him. There was a price to pay."

The Polonich clash occurred in Paiement's third year with Colorado, and in the fourth, ex-Bruins coach Don Cherry took over behind the bench. Cherry had a long list of players he'd had in Boston who could frighten opponents into docility—John Wensink, Wayne Cashman, Bobby Schmautz, Terry O'Reilly, Al

Secord, and Stan Jonathan—but for him, Paiement ranked as the scariest guy he coached.

"The guy that nobody really fooled with was a guy that played for me in Colorado, Wilf Paiement. The guy had those eyes like Schmautzie, and I'll tell you, you didn't fool with this guy. He was the nicest guy off the ice, as a tough guy usually is, but nobody fooled with him," Cherry told author Al Strachan for *Hockey Stories Part 2*.

Cherry would finish the season with Colorado without Paiement—the Rockies traded him in a blockbuster deal for Toronto Maple Leafs sniper Lanny McDonald. Paiement had turned 24 and initially felt rejected, but he came to see the move as good for his career.

"Toronto's a mega city for hockey. Colorado and Toronto, you can't compare the two cities for hockey. I was coming to a hotbed of hockey," said Paiement. "When you're a kid and you watch the Toronto Maple Leafs or Montreal Canadiens on TV, obviously your dream is to play for them. Luckily, I was able to play for the Leafs and stay there for about four years and had a great stay there and loved every minute of it."

But the Canadiens and Maple Leafs couldn't be much further apart in the 1970s. Whereas the Habs spent the decade capturing Stanley Cups and setting records for wins, the Leafs seemed to be continually rebuilding. By the time Paiement arrived, the players were gearing up for an open revolt against general manager Punch Imlach. If that wasn't enough, Paiement was faced with the unenviable task of replacing McDonald, one of the team's most popular players.

"The only thing is I was really replacing a fan favourite and a hell of a hockey player . . . Lanny's a legend in Toronto and across Canada," Paiement said. "Toronto was playing a lot more competitive a year or two before I went there and, when Imlach came in there, he decided to build his own team, I guess."

Despite the turmoil, Paiement's talent still managed to shine.

Fan resentment over the trade and loss of McDonald waned when Paiement, donning No. 99, scored 40 goals and 97 points in his first full season with the lowly Buds, edging out all-time Leaf great Darryl Sittler by one as the team's leading point-getter.

"Wilfie was a real big power forward. The guy was probably one of the strongest men I had ever seen in the game," said Paiement's teammate Dan Maloney. "Wilfie was a good, solid team player and a lot of fun to be around. He played hard."

The next year, however, Paiement's numbers slumped amid the deepening Leaf morass, and he was dispatched to Quebec for Miroslav Frycer. It was a good move for both Paiement and the Nordiques as he performed brilliantly immediately upon his arrival, scoring seven goals in eight games.

With Quebec, Paiement was finally playing for an NHL contender. In the playoffs, he managed 12 points in 14 contests as Quebec edged out the Montreal Canadiens and Boston Bruins before bowing out in four straight to the New York Islanders, who were on their way to winning their third of four straight Cups.

Paiement said, "We had Peter [Stastny], who was a great, great player and in the '80s was second to Gretzky. We had a real exciting team. We had speed, we had talent, we had grit. We had a little bit of everything. We had a great coach—I think [Michel] Bergeron was a hell of a coach. And we were sold out every game."

In 1983–84, Paiement fell one goal short of recording his third career 40-goal year, in spite of often seeing time on the third line. "We had the Stastnys [Peter, Marian and Anton] on the first line, and we had Michel Goulet, Dale Hunter on the second, and I was playing with André Savard and Tony McKegney."

The 1984–85 season was a mixed one for Paiement. His scoring was down from the year before, and he'd made headlines again, this time for a high stick to Boston's Charlie Simmer, which broke Simmer's jaw. But he and the Nordiques again went deep into the playoffs, reaching the conference finals before losing in six games to the regular-season champion Philadelphia Flyers.

Paiement was sent to the New York Rangers before the playoffs began the following season, but he somehow managed to reach the conference finals for the second year running. Ironically, even though he was out of Quebec, Montreal still found a way to block his path to the Stanley Cup. "They had a guy between the pipes, what was his name, Patrick something?" Paiement joked about Patrick Roy, the Canadiens rookie who would guide the Habs to the Cup and win the Conn Smythe Trophy as playoff MVP that year.

In spite of Paiement helping the Rangers get past the NHL's second-best regular season squad, the Flyers, and the third overall Washington Capitals during the playoffs, he wound up in Buffalo for 1986–87. At first it seemed like a positive move, as Paiement began the season scoring at a blistering pace. But it wouldn't last.

"In the first 20 games, I had 13 or 14 goals playing with Gilbert Perreault," Paiement remembered. "And then he retired after 20 games. What a clown!"

With the Sabres rebuilding, Perreault decided to hang up his skates, leaving the team and Paiement without a number-one centre. Paiement ended up with 20 goals before missing a chunk of the season to injury.

Without a contract, Paiement ended up signing with Pittsburgh. It turned out to be his final NHL destination, and he split the year with the Penguins and the AHL's Muskegon Lumberjacks before retiring.

"I wish I would have been seven or eight years younger, I could have played with Mario [Lemieux] on a regular basis. [Three] years after that, they won the Cup," Paiement said, chuckling at his own bad timing. "Once you're retired, you look at the big picture and say, what's missing? Obviously it's a Stanley Cup. Not everybody has that chance to claim it. You gotta be a little lucky to be on the right team at the right time and be able to be part of that puzzle."

He pointed to Bob Bourne, who was taken by Kansas City the same draft but in the third round. Bourne refused to play for the Scouts and ended up getting traded to the Islanders, where he stockpiled four Stanley Cup rings.

Then there's Doug Risebrough, Rick Chartraw, Mario Tremblay and Gilles Lupien, who were drafted after him in '74 by the Canadiens and who'd go on to play on Cup-winning teams.

"That's just the way it ends up. I could say I wish I would have been on the Montreal Canadiens. They won five Stanley Cups while I was playing in the league," said Paiement, who now manages residential properties he owns around Toronto. "But I'll be honest, I'm not sour about my career. I'm proud of what I did and we'll leave it like that. What are you gonna do?"

Paiement isn't seeking absolution for his transgressions. He'd prefer to be remembered as a productive two-way player who outscored a number of his contemporaries who'd wind up in the Hockey Hall of Fame. But he's realistic: "Just to give you an example, who won the Super Bowl last year? I gotta think about it. But if something really negative comes about, it seems to stay in your mind."

In the end, he'd rather leave the negatives in the past and has no desire to dwell on them. "I don't want to be remembered for what happened at the World Championships . . . And what happened with Polonich, it's too bad it happened but it happened, and it's there and you can't do nothing about it. Whatever happened with Simmer, it happened, and you can't do nothing about it either."

JIMMY MANN Keeping clear of an angry Jimmy Mann came at or near the top of most hockey players' tips for self-preservation.

"Junior was great: I scored a lot of goals and was the toughest kid in the league . . . nobody even wanted to come near me," said Mann, a native of Laval, Quebec, who scored over 80 points in each of his last two years with the Sherbrooke Castors.

In their first-ever NHL draft, the Winnipeg Jets used their first-round pick to select Quebec Major Junior Hockey League terror Jimmy Mann. The Jets' roster had been decimated going from the World Hockey Association to the NHL, and general manager John Ferguson seemed to believe the team needed someone who could

Dave "The Hammer" Schultz of the Flyers assumes a familiar seat in the penalty box. (Courtesy of thesportgallery.com, copyright SPORT Gallery Inc.)

Pierre Pilote, Reggie Fleming, Stan Mikita, and Moose Vasko don boxing gloves for a photo shoot in the early 1960s. (Le Studio du Hockey/Hockey Hall of Fame)

"The Grim Reaper" Stu Grimson of the Mighty Ducks takes a swing at Nashville's Patrick Côté during the 1998–99 season. (IHA/Icon SMI)

Ken Daneyko of the Devils loses his jersey and his composure, mauling Steve Leach of the Bruins in January 1996. (AP Photo/Dan Loh)

Tony Twist of the Nordiques gets his dukes up against Craig Berube of the Capitals in January 1984 at Le Colisée. (IHA/Icon SMI)

Paul Laus of the Panthers gets one on the nose from Darcy Hordichuk of the Thrashers in December 2001. (AP Photo/Wilfredo Lee)

Georges Laraque, right, and P.K. Subban face off at Grace Children's Hospital in Port au Prince, Haiti, in July 2011, after Laraque spearheaded Hockey for Haiti to help rebuild after the 2010 earthquake. (CNW Group/World Vision Canada)

Kelly Chase and Kyoko Ina were paired up for the second season of CBC's *Battle of the Blades*. (Courtesy CBC Television)

Bob McGill and Jimmy Mann work out some issues. (Graig Abel)

grab the other teams' attention the way Ferguson did with the Montreal Canadiens.

"Fergie had mentioned to me, 'Jim, we don't have that tough a team and we need you to help us play that role,'" recalled Mann.

The newcomer made an immediate impression on Curt Keilback—the original voice of the NHL Jets—as well as Keilback's wife. "My wife told me one time, she was sitting in the stands when Jimmy was out there, and he went to go fighting with some guy and his eyes turned black. And some people do—I've seen people whose eyes would go black when they really get mad," said Keilback, who remembered Mann as a young kid who could have used a bit of seasoning before being thrown into the lion's den.

"He had been a goal scorer when he played junior, but he wasn't ready for the NHL's skill level. But he certainly was ready for the NHL's tough level," Keilback said, adding that a stint in the minors might have helped Mann's hockey development.

Mann agreed, but reiterated that Winnipeg was desperate for toughness. "On that team, if they would have let me play, I would have developed. I know what I could have done—I did it in junior. The style I played, they had to let you play more. Chris Nilan was in the same situation as me, but Montreal gave him a chance."

Keilback believed that there was never a tougher Winnipeg Jet, no small feat given that the team would feature hard men like Jim Kyte, Shawn Cronin, Tie Domi, Kris King, and Jim McKenzie over the years to come. He recalled a game against the Boston Bruins at the Winnipeg Arena in which the rookie Mann took on three of the league's most ornery in Terry O'Reilly, Al Secord and Stan Jonathan—and beat them all. The fans went nuts and so did Fergie. After that, Mann's role was established.

"I didn't mind fighting, I'll tell you that much, especially for my teammates . . . But you get into a track and that's what's expected after a while. You get into that rut and it's something that's really hard to get out of," said Mann. "But I did what I can, I worked at it, and I said if this is what I have to do to be here then that's what I'm going to do."

By season's end, the rookie led the league in penalty minutes with 287.

"You go into Philly, you go into Boston—it was a league that was tough, there were tough guys on every team. And I was the one that had that job in Winnipeg," said Mann. "We had Scotty Campbell who didn't play as much, and Dave Hoyt who was on his way out, so I was pretty well on my own. I was the one that had to take care of the team."

He did it well, and many were taking notice. Keilback said you had to be ready for anything when Mann's eyes started rolling around in his head, and the Red Wings' Dennis Polonich, who'd already tangled with the game's most penalized players, recalled the horror he felt after making the mistake of knocking Mann down in front of the net: "I knew of his reputation and how tough he was, so when he got up I went, 'Oh my God, what have I done?!'"

Larry Playfair, a tough customer when he played for the Sabres and Kings, said that given the right opportunity and circumstance, Mann was effective. "But I think Jimmy Mann was a little off his rocker," Playfair added. "Jimmy was left-handed and it was a little scary. What I mean by scary is you never knew if he was going to spear somebody on your team; he was one of those guys you always had to be a little bit leery about."

To this day, Mann is still remembered for annihilating Pittsburgh Penguins forward Paul Gardner as both teams were skating into position for a faceoff. Many denounced his attack as nothing more than a blatant cheap shot, but Mann insisted he was sticking up for an injured teammate, Doug Smail, who was recovering from a broken jaw and whom Gardner had cross-checked in the face so hard his stick broke.

"In those days, to break a stick, you had to cross-check pretty hard. Dougie was one of our good players and wasn't a trouble-maker, and I went on the ice and suckered [Gardner]. And I don't regret it at all," confessed Mann.

After the game, reporters converged on Mann's dressing room

stall to discover coach Tom Watt's instructions prior to sending him out for the puck drop. "Jim, come and tell me what Tommy said," Ferguson demanded. "He told me to take his face off; that's what I did!" replied Mann. "No, no, no! He said to take *the* faceoff!" an exasperated Ferguson cried.

"I don't think it was a coincidence that Tom Watt sent him out. But Tom was strangely mute on the whole thing afterward," said Keilback.

Unfortunately for Mann, a provincial Attorney General's office official was in the crowd, and before long, Attorney General Roland Penner charged Mann with assault. Mann eventually was forced to pay a $500 fine. "He didn't have a clue what the game of hockey was all about. He probably never saw a game in his life," Mann groused.

As feared as he was on the ice, away from it Mann was one of the game's biggest softies.

During one flight, he met a boy who'd been set on fire by his own father. When Mann learned the boy was a big Jets fan, he hired a limo and brought him to the games. It wasn't an isolated gesture, as Mann regularly brought kids with special needs to practices and games as well. "Jimmy was one of the nicest guys. He used to come [to] almost every practice with one or two handicapped kids. He wasn't much older than them himself and he'd be bringing guys out to practice and to games. He was a really, really good citizen in that way," said Keilback.

Mann also worked for numerous charities in the city and was on the board of the Special Olympics. "We had a floor hockey team and took care of the kids. That's fun, that's what it's all about. It's fun to be able to put a smile on someone's face," said Mann. "It's really great for me, the feeling to help and go to hospitals and see the kids. I was very active in that part of it and we are still today. Anybody that tells you that's not important, they're wrong. Everybody in the National Hockey League and any other sport, they all do it and if we can give back and make some little kid smile, then my job's done."

At one point, Mann noticed that the parents of kids with Down's syndrome would drop off their sons at floor hockey and then promptly leave. He soon had a meeting with the parents and sorted that right out.

"Everyone was staying after that. They were all there. And I would get the parents involved in the practicing and playing with the kids. I would put parties and dances on. And you would see the change in the kids," he said. "I wanted the kids to feel like I did when I had my parents there."

About midway through his fifth season with the Jets, Mann was traded to the Quebec Nordiques. Years later, his new teammate Wilf Paiement would rank him among the league's top enforcers.

"Chris Nilan, I don't think could deal with Jimmy Mann," Paiement said of provincial rival Montreal's top cop. "I remember Larry Playfair and him went at it quite a bit. Jimmy held his own for sure."

Paiement stressed that Mann would only play six or seven minutes a game, sitting on the bench most of the night before being sent out to face the other side's biggest bruisers.

"That is tough. As an example, I was playing an average of 20 minutes a game. Every once in a while I had to fight, but you're warmed up, you're out there, it's not as tough," Paiement said, pointing out he didn't experience the additional pressure of having to sit and think about an inevitable clash with a designated fighter. "[Mann] worked hard; he had a good attitude. As far as being a good team man, he did a hell of a job."

Mann missed the 1986–87 season and even pursued a police career, but the NHL wasn't finished with him, as teams sought to add muscle to their rosters. Mann would choose Pittsburgh as his return destination, where superstar Mario Lemieux was looking for more protection. But other prospective enforcers there, like Carl Mokosak and Mitch Wilson, were less than welcoming to Mann— they felt he threatened their jobs.

"There were these two or three guys who were really pissed off because they figured because they're in the organization, they were tough kids that were going to get the job. But they signed me. So I was on my first shift—first shift of the whole training camp—and I had four fights. [Head coach] Pierre Cramer says, 'Jim, you're done for the day.'"

Mann suffered some injuries—broken elbows in training camp and a torn groin—that kept him out most of the season. He rehabilitated from elbow surgery, played for the Muskegon Lumberjacks of the IHL, came back to the Pens and did enough for general manager Eddie Johnston to be ready to sign him to an extension. But then Tony Esposito was hired to replace Johnston, signalling Mann's end.

"I don't even want to get into it about him. He didn't really want me around and I said too bad, you're gonna pay me anyway. We didn't get along very well; I got along with everybody but I didn't get along with him," said Mann. "He almost killed that franchise anyway. So that put a kibosh—I was ready to go, injuries [weren't a problem]. I wanted to play a couple more years, and in Pittsburgh too. Maybe I would have won a Stanley Cup. But Esposito didn't want me around so I ended up in the minors, but he was still paying me."

Mann finished the 1987–88 season with the Lumberjacks and closed out his career with the IHL's Indianapolis Ice.

"I scored, I fought, but then I got to a point where I was so tired of it and I didn't want it any more. I was really, really tired of it, fighting all the time. I was 30 years old, so I thought, 'I don't really need this.'"

A decade of taking care of his teammates and giving them room on the ice had finally worn him out: "The mental part of it, after a while, it takes a toll on you. . . . You're getting a little older as you get down the road and the kids are coming in, and you got to be at your best. Whenever you're playing the game, you have to do it right—the right thing at the right time. Whether it's going out there and playing a couple shifts and telling a guy if you touch him again you're gonna have to deal with me, or take it in your hands right away."

But Mann wasn't yet through with hockey, and would begin his second career, this time with a travelling old-timers team, where he's gotten to personally know ex-pros like Nilan, Bob Probert and Tiger Williams. Besides playing well over 1,000 games with the team, Mann is also in charge of its travel and logistics. But as much work as it's been, he's also had a ball.

"It's all charity work and the guys come out and we get closer to the fans. I think today it's harder for the fans to get close to the players; they're always in charter flights, never in the airports. . . . We do the Legends game, we do autograph sessions, pre-skate before the game. It's just fun. Again, that's part of giving back to what we got out of the game. And we have an unbelievable bunch of guys," Mann concluded.

KEVIN McCLELLAND A natural scorer in the juniors, Kevin McClelland would have to accept a completely different role in order to make the transition to the big leagues.

He scored 50 goals and 124 points with the Oshawa Legionaires at 16 and was drafted 18th by the Hartford Whalers. Continuing his scoring exploits in major junior with the Niagara Falls Flyers, he potted 36 goals and 108 points in 68 games during his second year. McClelland never played a game for Hartford, going to the Pittsburgh Penguins as part of the compensation package the Whalers gave up for signing goaltender Greg Millen.

In his third and final year of junior, McClelland scored another 36 goals and reached 83 points—in only 46 games—and had a 10-game trial with Pittsburgh. But rather than take centre stage in the Steel City, he would take it in Canada's oil patch.

Wayne Gretzky said Edmonton Oilers coach and general manager Glen Sather wasn't afraid to take chances on players who'd been "left for dead." "Guys most teams were willing to sell for scraps, Sather picked up, polished and set back on the ice, where they played their hearts out," Gretzky said in *Gretzky: An Autobiography.*

"Kevin McClelland couldn't make it with Pittsburgh, the last-place team in the league. He came to us and really contributed."

After scouring the league for grit, Sather found and acquired McClelland in order to match the dominant team of the day, the New York Islanders.

"When I got traded to Edmonton, there were already guys that could score left and right, and I didn't think that I was going to fit in on a scoring role, so I had to change," said McClelland. "If I wanted to play in the NHL, I had to accept that role. And to be part of that team—who wouldn't want to be part of that hockey club?"

Playing under coach Bert Templeton in junior prepared McClelland for the tough-guy role he'd take on for the Oilers. "He was a great coach, and he made you accountable. He had such a big influence on me getting to the next level—I think he instilled a little of that toughness in me and got me ready."

McClelland landed in Edmonton just as the Oilers were becoming a dynasty. In '81 the Oilers lost to the Islanders in the second round, and in 1983, the year before McClelland arrived, they reached the Stanley Cup Final but were swept by the Isles, who captured their fourth straight championship.

"They were looking for someone who could play physical against the Islanders. [Bryan] Trottier was a pretty physical guy and they needed someone who could slow him down. They brought me in as a third line checking centre, and then I took it beyond that."

The Oilers met the Islanders again in the 1984 final, and McClelland scored the only goal in a rare Edmonton victory at Nassau Coliseum. McClelland deflected the credit to his linemates Dave Hunter and Pat Hughes, the corner men whose game was to jar pucks loose.

"They did that, and happened to find me in the slot and I just shot it at the net. I didn't really have an idea where it was going, I just wanted to put it on the ice and it ended up going in," said McClelland. "That's what we were looking for, a split there, because that was back in the 2-3-2 era. . . . It was just a big relief to get that win in game one of the Stanley Cup Finals."

Many still believe the goal was one of the most if not *the* most important single goal in Oiler history, and Kevin Lowe is no different.

"That goal and that win was the defining moment for our team," said Lowe to the *Edmonton Journal* in 2004. "We proved we could win a low-scoring game. We'd also had zero success against the Islanders."

The Oilers would get blown out 6-1 the next game, but they then knocked off three straight wins in Edmonton to earn their first Stanley Cup. McClelland would go on to win three more Cups with the Oilers. "I was a role player . . . but it was great to be a part of it and be a piece of the puzzle."

Although best known for their high-powered offence, the Oilers were also one of the toughest teams in the league and could play the game any way the opposition wanted.

"We had myself and when I first got there, there was Dave Semenko and Don Jackson. And when Sammy [Semenko] was getting towards the end, they brought in [Marty] McSorley. And when I was about to get traded, they brought in Dave Brown. So Slats always had his physical guys—with all that talent around, you didn't want [the opposition] taking liberties," said McClelland. "I think we did a pretty decent job and allowed them to go out and do what they did. And what they did was put four rings on my fingers."

Unlike many enforcers, McClelland actually enjoyed fighting, and he became the second-most penalized Oiler in history, trailing only Kelly Buchberger.

"It was fun. I never really wanted to let my teammates down by taking a beating . . . so I was always ready and focused for whoever was going to come up and test me."

McClelland took on all the heavyweights, players like Clark Gillies, Joey Kocur, Bob Probert, Stu Grimson, Tim Hunter, and Larry Playfair. To have a chance against the larger men, McClelland spent a good deal of time in the gym.

"I was only 192 pounds so I was fighting a lot of guys heavier than me," McClelland said. "One year, Kenny Lakusta and Willie de Wit, those guys were Canadian champion boxers, and myself, Semenko and Pat Hughes and maybe Hunter went in there for training. Not for the purpose of taking it out on the ice, but I think that helped a little bit too."

"Pound-for-pound, Mac was the toughest player I ever played with," said Lowe, "and the meanest guy. He would run roughshod over players. A lot of times he looked after Mark [Messier], too—not that Mark couldn't handle himself."

When McClelland was traded to Detroit, Oilers captain Mark Messier, for one, was sad to see him go.

"I've found it extremely difficult seeing a guy of Kevin McClelland's nature have to leave the hockey club," Messier said to the *Journal*. "I think when he was traded here, it was one of the most instrumental deals we ever made. He provided what we needed, a big, strong centre." McClelland's NHL career wound down after the trade; he played one season for the Red Wings before playing most of the next with Detroit's farm team in Adirondack. Signing with the Toronto Maple Leafs didn't get him much more big-league time, as he spent the majority of the next two years skating in St. John's, Newfoundland. "When I was in Toronto, I went up and down from St. John's, and I just got called up on weekends because we were playing Chicago and I had to fight [Mike] Peluso and [Stu] Grimson and then I go right back to St. John's."

His last NHL appearance came with the Winnipeg Jets in a game in which he found himself dropping the gloves against an old Stanley Cup teammate.

"Tie Domi went out and fought [Cam] Russell from Chicago, and we were trying to change the momentum and I'm saying, 'Jeez, who else is left to fight?' Smitty [Steve Smith] was the next biggest guy, so I went out and I bumped him a little bit and said, 'Let's go,' and ended up having a fight," McClelland said. "We spent a lot of time there [in Edmonton] and me and him were pretty close, but when you're on the ice, you know that you might have to drop the gloves with friends, and that's what you had to do to keep your job."

McClelland retired with 1,672 PIM and 188 career points in 588 NHL games. Going from rusher to crusher had its impact on his physical well-being. "Maybe still got a couple side effects from concussions. I don't know what the heck it's done. I got two plates in my jaw, my knee's all rebuilt and I had both shoulders done."

But just as he was preparing for life after hockey—he got his licence to sell insurance—a figure from his past returned to pull him back in. "I got into coaching sitting around after I retired, wondering what I was going to do. I got a call from the late Bert Templeton," said McClelland. "He gave me an opportunity to be an assistant coach in Barrie, and that's how it started. It was a lot of fun starting coaching; it's so hard to do something [new] after you've done something for so long. I thank Bert Templeton for that opportunity."

After a season as an assistant with the Barrie Colts, McClelland took over as head coach with the Prince Albert Raiders for two seasons. His rise continued when he became assistant for his alma mater, the St. John's Maple Leafs. But after five years, the team moved to Toronto, and McClelland looked elsewhere to coach.

"[Leafs GM] John Ferguson Jr. offered me to go with the team but I decided to go down to Memphis, where I had something lined up," McClelland said of his move to the CHL's Memphis Riverkings. "I don't like flying first of all—it really bothers me nowadays, and I don't have to fly in this league. So I've had opportunities to go to the next level but I just like doing what I'm doing right now." McClelland spent three years with the Riverkings and another two with the Colorado Eagles before he landed in Wichita. There, he's coached the Thunder and implemented the lessons taught to him by Sather.

"I learned a lot from Glen Sather as far as his style and the way he runs his practices and his demeanor. He was just a great guy and he was almost like a second father to all of us in Edmonton. I like having a team that scores a lot of goals, and if someone wants to come in and play physical, I've got guys that look after that too."

THE DEFENDERS

Some of the game's toughest have come from the back lines, and as defencemen, they've had to shoulder responsibilities that extend far beyond fisticuffs. They're the ones counted upon to contain oncoming rushers and clear the net without regard for the size and toughness of whoever is standing there while also protecting their goalie and other teammates. Here are some of the game's finest bruising defenders.

LARRY PLAYFAIR

Larry Playfair swears that no coach ever instructed him to go out and fight. "I tell that to people and they go, 'Come on! There must have been one.' Never once," Playfair said. "I would like to think that I knew when it was time to go out and have a conversation with someone, and it worked for me."

At the peak of his pro career, which extended from 1978 to 1989, few were better at "conversation" than the 6-foot-4, 220-pound defenceman from Fort St. James, British Columbia. However, after Playfair made the Buffalo Sabres squad in the fall of 1978, he needed a little bit of schooling from his more veteran teammates before he truly knew the where and when of dropping the gloves: "I don't mean to be so uncouth as to call it an art, but there was a time and a place, and you needed to be smart about when that happened."

Long-time Islanders broadcaster Jiggs McDonald said Playfair was a master of knowing when the time for small talk was done. "My recollection of Larry is he didn't go looking for trouble. He didn't set out to cause trouble, but if there was trouble to be had, and something developed, he was right there. He would take care of matters."

An intelligent, articulate man who says that hockey, to him, was a job and not a driving passion, Playfair has given his past a lot of thought. "I've got zero problem with being an enforcer. The problem I have is when someone says, 'You're a goon'—they didn't watch me play very much. Was I the top one, two or three defenceman on our team? Absolutely not," he said. "I played a regular shift quite a bit. Don't feel bad for Larry Playfair because I don't like being called a goon. But it's not an accurate description."

Playfair was chosen 13th overall in the 1978 amateur draft from the Portland Winter Hawks of the WCJHL. During his final year in Portland, Playfair notched 13 goals and 19 assists to go with 402 PIM in 71 games. The rest of the team—and the league—were no slouches. "We had a really tough team. We played against New Westminster, who had a really tough team, Victoria had a pretty tough team. That league was a little more of that than it was anything else," Playfair explained. "You're 18, 19 years old, think you're bulletproof. That particular year, we had a pretty tough team. We had Perry Turnbull, we had Paul Mulvey, we had Doug Lecuyer, all those guys played in the National Hockey League—I'm talking about guys that would fight—Wayne Babych, Dale Yakiwchuk. We had a pretty big, impressive team. I'm not apologizing for any of that stuff. I did it and I'd probably do it again."

In Buffalo, right from his first game, he was paired with "King Kong" Jerry Korab, and they would play together for years. But Playfair had a very rough debut, November 23, 1978, when he met John Wensink of the Bruins.

I'd gone back to get a puck that had been dumped back into our end of the rink. Terry O'Reilly was on one side, Peter McNab was at centre ice for the Bruins and Wensink was on the left side. I went behind the net and I faked the pass up the boards to Craig Ramsay. Peter and O'Reilly went for the fake, so I went back behind the net thinking I had a little bit of time to set up, and I didn't see Wensink coming in. He hit me with a clean hit. That's the one vivid time I

Larry and Jim Playfair, who both made the NHL, flank their father, Al, in their home in Fort St. James, BC, in 1983. (Courtesy Larry Playfair)

remember having a concussion, because I had a headache for two or three weeks after that.

Once he was back in the lineup, Playfair's defensive game improved immensely through Buffalo's practices, having to stop the likes of Gilbert Perreault, Rick Martin, and Danny Gare: "I was playing against these superstars. I learned a lot in practice. I played in a few games, not many, my first year here. I started to feel comfortable probably by the middle of my second year."

Playfair knew early on it was his role to protect the stars, even if it meant a really tough challenge. In a game in Long Island, Bob Nystrom whacked Rick Martin over the head with his stick. "I saw what happened, so I jumped over the boards, either that shift or the next, and I confronted Nystrom. We had a real good battle. He beat me. But from that point on, Bobby didn't mess with any of my players. I'm not saying that that's why, but I think it is. I think I helped him understand that at least there was going to be a repercussion. Nor did I mess with his players. It was always a good battle between us, our two teams, the Islanders and the Sabres."

Nystrom sure remembered the brouhaha: "It was one hell of a fight, one hell of a fight. I came out of that, I had two black eyes," he said. "I'm not sure, but I think I broke his nose. But I've got to tell you what, I took my licks, that's for doggone sure. And we did have respect after that."

Away from the ice, Playfair, whose brother Jim also played in the NHL, knew that he couldn't befriend players he might have to fight; the friendship might make him second-guess the on-ice action that hurt his teammate. He cultivated an image as well: "I felt my best asset was for people to think, 'I don't know if he's crazy, I think he might be though, he's kind of a weird guy. I'll just stay away from him on the ice.' That's what I wanted people to think," he said. Not being a top-line player, Playfair felt he had to really struggle to keep his job: "I had to work hard, I had to be in shape because the next guy would have taken my job, I wasn't that far away from being out of a job. So whatever I could get as an edge, I needed to keep."

After his career ended—his last half-dozen seasons in Los Angeles and Buffalo having been marred by injuries, particularly a ruptured disc in his back—Playfair found himself in Ottawa for a three-on-three tournament. There, he was told the story of how Tim Higgins of the Black Hawks used to crack up his teammates in the visitors' dressing room at the Aud in Buffalo by putting baby powder on his face and hands to look scared and stuttering, "I-i-i-i-s-s-s-s L-l-l-l-a-r-r-r-r-y P-p-p-lay-f-f-air p-p-p-l-aying tonight?"

As Playfair noted, "The point was that they weren't in there talking about Gil Perrault or René Robert or Danny Gare or Rick Martin. They were in the dressing room getting ready for the game, worried about Larry Playfair. For me, that was like, 'Alright, maybe I got into their heads a little bit'... If they were that concerned about me, then they must have at least known I was on the ice, and I think that probably allowed me to play a few years longer in the National Hockey League."

Post-hockey, it took him a while to get comfortable. The Sabres let him try marketing, sales, and colour commentary on the radio, but Playfair didn't find contentment in any of it. The Sabres Alumni Association had only just started in 1988, and it soon fell into Playfair's lap, proving to be a perfect fit with his day job of building, leasing, and refurbishing commercial properties around Buffalo.

With the 40th anniversary of the team having passed in 2010, Playfair said, "It was heartwarming for me. I had less to do with that being put together than a lot of the other events that we've done around here, yet I got more credit for it, unearned." Playfair is proud of the team he has put together and the money they have raised for good causes.

And he can pinpoint the moment the association turned into something more than just getting together to tell stories. A letter came, addressed "Former players at Buffalo Sabres." It was from Nancy Kent, the sister of Brian Spencer's third wife. Shortly after Brian was killed, Brian's wife lost her life to breast cancer. They left behind two teenage boys, Jason and Jarrett.

Having a tough time with the boys, who had been moved from Long Island to Minnesota, their aunt was asking whether the Sabres did anything for the children of former players. The golf tournament now had a focus.

"We were able to get the boys each $2,000 for their college for four years," said Playfair. "That really became the start of our alumni association. It all came together for a single purpose. In our golf tournament now, we've put over 85 kids, I think, through school—not only alumni players' kids, I think we've only got a handful, maybe less than a dozen alumni's kids—the rest are just from southern Ontario and Western New York that we've helped out."

BOB GASSOFF The St. Louis Blues were obviously up to something when they drafted the defenceman Tiger Williams called "the toughest hockey player I've ever known."

The Blues, who already owned the rights to Steve Durbano, the Plager brothers, and "Battleship" Kelly, took Bob Gassoff, the holy terror of the WHL, in the third round of the 1973 amateur draft. Just for good measure, they also picked up John Wensink in the seventh round. The Blues were readying themselves for the violent nature of professional hockey in the 1970s.

Gassoff, a defenceman from the Medicine Hat Tigers, seemed like he'd fit right in after amassing 702 penalty minutes in two seasons.

Williams remembered Gassoff as the meanest player he'd ever met. In one junior contest, Tiger watched Gassoff take a penalty in the first minute of play and not-so-subtly suggest to the referee that he refrain from calling further infractions against him. "He skated up to the referee and said, 'You give me another goddamned penalty and I'll break your ankle.' Two minutes later Gassoff returned to the ice, and when he immediately drew a penalty, he just two-handed the referee and did break his ankle," Williams said in his memoir.

Gassoff would also leave his mark—literally and figuratively—with the Blues' farm team, the Denver Spurs, where he compiled an unbelievable 301 PIM in a mere 45 games. Promotion to the NHL did not soften him in the least.

In his first game in the big leagues, he took on two former Blues enforcers St. Louis had found expendable when they heard the reviews about "Gasser." His first opponent was Steve Durbano, now with the Pittsburgh Penguins.

"Durbie took his stick and went after Gasser. And Gasser dropped the glove and beat him. And beat him," remembered teammate Bob Plager, "and knocked some of Durbie's teeth right out."

Next came Battleship Kelly, who fared no better.

"Gasser won everything that night," Plager said in his memoir.

"He just showed them how tough he really was. And this is a kid who was just 5-foot-11 and 190 pounds." Gassof had established a reputation that he just kept building upon. His stick rearranged Toronto agitator Eddie Shack's features in retaliation for a previous game's encounter, in which Shack escaped a Blues' gang attack by skating backwards halfway around Maple Leaf Gardens before diving into his own bench. Gassoff's surgical strike left Shack with a gouge near his right eye, a lacerated forehead and cheek, and a lost tooth.

"Gassoff gave it to me behind the net," Shack commiserated to the *Globe and Mail*. "I fell down after colliding with Lou Angotti. Gassoff kept raking me with the stick."

In an exhibition game against the Winnipeg Jets of the World Hockey Association, Gassoff put future Hall of Famer Bobby Hull's wrist in a cast. He dislocated ligaments in Hull's wrist with a slash just after he was released from the penalty box for previously high-sticking the star left winger. "What really galls me is if the game had been officiated properly, Gassoff wouldn't have been on the ice," Winnipeg coach Bobby Kromm complained afterwards. "He would have been in the penalty box all night."

Gassoff certainly didn't pick his spots; he even challenged the bench of the Broad Street Bullies. And of course, he tussled many times against Toronto's own untamed tiger, Dave Williams himself.

"I fought Gassoff for about five years. We played together briefly in junior in Vernon, British Columbia. In practice we used to spear each other and guys would sit around drinking beer and debating which one of us was toughest," Williams said. "I played against him in junior, the minor professional league and the NHL, and he never got easier. He would do anything to get an advantage: gouge your eyes, kick, spear, even push his finger into your nose and twist it to increase the pain."

Teammate Garry Unger remembered Gassoff as "probably the toughest guy that I ever played with in the National Hockey League" in a 2002 interview.

"I don't like to hear that name," Wilf Paiement laughed. "Bobby

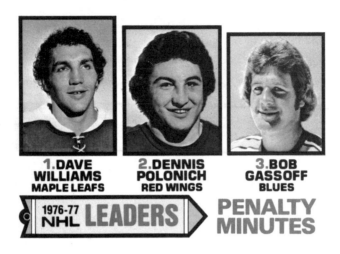

1. DAVE WILLIAMS MAPLE LEAFS
2. DENNIS POLONICH RED WINGS
3. BOB GASSOFF BLUES

1976-77 NHL LEADERS ▷ PENALTY MINUTES

Gassoff was quite a tough guy—holy, was he tough. He was probably one of the toughest that I can recall playing against."

Paiement remembered tangling with Gassoff early in his career with Kansas City and getting on the wrong end of the exchange. Teammate Larry Johnson came to lend a hand, and as Paiement and Gassoff were led to the penalty boxes, Paiement made a bit of a scene.

"He didn't say too much. He kinda looked at me and he says, 'You know what, in five minutes we gotta be out there again.' I say, 'Yeah, yeah, yeah.' Holy shit, the closer the five minutes got, the funnier I was feeling. When he came out, he came after me again," Paiement said. "That's the type of player he was. Bob Gassoff could go in any rink and raise some eyebrows. . . . Tough as nails and could compete against anybody. And he'd go after you too."

But once the game was over, Gassoff became a completely different person.

"There was a guy who on the ice was just a freak," said Blair Stewart, who played against Gassoff in junior and the NHL. He added, "And then I worked a hockey school with him in Banff and he was just the nicest, softest-spoken guy you'd ever want to meet. But you throw him out on the ice and something changes. Sometimes you see these guys and you look at them and there's nobody home. You get them off the ice, and they're just almost opposites of what you'd expect. [Dave] Schultzie was the same way. On the ice he was one way, and then off the ice he was pretty damn tame."

But besides wreaking havoc, Gassoff was also starting to show promise as a player. His coach, Emile Francis, called him the most improved player on the Blues in 1976–77. Sadly, after only four seasons with the club, a tragic accident claimed Gassoff's life. On Memorial Day weekend 1977, the 24-year-old native of Quesnel, British Columbia, was killed when his motorcycle hit a car head on. For years the memory would haunt Unger, who hosted the season-ending party Gassoff attended.

"The moment that I answered that phone call, at the moment that I realized what was going on, that question came to me like an arrow," Unger told BP Sports. "It could have been me or anybody. We were all driving and drinking and having a good time, and we were young and indestructible, and all of a sudden he was gone. That was kind of the start of my looking at this whole other side, the spiritual side of life."

Williams believed many pros slept easier when they learned they'd never have to face Gassoff again.

Not so in St. Louis. The players were devastated and the team collapsed, failing to reach the playoffs for two straight seasons and accumulating a lousy 48 points in 1978–79.

The club acknowledged his contributions by retiring his No. 3—the first number the club took out of circulation—at the start of the 1977 season.

DAVE RICHTER There was little mystery about why the Minnesota North Stars pursued collegiate defenceman Dave Richter, and it certainly wasn't for the B.Sc. in Education he earned from the University of Michigan. According to Richter, "I'm driving around in a car with a fellow by the name of John Mariucci, who's just a great guy, played in the NHL, and he goes, 'You know what? You created history with the North Stars.' I go, 'What?' And he goes, 'Yup, you're the first person that we ever drafted sight unseen.'"

Mariucci served as a special assistant to North Stars general manager Lou Nanne, and he explained to Richter how he had been coming to see a game between Richter's Wolverines and the Minnesota Golden Gophers. Arriving 10 minutes before the game was scheduled to start, he had missed a brawl that broke out during the pre-game skate. But the other scouts who'd caught it filled Mariucci in on the eruption and Richter's part in it, which convinced him to push for Richter getting drafted. The North Stars took his advice, choosing Richter in the tenth round of the 1980 draft.

It wouldn't be the first time Richter made an impression before the puck was even dropped.

Another time against the Gophers, Richter's father flew down from Winnipeg for the weekend to see his son in action. "In the pre-game warm up, I ended up getting into a fight on Friday night. So I was bounced for Friday's game and all Saturday's game," Richter remembered. "But I got to have a good visit with my Dad. He was ticked. Absolutely ticked that I got kicked out."

That's not to suggest Richter was some meathead who did nothing but get ejected from games in a league that barred fighting. He received the Carl Isaacson Award for the best student-athlete and the Vic Heyliger Trophy for outstanding Wolverine defenceman in 1982.

Richter's senior year would prove to be a monumental one. When the Wolverines were eliminated in the playoffs, the North Stars got in touch with him and urged him to come skate with the team, adding he might have a chance to play.

After getting a taste of the NHL, the towering 6-foot-5, 225-pound defenceman spent much of the following season getting his feet wet in the pros with the CHL's Birmingham South Stars.

"My first year I spent the majority of it in Birmingham, Alabama, but every time [Minnesota] played Chicago or Philadelphia, I'd get called up and I knew they didn't call me up to score a touchdown," he said, laughing. "You knew what was expected of you."

As a CHL rookie, Richter was an All-Star, but he saw a brand of hockey he'd never experienced in college: "When I played in the minors, there were a bunch [of games] that were absolutely bizarre, whether it be the benches emptying, guys standing in other teams' benches fighting; those days are gone. You'll never see those again," he laughed.

Richter saw action in 42 games with the parent club in 1983–84 and another 55 the next year, in which he took on some of the game's top guns in Terry O'Reilly, Joey Kocur, and Jeff Brubaker.

"He intimidated a lot of people just with his size and his look, and then he could also back it up too. He was a really tough kid," said teammate Brad Maxwell, noting many were surprised to find Richter mild-mannered off the ice.

Richter considered Norris Division games great hockey, with every contest played as though it was the playoffs. "It seemed like a small division, you didn't have to fly very far, the rivalries were there, the cities weren't far apart. That was great. The old Chicago and Minnesota and Detroit rivalries, that really I think was the heyday of hockey," said Richter. "They were hard-hitting, aggressive games."

Richter was happy he wasn't alone in what was a very, very tough division, with Maxwell, Willi Plett, Bob Rouse, and Harold Snepsts backing him up. "Sometimes you're playing and your shoulder might be hurt, and of course you don't let the opposition know that. It's just like some days you wouldn't be able to drop 'em and go as good as you could, and it's more the merrier is one way to put it," he said.

Richter and friends also helped alleviate Minnesota's past problems of failing to stand up to teams in their home rinks, like the Bruins in the Garden and the Flyers in the Spectrum.

The Flyers, perhaps looking to again physically dominate the league, traded for him in 1985–86. "He hasn't lost a fight," North Stars GM Lou Nanne said at the time. "He might lose one someday, but he's not going to lose many. And with him and Dave Brown, nobody is going to mess with the Flyers."

"He can fight and, obviously, we like tough guys," said Flyers general manager Bobby Clarke, adding the team had been considering acquiring Richter for a while. "We've been impressed with his strength and defensive ability."

But Richter didn't seem to have a smooth relationship with Flyers coach Mike Keenan, so Clarke, who traded Ed Hospodar to the North Stars for Richter, ended up re-signing Hospodar as a free agent and trading Richter to Vancouver for J.J. Daigneault.

Richter lasted two seasons on the West Coast. His last game with the Canucks came in March 1988 against the New York Islanders, during which he earned a 10-game ban for leaving the penalty box at the end of the second period to confront scrappy goalie Billy Smith, with whom he engaged in a shouting match.

By the start of the 1988–89 season, Richter was suiting up for the St. Louis Blues, who had also added Craig Coxe to beef up their lineup. "When you have size, you have presence," Blues star centre Bernie Federko said of the additions.

Federko must have been happy to finally see Richter on his side, having faced him as an enemy player and suffering a whack in the face from Richter's stick in '85, when Richter was still a North Star.

"I want our team to be a team that has respect," said Brian Sutter, who'd just become the new coach of the Blues. "He's known for sticking up for his teammates, and he's a big guy."

Having played for several teams in so short a period, Richter said he often ran into ex-teammates but found no difficulty in sorting his priorities.

The whole thing is you're playing for whose jersey you're wearing and you want that team to win. And you did whatever you did to help the team win. Some people think fighting is how are they doing in the fight or how many times are they fighting. The more important thing is can you pick a time that's going to change the flow of a game, or help your teammates with the final outcome. Is that going to help that team in your long series against the opposition or for that specific game? Is it going to help you win that game?

The Richter-Coxe experiment in St. Louis lasted only one season. Richter spent the next couple years bouncing between IHL and AHL teams before retiring. But his exploits haven't been forgotten, even if he might prefer they remain in the past. "The funniest thing is I'm coaching my son now and he's 12. A couple years ago, I told them, 'You don't take silly penalties; if there's pushing after the whistle, just get out of there.' And he and his teammates looked at me when I was giving the speech, and he goes, 'Yeah, but Dad, we Googled you at school today,'" Richter said.

A number of his scraps have been preserved on YouTube, which has given not only the kids but his fellow salesmen at the office a chance to see the previously unknown side of the seemingly gentle giant. "If you have a short memory, someone at work will say, 'Hey, look at this!' So it gets brought up probably more frequently now for my generation than it did for people that played previous to me."

Richter is reminded of his past career on a daily basis, as he still carries the battle wounds he collected in the course of his journey. "Every time it gets cold, a couple [fingers] aren't useful. I've been told that they have very good joint replacements for your thumbs now. Every time I see the doctor, they look at that and they go, 'When do you want your nose done again?' It comes with the game. You have the bad back, bad knees, bad shoulder, bad hands, bad nose. That's all part and parcel of it."

DAVE MANSON His opponents might have thought he
lived up to his nickname, "Charlie," but Dave Manson was far from enthused about it.

"It was an easy nickname to give," Manson said in his distinctive raspy, loud whisper that came courtesy of a punch to the throat.

"It's not one that you're proud of by any stretch of the imagination, given the history of the man. It didn't reflect in any way shape or form the way I played—I hope, anyway."

"I'll say this, if given a choice between two nicknames, one's 'The Grim Reaper,' one's 'Charlie Manson,' I'm glad I got stuck with mine," said Manson's Blackhawks teammate Stu Grimson.

The nickname, after the leader of the California cult-like criminal Manson Family of the 1960s, came in the juniors, where he developed his physical brand of hockey.

"I think we played the game hard in junior and sometimes maybe you cross the line," said Manson. "Some guys were looking for a night off and there were no nights off. If somebody came down the ice with their head down, they got hit. It was a lot different game than it is today."

Years into Manson's professional career, Terry Simpson, his head coach with the WHL's Prince Albert Raiders, still enthused about him. "He plays with aggressive passion; it's something you'd like to see in all players. He commands room on the ice," Simpson told the *Edmonton Journal*.

Manson's most rambunctious years in the NHL came with Chicago, where he carved out a reputation as a dangerous, unpredictable defenceman.

"You could always tell he was wound up when his eyes started spinning," said Simpson.

"Dave was the guy that you were nervous around because he had that 'snap factor,'" said Kelly Chase of Chicago's most hated rival, the St. Louis Blues, adding, "He doesn't mind dropping the gloves, yet he might slash with the stick first or cross-check you or whatever it was. . . . He was one of those guys with a short fuse and he was tough and he'd fight anybody. You never knew with Dave exactly what he was thinking, which is always a good way to have a tough guy because they keep you off balance."

Tony Twist, another Blue, said, "He could fight. He wasn't afraid to fight, use his stick, the body. He intimidated a lot of guys from positioning up in front of the net. . . . I had a lot of respect for him because he played a tough, hard-nosed game. He was one of those guys that every team wants to have."

"It didn't matter who it was, he didn't hold back; he'd hurt you," said Curt Keilback, who observed Manson as play-caller for the Winnipeg Jets and Phoenix Coyotes.

Not even a perennial All-Star, Norris Trophy winner and future Hall of Famer like Boston's Ray Bourque got special treatment, as Bourque discovered one night in Chicago Stadium. Attempting to gain the Chicago zone, Bourque was unceremoniously straight-armed by Manson and dumped onto the ice.

"It was just a case of it didn't matter who's coming across the blue line. You're young and want to make sure you protect your territory. And at the time, it just happened to be Ray Bourque. It's one of those things, you play the game hard and that happened," said Manson, chuckling. "There were no free passes in those days."

With one exception: Ken Baumgartner.

"We had a mutual respect there. We won the Memorial Cup together," said Manson of their playing days with the Raiders, adding:

> There was one time in Toronto he laid a bodycheck on me, I had my head down, but Kelly Buchberger had already come in there, so that was the only time it was even close. Ken played pretty honest at the NHL level, never took advantage of anybody on our team, and I tried to show him the same respect. If the line was ever crossed where you had to do something, you crossed that bridge when you got to it. But Ken and I were fortunate enough to play together and win a Memorial Cup and that's something that you carry with you for a long time.

"There are certain players that you have an understanding with," Baumgartner confirmed in an interview with the *Toronto Star*. "We're friends. The day I hurt my friends is probably the day I'll get out of the game."

Dave Manson of the Toronto Maple Leafs does his best to stop Sandy McCarthy of the New York Rangers during the 2000–01 season. (IHA/Icon SMI)

Besides a significant physical presence, Manson also brought a touch for the net to his game. In 1988–89, Manson not only racked up a massive 352 PIM but also drove home 18 goals—after scoring only two in his first 117 NHL games—with his wickedly heavy slapshot. He also ended up appearing in the All-Star Game. Thanks to all the attention his partner Doug Wilson garnered from opponents, Manson found himself with room to shoot. He said, "My job was pretty simply—get pucks to the net and I was fortunate enough that some of them went in."

Mike Keenan, his coach, would liken Manson to Islanders stalwart Denis Potvin. "He's got all the attributes of Potvin," Keenan said that year. "He can skate and shoot and he's tough both physically and mentally. The big thing with Potvin was that he was a tough competitor."

Statistically, that season would prove to be Manson's highwater mark. By the time he was traded to the Edmonton Oilers, Manson had become a steady defender rather than a bomb waiting to explode. But he still could score and boasted 200-plus penalty minutes, saying his offensive strategy didn't change much from his Chicago days when Wilson led the attack: "No different in Edmonton, where we had Norm McIvor . . . he was a playmaker back there. When you can shoot the puck, the best thing to do is get the puck at the net."

After Manson's first 15-goal season with the Oilers, the Washington Capitals came along with a $5.1 million four-year contract, a huge rise from his $300,000 annual salary. The Oilers' GM Glen Sather matched the offer and kept him on the roster.

"Tell Slats Dave's worth it. He's a bargain," said Simpson, who by then was an assistant coach with the Jets. "He's going to be a great player."

With his new contract in hand, Manson managed another 15 goals to go along with 220 minutes in penalties.

"So much talent . . . then you throw in that mean streak," Oilers assistant coach Ron Low said to the *Edmonton Journal*. "Not too many tough guys can skate like Charlie or make plays like him. Bob Probert, maybe. The thing about Charlie is the more you play him the better he gets. Against Winnipeg the other night he had to play about 40 minutes because we lost some defencemen, yet he was the best player on the ice by a mile. He's turned into a leader. If he keeps his cool, he can be a star in this league."

Low explained the coaching staff tried to get Manson to act instead of react, pointing out teams sometimes took advantage of him in Chicago by goading him into taking bad penalties. A dirty look by this point in his career was often enough to put players in their place.

"His presence arrives before he does. The first time I met him . . . well, you didn't want to say anything to upset him. . . . Especially with that Clint Eastwood voice now," said Oiler goalie Norm Foster, who added Manson was in fact soft-spoken when you got to know him. "There's intimidation there with Charlie. There's the element of the unexpected. That plays in his favour."

Another move, this time to Winnipeg, and Manson became almost tame compared to his Chicago days: "Everyone thought he was a lunatic [in Chicago]. He said the first year he just went a little crazy, the guys got scared of him and after that his reputation carried him," said Keilback. "You didn't see those vengeful attacks on anybody when he played with the Jets and I don't think you saw many of them when he played in Edmonton either. When he was in Chicago his rookie season, that's where he established his territory."

Chase agreed, saying Manson had already earned his space on the ice.

"He made his point lots of times early in hockey. He got respect from guys; they didn't act up when he was out there," Chase said.

After following the Jets to Phoenix and playing as a Coyote for a season, Manson would spend time with the Canadiens, make a return to the Blackhawks, and then take a run all the way to the final with the Dallas Stars before signing with the Toronto Maple Leafs, where he played his 1,000th game.

Manson's efforts would encourage a new generation of players coming into the league. On WadeBelak.com, the late enforcer would list Manson as one of his hockey heroes. He was thrilled to play with him in Toronto and called Manson his favourite road roommate.

"Wade's a western kid and he's a great kid. . . . It's great that younger guys look up to you and Wade plays the game as honest as it can be played in today's game," Manson said prior to Belak's untimely death in 2011.

Others Leafs offered accolades for their teammate.

"He's one tough customer," Shayne Corson, who also played with Manson in Edmonton and Montreal, told Neil Stevens. "When you finished a game against him, you knew you'd been in a battle.

"As a teammate, he's a leader on and off the ice. He's always ready to back you up. He always works hard in practice and gives everything he has, game in and game out. Everybody has a bad night, but it's never a matter of lack of effort in Dave Manson's case. I know there is a lot of respect for Dave in this dressing room."

BOB MCGILL The Toronto Maple Leafs were desperate for just about everything in 1981–82—including toughness. They'd just traded away Tiger Williams when they promoted 19-year-old Leduc, Alberta, native Bob McGill to their struggling back line.

A second-round draft pick in 1980, McGill was thrust into a trial by fire, as were two other teenagers, Fred Boimistruck and Jim Benning, for what proved to be yet another horrendous season for the Leafs.

"Obviously, looking back, I wasn't ready," McGill told the *Toronto Star.* "It would have been okay with one of us teenagers, or maybe two, but with all three of us it was a very difficult situation. I bounced back, but a guy like Freddy never recovered."

After a respectable initial showing in 68 games—as respectable as is possible on a 20-44-16 club—McGill would spend more time with the farm team in St. Catharines, Ontario, than the parent club over the next couple years. In his sophomore season, McGill found himself getting booed out of Maple Leaf Gardens until the Leafs mercifully pulled the plug and sent him down to their affiliate, where he'd play 35 minutes a game and work closely with coach Doug Carpenter after practice.

His confidence returned and so did he, permanently, to the

NHL in 1984–85. The '80s were no place for meek defencemen, as defenders were often called upon to trade punches and the occasional head-butt too.

"I was suspended a couple times for head-butting, but nothing like the head-butt [Bob Probert] gave me where he cold-cocked me," McGill said, also recalling banging his head into Chris Nilan's when the latter had his arms completely tied up. "The other one was when I was in the American League, where I fought Dave Brown, and he knocked me down twice. Stupid me gets back up both times and continues to fight, and I'm friggin' bleeding all over the place, and I was pissed off so I kind of head-butted him and I got a couple games suspension for that."

McGill's reputation as a tough customer grew, so much so that Wendel Clark's agent gave him a heads-up about McGill before Clark arrived for his first Leafs training camp.

"Seems [McGill] was more interested in my penalty minutes with Saskatoon than he was with the fact that I'd been drafted No. 1. So he wanted to formally welcome me to the Leafs. As I would find out later when the season started, it was nice having Big Daddy on your side," Clark said in *Wendel: My Life in Hockey*.

McGill put together three more seasons with the Leafs after his 55-game stint with St. Catharines in 1983–84 before getting a reprieve. In 1987 he was sent to Chicago along with Steve Thomas and Rick Vaive in exchange for his chief Blackhawks rival, Al Secord, as well as Ed Olczyk in a blockbuster summer trade. It was a gift for McGill, who was used sparingly the previous season and seemed destined for a return to the minors. Apparently expendable for Leafs coach John Brophy and company, McGill was welcomed in Chicago, where he would become a pillar on an eventual first-place club's defence.

"It was pretty ironic because when I played with the Leafs, Chicago was a pretty heated rivalry, but Al Secord was kind of my nemesis on the other side. And we got traded for each other," said McGill. "So when I went to Chicago, they welcomed me with open arms. I remember meeting Denis Savard on the sidewalk outside the hotel the first day and he's like, 'Oh hey! How's it goin'? Glad to finally have you on my side!'"

Whether an enemy Leaf or hometown Blackhawk, McGill always felt pumped to play in Chicago Stadium, especially when Wayne Messmer belted out "The Star-Spangled Banner." "There was nothing like it. If you couldn't get up and be ready when the puck dropped in that building, then you weren't alive," said McGill, whose hair on the back of his neck would stand up as the crowd roared non-stop through Messmer's performance. "Even when I played with the Leafs in the early years, we always played well in Chicago because we used to go crazy on the bench while the national anthem was playing—you'd get jacked up and go. When you played there on a regular basis and you were winning all the time, it was the loudest building. You could never imagine."

McGill fit right in with the team, and the 6-foot-1, 205-pounder developed a fraternity with Chicago's other tough guys. "We had a real close team. The four years I was there we lost the [Conference Final] in '89 and '90, and won the President's Trophy in '91 but lost to Minnesota in the friggin' first round. But it was a tight group. It was kind of something where you went through the wars together so you stayed kinda close."

Chicago's chief antagonist was the St. Louis Blues, and one of their resident tough guys, Kelly Chase, respected McGill's aggressive style. "He was a guy that always came and played hard, that we knew was going to stick up for his teammates and was a team leader," said Chase.

In 1991 the Blackhawks lost McGill when the San Jose Sharks chose him in the expansion draft.

"We lost some leadership, some toughness and a real top team player," Chicago's coach and general manager Mike Keenan said at the time, adding he wasn't sure how the team would replace McGill's toughness. "It's obviously a real disappointment, but that's what expansion is all about. The new teams pay $50 million to get good hockey players and they got a good one in Bob McGill."

Mark Osborne, Bob McGill, Tessa Bonhomme and host Paul Hendrick talk hockey on Leafs TV. (Graig Abel)

The Sharks knew it too.

"In Bob McGill, we got the veteran defenceman we were looking for," Chuck Grillo, San Jose's director of player personnel, said in an interview with the *Chicago Daily Herald*. "We've got a crop of young defencemen who are going to need help with their careers and we think Bob is the right guy for that."

In spite of his value as a tough, dependable rearguard, San Jose couldn't turn down Detroit's offer of Johan Garpenlov and sent McGill to the Red Wings at the trade deadline for the talented Swedish winger.

"That was the weirdest feeling ever walking into the Detroit Red Wing dressing room for the first time because I was the hated guy, and I hated them because they were bitter rivals with Chicago and the Leafs my whole 10 years. And all of a sudden, you're walking into the dressing room as part of the Red Wings. It was a surreal experience," McGill said, noting his former sparring mate, Probert, was still there. "It was kind of neat to have him on my side for a change instead of having to line up against him and having to worry about getting killed."

Ironically, the Wings would be bounced out of the playoffs by McGill's former team, the Blackhawks, getting swept in four straight games in the 1992 division final.

The rest was a blur as he got drafted by Tampa Bay but was claimed on waivers by the Leafs after opting for salary arbitration. Unfortunately, his return to his original NHL club was cut short by a broken jaw. In 1993–94, McGill suited up for the New York Islanders and Hartford Whalers before retiring.

The following year, he did television colour commentary for the IHL's Chicago Wolves. But the itch to return to action overtook him and he would strap on the skates once more.

"When I quit, I hadn't played much my last two years, and I wasn't really happy with the game of hockey," said McGill to the *Herald*.

Ironically, McGill crossed paths with Secord again, but this time as a teammate, as Secord had staged his comeback the year before. McGill told the *Herald*:

We've become pretty good friends, actually. Al came back to Chicago for one year and we played together on the Hawks [in 1989–90]. It was kind of funny because we had about 10 different fights and we didn't like each other too much. But we became teammates, and we have a mutual respect for one another because we both come to the rink and battle hard. We've scratched and clawed for everything we have. I think you have mutual admiration for that type of player when you play with him on your team. We get along very well. We're a couple of older guys, so we've got to lead the way for the young guys and show them how it's done.

However, McGill only managed eight games before a shoulder injury forced him to finally call it a career as an active player. After trying his hand at coaching in the East Coast Hockey League (ECHL) AHL, and OHL, McGill returned to the broadcast booth, where he provides analysis for Leafs TV and radio colour commentary for Toronto's AHL affiliate, the Marlies.

BRAD MAXWELL Very few players got anything resembling a free pass in the 1970s. Even skilled NHL defencemen were called upon to settle scores against liberty-takers.

Today, Brad Maxwell could probably get by on his skating and puck prowess alone. But back in his salad days, Maxwell had to stick up for himself and the rest of his Minnesota North Stars teammates by taking on the likes of Stan Jonathan, Tiger Williams, and Dwight Schofield.

Fortunately for him, he had junior coach Ernie "Punch" McLean to get him ready for the wars.

"If you looked around the league at the time, in the three years that I played for him, the NHL was a much more physical game," said Maxwell. "Every team had five, six, seven guys that were really tough, and they had a mix too and guys that could play. And I think he saw that and that's what he was looking at. He got a lot of guys drafted that played in the NHL."

Maxwell played in three Memorial Cups in a row for McLean's New Westminster Bruins, losing the first two but winning in 1977. Although he racked up his share of penalties in junior, he was forced to pick up his physical game when he joined the North Stars.

"I didn't really want to play physical, but sometimes I just felt you had to stand up. Some guy comes in and gives you a cheap shot and you have to respond to it," Maxwell said, adding that the North Stars had their share of smaller players and Europeans who needed someone to stick up for them.

"He was a guy that looked after his teammates," said New

York Rangers great Harry Howell, who coached the North Stars in 1978–79. "I was happy to have him, and I'm sure all the other players were too."

Minnie's mettle was severely lacking at times, a glaring short-coming exposed during a December 1977 game against the Boston Bruins in which John Wensink issued an unanswered challenge to the entire North Stars bench.

"Boston was one of those teams that had a lot of guys—Jonathan, Wensink, [Terry] O'Reilly, Mike Milbury. And at that time, we were trying to be more of a playmaking team and not so much into that physical part of it. I know I was on the bench when he came over there and I didn't want to get suspended. I like playing the game."

Maxwell was a rookie at the time, and one of the few bright lights on a club that was on the verge of folding. Minnesota ended the season with the league's worst record and went through three coaches. His 18 goals that year set the franchise record for a rookie defenceman, and, although physically capable, he had no intention of leading a one-man charge against Wensink and the Bruins.

"That's always been such a controversial thing with what he did. But if you look at Wensink, he wasn't really much of a player. . . . To jump onto the ice, get suspended because you're coming off the bench, and do that for a guy like that, it didn't make much sense. . . . A lot of guys felt that way, that Wensink wasn't worth it," Maxwell said, adding the North Stars didn't have a designated enforcer to deal with an opposing player who just wanted to fight.

The new coach of the North Stars (who wouldn't last to the end of the season) didn't seem disappointed his players ignored Wensink's taunts.

"To me fights are going to happen in hockey," André Beaulieu said after the dust had settled somewhat. "There are frustrations and tempers. As long as it's a one-on-one situation, each player can handle himself. I don't think [responding to Wensink] would have helped. Why cause more trouble . . . I don't want any team to dictate to me how we are going to play."

That attitude in Minnesota would change in the coming years. When the league granted approval for the Cleveland Barons to merge with the North Stars, GM Lou Nanne ended up inserting a number of physical Barons players into his lineup. Through trades, the North Stars became a tougher team and were finally ready to defend themselves. With a new, pugilistic-minded coach in Glen Sonmor, the North Stars came looking for a fight when they visited Boston on February 26, 1981.

"Glen was a tough guy when he played. The North Stars had never won in Boston in 14 years and you go into Boston and it was a really small rink, and you can get intimidated with the physical players that they had," said Maxwell. "We had a meeting before the game and [Sonmor] says, 'We have tough players, and we have players that can play both ways. Tonight, we're just going to go to war. We're going to make it a battle. I'm tired of coming in here and losing games because we get physically outplayed.'"

The North Stars waited all of seven seconds before starting a fight as Bobby Smith took on Bruins agitator Steve Kasper. The first period took an hour and 31 minutes to complete after 341 penalty minutes were assessed.

Both teams ended up shattering six NHL penalty records, including total penalties for one game, with 406 minutes. Coach Sonmor even tried to go after his counterpart behind the Bruins bench, Gerry Cheevers. After tussling with fans on his way back to the dressing room, Sonmor challenged Cheevers to a fist fight.

"If he wants to check the heart of anybody in our organization, start with mine," Sonmor said about Cheevers having questioned Bobby Smith's courage. "We've got a corridor right down by our dressing room in Minnesota. Come right down there and I'll gladly accommodate him. And tell him when he does come to bring a basket to carry his head home. I've had it up to here with him."

Although the North Stars lost 5-1, Somnor was ecstatic that his team sent a message to the Bruins: They would no longer be pushed around.

"We're a little tired about this team laughing at us and saying, 'All you have to do is come out and push them.' Now let's see how they like it. Evidently, they don't like it when they don't win all the fights. . . . What is our alternative? Stand back there and take that and be sneered at and laughed at? No sir. It's over," said Sonmor.

The North Stars would also have the last laugh, sweeping the Bruins 3-0 in the first round of the '81 playoffs.

"It was like playing a whole different team," said Maxwell. "Boston wasn't quite as physical and wasn't as intimidating. Boston won a lot of games on intimidation. They had talented players, but they had more physical players than they had talent."

Maxwell remembered there weren't many fights in their playoff series and that Sonmor's idea worked out for the best: "We had a talented team in '81, so if you want to play with us, we'll beat you," said Maxwell.

The North Stars went all the way to the Stanley Cup Final before bowing out in four straight games against the great New York Islanders.

"I think what happened to us is we got in there as a bunch of young kids, and you're playing against Trottier, and Potvin, and Bossy, Smith, Gillies and these guys, and we were more in awe for the first few games, and we just stood around and were watching them play instead of playing," Maxwell remembered. "For us to get that far, that was a pretty big deal."

During Maxwell's years with the North Stars, heavies like Paul Holmgren, Jack Carlson, Willi Plett, and Dave Richter roamed the ice, ready to start or quell trouble.

"What they also did is give a little bit of leeway to some of the guys like Dino Ciccarelli and Neal Broten, knowing that they weren't going to get picked on and hammered on by some big tough guy because they had somebody behind them who would help them out."

The North Stars entered the Norris Division in 1981–82 and soon built up a rivalry with Chicago that's still talked about at Minnesota

Wild games, according to Maxwell. But the North Stars–Hawks game that stands out the most for him didn't even have anything to do with what was happening on the ice. This particular game occurred in Chicago Stadium, a rowdy place under normal circumstances—but this was a playoff game and the stadium was packed beyond capacity with a number of fans who felt particularly rambunctious.

"Something happened in the stands. It started behind our net—two fans started fighting and pretty soon the whole lower section from behind our goal to all the way behind the players' bench, they were all fighting. And they had all these security guards in orange jackets roughing up people. I don't know how it started—it wasn't like there were Minnesota fans in there. These people were all from Chicago and fighting with each other," said Maxwell, noting the game completely stopped when the brawl got out of control, with the players standing around for 30 minutes watching the proceedings from the ice and benches. "They're swinging and kicking; the women were fighting, the guys were fighting. Both teams just kind of stood there in awe and watched this. It was an incredible thing."

Besides holding up his end of the physical bargain, Maxwell could also score. No rearguard in franchise history has broken his personal best of 19 goals in a season. That came in 1983–84, when Maxwell also recorded a career-high 73 points and set a personal penalty minute record of 225.

Despite establishing career-high numbers, Maxwell was traded to the Quebec Nordiques the following season. He wouldn't find out why until years after his retirement, when Nanne came clean during an alumni gathering over a few beers—Maxwell's wife at the time didn't get along with the other players' wives.

"And I go, 'Well, Louie, I wish you had told me because I could have divorced her back then,'" Maxwell said of his first missus. "Because I liked Minnesota, I liked playing here. And you always want to stay on the team you started playing with."

After asking for a trade out of Quebec, Maxwell played for a struggling Maple Leafs outfit before being shipped off to the Canucks. Later he was picked up by Phil Esposito of the New York Rangers. From there, he'd return to the North Stars in what had to be among the strangest deals of all time.

"I went to New York and played 10 games and we won like eight of the 10 games that I played and then I got traded back to Minnesota in a card game," he said.

Nanne and Esposito were childhood friends and maintained their ties into adulthood, even purchasing Florida vacation homes that were next to each other and playing the odd game of chance.

"And what they're doing is gambling players—they're writing players' names down on a piece of paper and that's what they're gambling. That's what Phil told me. He caught me one night, I was in New York, and we were practising in the morning and he said he was gambling with Louie last night and he lost me in a card game. He said, 'I lost you to one of your old bosses,' and I said, 'Which one? I had a few.'"

Maxwell returned to Minnesota and played under "Miracle on Ice" coach Herb Brooks. His contract ran out in 1987, but he showed up for camp in '88 hoping to secure a spot. In spite of having a good tryout, Nanne had brought in other defencemen, and Maxwell was left the odd man out. His agent could have gotten him signed with the Washington Capitals, but the trades had taken their toll on his pride.

"When you're first drafted to a team—I was a first round pick—you're kind of like a T-bone steak. When you get traded, you're like a sirloin. You keep working your way down until you're hamburger," said Maxwell, who now questions his decision. "I should have went when I look back on it all. But sometimes what happens is you've been traded that much in the last three years, you lose a little bit of self-esteem, and I just thought maybe it's time I started looking for a real job."

KEN DANEYKO

Three Stanley Cups, 20 seasons with the same team, his number retired—pretty rarefied air for any hockey player, but especially for a stay-at-home defenceman who was drafted by an unnamed team that had been one of the league's punchlines.

The franchise was newly arrived in New Jersey, fresh into its latest move after having already bounced from Kansas City to Colorado. They'd eventually settle on the moniker "Devils," after being known as the Rockies and Scouts, although Wayne Gretzky once charged that "Mickey Mouse" was a more apt name for the struggling club.

Chosen 18th overall in the first round of the 1982 entry draft by New Jersey, Ken Daneyko couldn't find East Rutherford on a map but was thrilled to get an NHL opportunity, wherever it was. A broken leg in his first season set back the 19-year-old, but management was pleased with what they'd seen.

"Certainly the toughness didn't hurt," said Daneyko. "They were happy, especially the way the game was played then, that I was going to bring some toughness around the net and protect our goaltender, and do whatever it took to keep the puck out. That was certainly part of my role."

New Jersey only really began turning around its fortunes when it brought in Lou Lamoriello, who would become the team's general manager and eventually the longest serving GM of a single team in the league. Under Lamoriello, the 1987–88 Devils garnered the franchise's first-ever winning regular-season record with players like Daneyko, Kirk Muller, John MacLean, Pat Verbeek, and Bruce Driver making up the nucleus of a good, young team.

"Lou got here and gave us some structure and discipline, and for the last decade of my career, we were one of the elite franchises in hockey. I was very proud of that and glad I was around to be part of it," Daneyko said, adding, "When Lou came . . . he said if you wanna play five years or you wanna play 15, you gotta make your niche, to be a good solid defenceman who plays tough and protects his goalie, protects his teammates. And I listened to him."

Hot goaltending from rookie Sean Burke helped lift the Devils all the way to the 1988 conference final, where they eventually bowed out to the Boston Bruins in seven games. But it was the intensity of the Devils' seven-game division final against the Washington Capitals that remains most memorable for Daneyko.

"The game we beat them 10-4 at home, it was an all-out blood-bath. But the whole series was like that: both teams wanted to win," said Daneyko. "What stands out for me was every time at the end of the game, there were five-on-fives or bench-clearing brawls. It got crazy, but back then, that was part of it. And it builds team camara-derie. I know the game's changed somewhat, but when I look back, I enjoyed that part of it at times—with your teammates, ready to go to war."

The club took a massive step backwards the following season, and it wasn't until Jacques Lemaire arrived as coach and Martin Brodeur as goaltender in 1993–94 that the Devils were on the cusp of again being a serious challenger for the Stanley Cup. But they'd first have to wait for the New York Rangers to end their 54-year championship drought. The Rangers had taken a major step toward achieving that goal when they acquired Danyeko's childhood friend Mark Messier in 1991.

Growing up in Edmonton, Daneyko was taught what it took to reach the next level in hockey by his friend Messier, two years the elder, and his own brother. As adults, Messier would be in Daneyko's wedding party, and when the Edmonton Oilers played the Devils, Messier and Daneyko could often be found talking and joking before the puck was dropped. With the teams only facing each other once or twice a year, their rivalry was practically non-existent.

That all changed with Messier's trade to New York, which immediately revitalized the Rangers, and the improving Devils were anxious to shed their little-sister status.

"Now it was for real because the Rangers and us were rivals and both good teams. I remember having a lot of battles in front of the net with him," Daneyko reflected. "I had to try to slow him down at times, and if it took playing a little extra hard on him, battles are going to happen regardless of our friendship."

Every game between the teams became pivotal, and none were more hotly contested than their seven-game 1994 conference final. "Some hockey people say that may have been the best series in the history of hockey," said Daneyko. "It had everything—great goaltending on both sides, it was awfully nasty and physical, and great players involved with Messier and [Scott] Niedermayer and [Scott] Stevens. It was a great series and that creates a great rivalry."

Ultimately, the Rangers would take that series and the Cup. The next season, the Devils were ready to win their first ever championship, but Daneyko nearly missed his chance to hoist hockey's top prize after tearing his ACL in a fight against Ranger Joey Kocur at Madison Square Garden.

"He puts his whole body into it and I fell back awkward; this is in my Cup year and I ended up missing about 25 games with a torn knee ligament," Daneyko said, noting he refused surgery in favour of rehab, even though there was less than a 50% chance of recovering without going under the knife. "But fortunately, I was able to get back the last couple games and play in the playoffs—thank God—and we won our first Cup."

Daneyko would play in three more finals, winning two more Cups and playing his last shift during his third and final championship victory. He'd retire afterwards and later watch his No. 3 be lifted to the rafters.

"Hockey was my life. Since seven years old, I wanted to make it, that's all I dreamed and believed in. Certainly I humbly say nobody wanted to win more, and I think that made me successful. I understood my role and I knew I wasn't the most talented at times, but I did whatever it took."

Having never played for another team in his 20 NHL years, New Jersey fans would anoint him "Mr. Devil."

"I built a great rapport with the fans. I appreciated it and never turned a fan down for an autograph. That's what it was all about to me as far as being in New Jersey so long, I appreciated them supporting me on and off the ice," said Daneyko. "I do a lot of charitable work and that's stuff I take pride in. . . . Doing whatever I can in the community to make sure they understand I appreciate everything that was given to me here in Jersey."

You might not believe it if you've ever witnessed his stern, at times fierce countenance on the ice or watched him clearing the front of the net like a bouncer throwing out rowdy patrons, but Daneyko laughs a lot off the ice. When he offers self-deprecating remarks and jokes about life as "a frustrated golfer," one is reminded that things aren't always as they seem and one cannot possibly know the NHL's toughest men by simply judging their on-ice conduct or disposition.

"Most of them are real gentlemen and guys you'd love to have a cup of tea with. But when you're playing at the time, you're like, 'Man, I didn't know this guy's such a good guy.' But a lot of them are very respected," said Daneyko.

He'd found that out in person when he got to know two of the toughest, Tie Domi and Bob Probert, when all three were chosen to compete in the inaugural season of TV's *Battle of the Blades*.

"We spent a lot of time together—three months, five days a week—in Toronto. So that's when I got to know these tough guys and how good guys they are, and it was so sad what happened to Probert," said Daneyko, lamenting Probert's death in 2010. "Probie was probably top five, maybe best of all time. And just a great guy, a big teddy bear. You can't believe with what he's done in battle, how good a guy he is."

All three former ruffians were apprehensive about doing the show, worried they'd embarrass themselves and that no one would even watch. Daneyko chuckled at the thought of the three looking more like fish out of water than ex-pugilists, as they struggled to look graceful alongside Olympic-medalist figure skaters. It was a humbling experience, and one that gave them a deeper appreciation for the sport and the sacrifice it requires. Perhaps most enjoyable for Daneyko was a return to a familiar routine.

"It was like we got to reminisce and go back to our old days as far as being in the dressing room. I think a lot of players will tell you when they retire, yeah you miss the game, but you miss as much the camaraderie in the room. And we got to go back to those days a little bit," Daneyko said. "It was a great time, they did a great job up there, and it got huge ratings in Canada. Our ratings were as high if not higher than *Hockey Night in Canada*, and that says something."

PAUL LAUS League expansion has driven many a hockey purist to decry the watering down of the professional game. But without expansion, Paul Laus might never have escaped the minor leagues to become an integral part of an underdog squad vying for the Stanley Cup.

Laus seemed destined to be buried in the minors, unable to crack the lineup of a Pittsburgh team that would capture two consecutive Cups before winning the President's Trophy. It wasn't until the Florida Panthers entered the league that Laus was able to become a regular NHL blueliner.

In only their third year, the Panthers not only made it to the playoffs, but they surprised the hockey world by marching all the way to the final. Laus, who had always filled his team's role as enforcer, became a workhorse for the club, playing his first full NHL regular season and logging important minutes in the playoffs.

"Right before the playoffs, I messed up my hand pretty bad so I couldn't fight . . . I had to actually play," Laus said. "But you look at it now, there's not a ton of fighting in the playoffs. It's all about the grind game."

Coach Doug MacLean raved about Laus, comparing him to Devils stalwart Ken Daneyko.

"He's improved as much as anybody on this team. Halfway through the year, we saw him make a big jump. He's so well respected in the league as a tough guy. But he's become a much better player," MacLean told the *Miami Herald*.

Always a tough, physical defenceman, Laus established his style of play early on, hitting the opposition from the time he started playing organized hockey. He went from playing against boys to men when he turned 16 and skated for the Junior B St. Catharines Falcons. Luckily, he inherited some of the genes of his 6-foot-6 father, "Big John," and already stood 6-foot. Still, he says, the experience of competing against players as old as 21 was "quite an eye opener."

The following year, he was defending Hamilton Steelhawks territory in the OHL. The team moved to Niagara Falls the next season, 1988–89, after which Laus was drafted in the second round by Pittsburgh. It was a memorable event and a curious process to say the least.

Laus sat in the stands with his agent at the Met Center in Bloomington, Minnesota, waiting for his name to be called. Prior to the selection process, Laus had found himself thoroughly interrogated at big boardroom tables by men in suits who lobbed psychological testing questions, among others, to determine every possible personality facet.

"We met with every team and that was quite the experience . . . they're asking you questions about everything. The weirdest questions, but supposedly that tell you that you're a certain type of person and player."

Laus played one more OHL season, and it was by far his best; he scored 13 goals and 35 assists in 60 regular season games while also accumulating 231 PIM. But he saved his best for the playoffs, exploding for six goals and 16 assists in 16 contests.

The high was brief, as Laus turned pro just as the Penguins were embarking on a two-year championship run, winning the Cup in 1991 and 1992. With no spots open on the big club, Laus had the choice of returning to junior as an over-age player, sitting on the bench in Muskegon of the IHL, or playing in the ECHL.

Choosing the ECHL, Laus played just 20 games with the Knoxville Cherokees before injuries in Muskegon resulted in him getting called up: "It's funny how things work out, but looking back at it, it was an opportunity for me to move up. I went to Muskegon and played the rest of the year there. It's one of those things where opportunities knock and you've just got to take advantage of it."

Held off the goal-scoring sheet for the entire next season, Laus then followed the club to Cleveland when it relocated, and ended up scoring eight goals while earning the second-highest penalty-minute total in the league, with 427.

"The IHL back then was a very physical league and it suited me. My coach at the time, Phil Russell, who kind of played the same way I did, helped me tremendously with dealing with on-ice situations and how to handle myself."

Given Pittsburgh's success, it seemed like Laus could wind up buried and forgotten in the minors. That is until the league added two new Sun Belt teams. While on his honeymoon, he received a call from his mother, who told him his agent was looking for him.

"I talked to him and he said I got picked up in the expansion draft by Florida and I go, 'There's a team in Florida?' I didn't even know at the time. But obviously that changed my life in a huge way, going down there and playing there the rest of my career."

Looking back at his minor-league experience, Laus said his three-year apprenticeship helped him immensely. But in 1993–94, he was just looking to get a second chance at the NHL.

Not only did he make the club, but the Panthers recorded the best regular season ever by a first-year NHL expansion team, earning 83 points in 84 games and just missing the playoffs by a single point.

"We had a great core of veterans, from Brian Skrudland, Scott Mellanby, to John Vanbiesbrouck," Laus said, explaining he wasn't surprised by Florida's initial success. "They all were proven guys that still had good years left in them."

Also contributing to the club's good fortune was its first coach, veteran innovator Roger Neilson. The long-time Peterborough Petes boss had extensive experience in the NHL, having stood behind the benches of the Toronto Maple Leafs, Buffalo Sabres, Vancouver Canucks, Los Angeles Kings, Chicago Blackhawks, and New York Rangers before he landed in Miami.

"You couldn't ask for a better coach starting up a new organization," Laus said. "He instilled defence-first and played a system that, he knew if everybody bought into, we would be successful. The trap, it made teams frustrated—but at the time, we weren't a very skilled team. We weren't going to score five, six goals a game. But if we did get one or two goals and we shut down everyone else, we had a chance of winning."

At the time, Laus was building a reputation as a fighter. Hockeyfights.com reports he fought 11 times in only 39 games that year.

As Laus himself said, "Anytime that you're that type of [physical] player, it goes hand in hand with fighting. It's a by-product."

But the team looked for more from Laus than just his handy fists, and he spent a good deal of time with assistant coach Lindy Ruff, working on his agility and conditioning. It would pay off.

"You focus so much on his aggressive style, you tend to overlook his developing skills," said Panthers GM Bobby Clarke to the Palm Beach *Post*.

"There was a stretch when we had to put him in there and he came through. The future looks pretty good for him," added Neilson.

The Panthers missed the playoffs by one point *again* in the following, lockout-shortened season, but the club proved it was only getting better.

By 1995–96, Florida's first-ever draft pick, Rob Niedermayer had a career year, and youngsters Ed Jovanovski and Rhett Warrener, both drafted in 1994, were already playing like veterans by playoff time. "We had a bunch of young kids with veteran older guys that gelled at the right time," said Laus.

The club's 1996 Cinderella run took them all the way to the final, but they didn't have enough to overcome a very deep and talented Colorado Avalanche team. Although the Avalanche swept the series, only the second game was a blowout, and the fourth and final contest needed three overtimes.

Florida, unfortunately, never came close to repeating the success of the 1996 playoffs. The Panthers got bounced out of the first round in 1997, failed to qualify for two years thereafter, and got swept in the first round in 2000.

Laus, however, remained a significant contributor, and in 1996–97 he often saw ice time of nearly 20 minutes a game, including turns on the penalty kill and other crucial situations.

"He's a huge luxury because he's one of the best fighters in the league, plus he's a good player," MacLean said. "He may be one of the most improved players on the team the last two years."

"His value to the team has increased so much," Vanbiesbrouck agreed. "I know he's a hero to most of our fans, but the rest of his game has matured."

While Laus's role expanded, his fighting numbers actually rose as he got into 39 fights in 1996–97. It made him a favourite with fans, evidenced by the hit that was produced by a local DJ, who changed the lyrics of a classic rock song to "I fought the Laus and the Laus won."

The adulation was a nice bonus, but being the main enforcer for the team was tough, Laus admitted. "A lot of teams had at least two or three guys back in the '90s who would fight, so it was very difficult," said Laus, who, at 6-foot-1 and 215 pounds, was smaller than a number of the super heavyweights he faced. "But we had guys who weren't necessarily the type to fight every other game, but I knew that they had my back."

It wasn't until Peter Worrell joined the team full time in 1998–99 and Todd Simpson was acquired the year after that Florida had two other fighters who could take the burden off Laus's shoulders.

"They made everyone on the other team accountable. If I was

gone for the game or had a major and was in the box for five minutes, if something else happened, I obviously couldn't get at it. But now you have Peter there and you have Todd, they would answer the call."

While many enforcers lost sleep suffering and stressing about their next fight, Laus rarely missed an afternoon nap.

"Having a couple kids wore me out, so that was good," he said. "I didn't worry about it. I left whatever I did at the rink and that's probably what kept me sane all these years."

His relaxed philosophy about fighting didn't hurt either.

"I always used to say where else can you do that, get five minutes, and you're back at it. You do that on the street, you're in jail. Some guys that I played with would watch fights before games of teams we were playing, study it. And I just went out, did my job and left it at the rink. People couldn't believe when I would go home, they'd see me out in Florida with my kids and they'd go, 'You're the same guy that's doing that?'"

Fighting may have gotten Laus into the pros and helped keep him there, but it also prematurely ended his career.

Injuries limited him to a combined 70 games over his two final seasons. A wrist injury sustained in a fight with Atlanta's Jeff Cowan on January 19, 2002, led to the operating table, which cost him the rest of the 2001–02 and entire 2002–03 seasons.

"I got in a fight, punched the helmet and drove the hand through my wrist and my wrist split in half," Laus explained.

Over the next year and a half, he had three surgeries, with the last one totally fusing his hand and wrist. "I have a steel bar from just above my knuckle to about four or five inches down my wrist on my arm," said Laus. He took one last shot at playing, arriving at Florida's 2003–04 training camp, but his wrist was totally inflexible, and he was unable to shoot or pass. His playing career was officially over.

Still Florida's all-time penalty-minute record-holder, with 1,702 minutes, Laus returned to his home province of Ontario and joined the family business, Cal's Sales and Service. He also tried his hand at coaching, but he soon found he preferred watching the game as a spectator: "I was coaching my son's team but it's a whole different ballgame, dealing with parents and everything. I just sit back and enjoy him playing now [from the stands]. I enjoy it a lot more—less stress."

Watch Your Mouth

A big part of hockey—or any competitive sport—is getting under the skin of your opponents, angering or frustrating them to the point of distraction. Announcers call it "throwing them off their game."

But what is acceptable and what isn't? Has that line changed over the years?

Those are questions that Mark Norman—a Ph.D. student at the University of Toronto who is studying the sociology of sport and is the editor of the blog HockeyInSociety.com—has been asking as he researches and teaches about hockey in Canadian society.

"There's a culture where you take every inch that you can and press every advantage. I guess there's an arbitrarily drawn line somewhere, but it's considered acceptable to get under the opponent's skin," he said. "I think these days racist taunts would not be considered an acceptable way of doing that, but certainly in the past, that definitely has been the case."

Figuring out who can say what and when is tricky. In 1999, Bryan Marchment was suspended for one game for calling Vancouver tough-guy Donald Brashear a big monkey, which the NHL head office called "an inappropriate" comment. Marchment argued that he called a lot of opponents "big monkeys" and it had nothing to do with Brashear being black.

Marchment's agent Rick Curran was up in arms. "If this league wants to publish a dictionary with what things or words are appropriate and what ones aren't and the players look at them and they sign off on them, then fine. . . . Then they deserve what they get, if they say the wrong thing," Curran said. "I just don't think the league can arbitrarily step in and say what's right and what's wrong. That's how I feel."

Colin Campbell, then the NHL's discipline czar, said where the line was drawn changes. "It's an ongoing issue in society. What's acceptable tomorrow might not be acceptable next year."

Public acceptance of any racial or homophobic slurs is a major deterrent today, said Norman. "The shame that a player will face if he is caught using racist language is almost worse; the NHL will give a fine or suspension, but it's not usually something too significant. It's hockey reflecting broader cultural shifts in North America. There is still racism, but it's not socially acceptable."

While the NHL can, to a degree, control the on-ice language, off the ice is something else.

Arron Asham, who is of Métis heritage, said he was often called names in minor hockey, less often in the WHL, and that it subsided once he got to the AHL and hasn't been an issue during his NHL career. "There's no place in hockey for racists . . . You go out there and you've got a job to do and you do it. I think it's worse from the fans."

Some of the most recent incidents have come out of the stands, like Wayne Simmonds of the Flyers having a banana hurled at him during a September 2011 exhibition game in London, Ontario. "I've never had a banana thrown at me before," he said after the game. "I guess it's something I obviously have to deal with—being a black player playing in a predominantly white sport. I've grown a lot playing in this league and throughout my whole life. I'm not going to dwell on that. It's over with now." (Christopher Moorhouse was fined $200 for the banana toss.) A year later, while playing in the Czech Republic during the NHL lockout, fans of the Chomutov team chanted "opice" (which means monkey) at Simmonds. As much as the leagues may try to legislate any inappropriate language from the rink, it will be societal changes that really dictate things.

THE FAVOURITES

Fans have always embraced the toughest players, cheering for the men who'll stick up for their favourite team and, by extension, the supporters of the home side themselves.

EDDIE SHACK Known by a variety of *noms de guerre*—Eddie the Entertainer, Fast Eddie, and Clear the Track Shack—Eddie Shack outlasted most other hockey outlaws. From Sudbury, Ontario, Shack was a junior sensation with the OHL's Guelph Biltmores, his name being mentioned by scouts alongside those of future Hall of Famers Frank Mahovlich and Bobby Hull. All three graduated to the junior ranks in 1956–57, and Shack, an All-Star, would score more goals than Hull and tally more points than Mahovlich that season.

"Eddie was physically dominating—big, strong, and tough. And he could skate and had a great shot. If he were coming up today, he'd be drafted in the first two without question," said Bob Nevin in Ross Brewitt's *Clear the Track*.

"He was such a powerful skater. I wish I could have skated like Eddie," added Shack's long-time nemesis, John Ferguson. "Shack would be in the top five of any draft year."

Bursting out of the juniors as a can't-miss, blue-chip prospect, Shack flopped in New York, managing only a combined 15 goals in his first two seasons with the Rangers. Management was unimpressed. When general manager Muzz Patrick was on the *Hot Stove Lounge* radio show one night, journalist Scott Young proclaimed Shack the best Ranger on the ice. But Patrick simply dismissed Shack as "a river skater," suggesting he was the type who could skate all night, clueless about the way the river wound. But Bobby Hull couldn't have disagreed more. In the two years he played against Shack in junior, he observed a premier player, a talented skater and shooter who also had real size and strength. "He was a goal scorer.

I would have liked to have had him on the Black Hawks anytime. He'd have been a 50-goal scorer absolutely," said Hull. "[Rangers coach] Phil Watson likely did ruin him."

Shack's career prospects didn't look good. He was traded to Detroit for Red Kelly, but the deal was scuttled when Kelly refused to report to New York. A second chance would come from Toronto, where coach and general manager Punch Imlach saw potential for little risk.

Becoming an immediate favourite with Toronto fans—what was intended to be a novelty song, "Clear the Track, Here Comes Shack," became an instant radio hit—the Entertainer would pick up the normally conservative Toronto crowds, bringing them out of their seats with his distinctive bursts into enemy territory. "When Punch didn't play me, they used to yell, 'We want Shack! We want Shack!'" he said. "Imlach used to say, 'Well, if they want you that bad, go up there and sit with them.'"

On a very deep Leafs team, Shack essentially became a 10th forward—set loose every now and again, either to settle the other team down or get his own going.

"A lot of people were scared of me," Shack said. "Just push by and shoot the puck, keep your head up, when somebody comes through centre, hit the cocksucker!"

When the 6-foot-1, 195-pound Shack was on the ice, everyone else needed to be aware of where they were at all times, according to Red Wing centre Norm Ullman, who was taken aback by how often Shack targeted his linemate Gordie Howe, a dangerous player in his own right who was normally given a wide berth. "Eddie would run him all the time. Of course, he also knew how to get out of there quick, so he'd start all kinds of things and be gone, just like that. Not too many guys gave Gordie a tough time, and Eddie was probably the only player who never got it back," Ullman said.

"I had felt a lot of those thudding Shack checks and never regarded him with the amusement that others did," John Ferguson

"The Entertainer" Eddie Shack, playing here in Buffalo, leaps past Gump Worsley in the Minnesota North Stars net, during the 1970–71 season. (IHA/Icon SMI)

said in his memoir. He was also not amused when Shack head-butted Henri Richard in the 1965–66 semifinals or when, later in the game, he nailed Jean Béliveau into the boards, knocking the hockey legend out for two games. "Lots of times he would take flying leaps at our players, picking on some of the less rugged Canadiens. When that happened, I made it a point to go after him, so we had something going right from the start. Shack climbed to the upper reaches of my 'Most Wanted' list," Ferguson said.

Shack's teammates also weren't chuckling when he sent them flying. Ferguson added: "A lot of people couldn't figure out if Shack drove his own team crazier than he did the opposition."

Once Bert Olmstead, a Maple Leaf teammate, got in Shack's flight path and got creamed as a result. After regaining his senses, Olmstead tried to get through to Shack that he needed to change direction the next time he came upon a player wearing the same colour of sweater. The message seemed to miss the mark, as Shack raced headlong into Brit Selby to celebrate after Selby scored a goal on Shack's set-up. Selby would be out three games with a bad ankle thanks to what one reporter described as the "hardest check of the night."

Shack could also drive Imlach to distraction, and their relationship was up and down.

"You never knew what was going to happen with him in a dressing room," Imlach wrote in *Hockey Is a Battle*. "I was always mad at him or laughing at him or giving him hell about something, either for something he'd done out on the ice or for something he was doing right then."

After playing on the Leafs' final Stanley Cup winner, in 1966–67, Imlach decided he wouldn't protect Shack in the expansion draft. But instead of losing him to one of the six new teams, he arranged a sweetheart deal that sent Shack to Boston in return for $100,000 and Murray Oliver. After a couple years in a Bruins uniform, Shack found himself traded to Los Angeles.

"Eddie, he was different," said Dennis Hextall, who briefly played centre on Shack's line in L.A. "He was a big, strong, powerful skater; very strong physically. I think if Eddie would have stuck to hockey and less showboating, he would have been a better player. He liked the limelight. But he was talented. Eddie Shack, he was stupid like a fox off the ice. He knows what's going on. Eddie was a smart individual. He was pretty street smart, I'll put it that way."

According to Hextall, Shack's coaches were among those whom Shack aggravated the most, which might explain why he was traded so often. "You never knew what he was going to do. Eddie just did what Eddie thought was appropriate," Hextall said.

Imlach obviously thought enough of Shack to get him when he returned to the NHL as general manager of the Buffalo Sabres. In his first year there, Shack potted 25 goals.

"Eddie the Entertainer was one of my favourite people," Imlach wrote in his follow-up to *Hockey Is a Battle, Heaven and Hell in the NHL.* "Even when he made me maddest, I couldn't help laughing at him."

Shack proved to be a great commodity for Imlach once again, as Imlach traded him to Pittsburgh for René Robert, who, with Gilbert Perrault and Rick Martin, would go on to form one third of Buffalo's vaunted "French Connection" line. After Pittsburgh, Shack would return for his swan song in Toronto.

Looking back, many of Shack's peers believed he could have been known more as a star than an entertainer—or a huckster, whether it was for the Pop Shoppe, his doughnut franchise or his wine.

Shack occasionally demonstrated the touch around the net that he'd had in junior. He notched 26 goals one season with the Leafs, scored 20 or more goals for five different teams and made three consecutive All-Star appearances from 1962–64. But generally speaking, he didn't set the NHL on fire.

"He could easily have scored 300 goals in his career. Truthfully, if I had him on my team, he would have been a big-time offensive threat, and I mean it," said Bobby Hull.

Rangers star Andy Bathgate also thought Shack's scoring stats didn't tell the whole story about his offensive abilities.

"Hell, of the 239 he got over his career, most of them were even-strength goals," he said, explaining Eddie rarely played the power play. "In today's game he'd be more than a force. He'd park his ass in front of the net and be too tough to move out of there. I don't care how big these guys are now. You can't move a player of Eddie's leg power, strength and size."

Shack said he played all out, all the time, but knew the value of being remembered as well: "I kibitzed around a little bit. I liked to have fun. We're not here for a long time, but a good time. There's so many dull hockey players. They're boring," he said.

Jerry Toppazzini, a Boston Bruin who played with Shack on a 22-game European tour at the end of the 1958–59 season, remembered Milt Schmidt once speculating Shack's problem was that he "lost the game plan somewhere between the dressing room and the bench." Toppazzini added, "With all his ability, I'll bet if he had to do it all over again he'd forget that clowning crap, because it'd be so goddamn easy to be remembered and respected as a great player.... Make no mistake, he could do it too."

Hull, who also played on that tour, recalled having to repeatedly tell Shack to stay wide and go down the right side and not the middle. And Shack would do it with grand results, but as soon as Hull left him to his own devices, Shack would return to flying all over the ice.

But Harry Howell, who played with Shack on the Rangers, said Shack's loveable buffoon reputation was overblown.

"He became a hockey player as soon as he hit the ice," said Howell. "I knew him well enough that I knew when he was going to do something crazy. But he really didn't do any of those things. I think a lot of it was in the newspapers . . . he would do this, he would do that. But he wanted to back up all his teammates all the time, and he played good hockey for us."

Don Cherry, who crossed paths with Shack down in the AHL, also recalled him being an effective player: "He was tough and he could play. Jeez, when you hit him, it was like runnin' into a bag of anvils, all elbows, knees, stick and everything. After, you'd be skating away, limpin', hurtin' worse than him. . . . As a hockey player, he was a lot more than an entertainer."

TIE DOMI Like his idol Tiger Williams, Tie Domi rarely met a microphone he didn't like. But when he quit the game, Domi had surprisingly little to say about how he came to serve over 62 hours in NHL sin bins.

"I never talk about fighting, ever. I'm not comfortable talking about it. Mentally, it was tough, tough on me," Domi said, telling the *Toronto Sun* that his job came with the kind of anxiety and pressure he didn't miss once retired. "When I played I didn't talk about it. I can remember Keith Tkachuk as a youngster in Winnipeg saying to me: 'They've got so-and-so on their team.' And I just looked at him and said, 'I don't like talking about it.' He didn't understand."

But few enforcers ever got more attention or better compensation for playing their role. And fewer still who were Domi's size were as successful.

"He was all of 5-foot-10," said Domi's former teammate Dave Manson, chuckling about Domi's officially listed height, which could also bring guffaws from teammates. "But Tie wasn't necessarily a smaller guy—he was 210 pounds. And he was strong. He had a low centre of gravity."

Some announcers, and even former teammate Adam Graves, thought he was closer to 5-foot-8, and New Jersey's Ken Daneyko put him somewhere around 5-foot-9.

"He was built like a fire plug; he was very thick and very strong, one of the strongest guys pound-for-pound for his size, no question about it. And he took on all the heavyweights and acquitted himself pretty well," Daneyko said. "It's not always the size of the dog, it's the size of the fight in the dog, and not many guys had more fight than Tie."

Domi fought bigger men his whole career. He was drafted at 16 by the Peterborough Petes, who made him their designated hit man and gave him former Pete and legendary Boston Bruins bruiser Stan Jonathan's No. 8.

"Stan Jonathan was one of the toughest guys I've ever seen,

but after a fight his face would look like it had gone through a Mixmaster. Tie never got a scratch on him," Petes coach Dick Todd told the *Waterloo Region Record.*

"I was born a fighter," Domi told the *Record* about his early days living in Toronto's west-end Junction neighbourhood. "When I was 14, I was fighting guys who were 20 and I wasn't losing."

That toughness rubbed off on others, giving Domi's teammates more confidence—and robbing his opponents of theirs. "We won a lot of games before teams got off the bus because they didn't want to face him," Petes general manager Jeff Twohe said in Domi's video, *What It Takes.*

The Toronto Maple Leafs, the same team for which his childhood favourite Tiger Williams wreaked havoc in the 1970s, drafted Domi in 1988. He spent most of his time with Toronto's farm club in Newmarket, seeing only two games with the Leafs—in which he drew 42 minutes in penalties—before being shipped off to the New York Rangers.

Daneyko played for the Rangers' chief rival, the New Jersey Devils, and knew going into a game against New York that he'd have to face a Young Turk who was trying to establish himself.

"I had some pretty good battles with him. He was a very, very tough guy," Daneyko said.

It was with the Rangers that Domi's fame grew, in no small part thanks to his heavily publicized fights with Red Wings resident champ Bob Probert, feuds that have been repeatedly reviewed, analyzed, and dissected ever since. Little did Domi know that his high-profile contests against Probert would contribute to his moving from the bright lights of New York to the relative tranquility of Winnipeg. According to Domi, a lack of playing time in New York resulted in him asking Rangers GM Neil Smith for a trade. The only caveat? "Don't trade me to Winnipeg."

But Mike Smith, general manager of the Winnipeg Jets, witnessed the electricity Domi's rivalry with Probert brought to Madison Square Garden, and he coveted the same for his club. "Tie

Domi can help us in Winnipeg. If the chance comes, I'll trade for him," Smith later remembered thinking in a *Hockey News* blog.

With an abundance of scoring talent but a lack of grit in Winnipeg, Smith felt comfortable sending forward Ed Olczyk to New York for Domi and Kris King after the Christmas trade freeze of 1992. The move was immediately lampooned. Smith recalled one critic describing it as "the dumbest trade of the year, maybe the decade." The *Winnipeg Sun* had a front-page headline decrying "Goals for goons." But the fans felt differently, and tickets for the struggling Jets suddenly became a hot commodity. Domi and King's arrival paid immediate dividends. Although the Jets lost their first game with the two new players, the team went on a 14-game run without a loss. "This trade made the Jets a much more competitive team," Smith said.

Long-time Jets play-by-play announcer Curt Keilback said that before Domi and King joined, Winnipeg was considered soft, and that after they arrived, the Jets stopped being pushovers: "They added an element of toughness, and King added an element of leadership, becoming captain later on. And King fought a lot of battles in those days too—he fought as much as Tie did in the first year and he was a good fighter."

Domi's popularity skyrocketed—to the point that management put him on the cover of the Jets 1993–94 media guide, despite Teemu Selanne having won Rookie of the Year honours *and* scoring 76 goals the year before. The unprecedented attention Domi garnered would rub some of his teammates the wrong way.

"I had confrontations. We didn't try to make it the 'Teemu and Tie Show.' The fans liked us so much, what were we supposed to do? Tell the fans get lost? Don't cheer for us? Don't chant our names? What the hell? That's part of our business. And if guys didn't like that, then tough. And I had confrontations with guys, more than anybody my whole career, with teammates," Domi said in *What It Takes*.

After the *Sun* put Domi on its front page about a half-dozen times, coach John Paddock actually asked the media to pay a little less attention to him to stem the growing ill will in the dressing room, Keilback remembered.

"Domi brought a mixed reaction. Tie also loved the spotlight and who was getting the spotlight was Teemu. So Tie was able to get some of that by being in the company of Teemu," Keilback said.

But Dave Manson, who played with Domi in Winnipeg, didn't begrudge Domi's public prominence. "Tie was a great personality and he went out there every night and did his job and he was good at it," Manson said. "And if he stole somebody's thunder because of that, good for him, because he paid the price night in and night out for the scorers—he defended them."

Eventually, however, Domi asked to be traded. And it would be Toronto that came seeking his services once more, with GM Cliff Fletcher bringing him back to the Leafs, partly at the urging of coach Pat Burns.

Domi would shine in Toronto, not only fighting but playing a regular shift. He was recognized as a terrific skater who could shoot, pass and hand out devastating bodychecks.

"He got the gold ring, like a Clark Gillies, he got a chance to fight and got a chance to play," said Todd Ewen. "That's what every tough guy goes for. It's great to go out there and do your job, but when you get the bonus of a regular shift, what a difference."

"He was a good player. He could skate; score a few goals," said Manson.

Domi also had a long memory, which occasionally landed him in trouble.

He was suspended for eight games in 1995 for sucker-punching and knocking out one of the league's most-hated players, New York Ranger Ulf Samuelsson. At the time, Domi called it a "reaction, spur of the moment. . . . He said, 'C'mon, Tie Dummy, let's fight'—three times. We were down 2-0 in the last minute and he was rubbing my face in it," Domi said after the game.

Domi recalled that when he was a Ranger, Samuelsson, then a

Penguin, broke his stick across his head. Then while playing with Winnipeg, Samuelsson sacrificed another stick by spearing Domi in the stomach. So Domi reasoned that when Samuelsson goaded him in Toronto, he was looking to start something again.

Criticism over that offense would pale in comparison to when Domi lost his cool and knocked out superstar Scott Niedermayer with an elbow to the head with only seven seconds remaining in a playoff game against New Jersey—a game Toronto was leading 3-1. On *Hockey Night in Canada*, Don Cherry rationalized that Domi's actions came down to retribution for Niedermayer raking Domi's face with his stick in Game 2, an infraction that went uncalled.

"It festered," Cherry said. "I knew there was going to be trouble, when no penalty was called on this. Watch Niedermayer take the stick, rub his face on it, cut him twice on the thing—no call! Four [officials] never saw that!"

Besides getting him suspended for the rest of the playoffs—he would also sit out the first eight games of the next season—Domi's attack seemed to fire up New Jersey while also creating a media uproar that may have distracted the Leafs. Although Toronto won the following game, they lost Game 6 and were dominated in the finale as the Devils advanced, eventually all the way to the final.

"It was one of the worst hockey games I've ever had a team play," said coach Pat Quinn. "I felt terrible—not to have your team show up—I don't know what happened to this day, but from the goal on out, we were no-shows."

But more often than not, Domi's style of play was an asset. "Nobody got taken advantage of when Tie was on the ice," said Manson.

"When Tie is around, things just seem to have a little more order," one-time linemate Alyn McCauley told CBC Sports.

"Tie has a presence," Quinn added. "Some of our guys gain from that presence in how they play."

Keilback said Domi could not only throw punches but also take a barrage of them without showing any visible signs of getting hurt, noting he could get punched in the head and not bleed. "Cement, I guess," he cracked.

"You could hit him with anything you wanted to, and he'd still come back and want some more," agreed Bob Nystrom.

"Tie shied away from nobody," said Stu Grimson. "He'll probably go down as one of the toughest guys in the NHL."

"How can you not give Domi credit for being a small guy with a huge head who could throw bombs? It's just phenomenal," Ewen said.

In *Tough Guy*, Bob Probert explained Domi had a unique but awkward fighting style, a necessity brought on by his relatively diminutive stature and lack of reach. "His style was to kind of spin and throw with the left. He tried to pull you down and throw you off-balance. If you stumbled forward, he would try and throw a punch at you. It obviously worked well enough so that he made a career out of it."

Manson, who also played with Domi in Toronto, remembered fighting Domi as a Blackhawk in the final game at Maple Leaf Gardens.

"He had a style all his own and he got the better of me, but it doesn't matter—like we used to say, you never lose any as long as you show up. But for those big guys to fight the smaller guys, it was a lot tougher for the bigger guy because you had that added pressure of if you get beat."

Tie Domi would surpass his hero Tiger Williams as Toronto's all-time penalty-minute leader, and Williams was gracious about losing his crown.

"I'm glad it's him and not some other puke. I like the man. He shows up. It's not an easy job, in fact it's the worst job in the world," Williams told the *Toronto Sun*. "But he has done it since he came into the NHL. He answers the bell and that's all anyone can ever ask for."

Domi ended his career in Toronto, finishing with 1,118 combined regular season and playoff games and over 3,700 penalty minutes.

DENNIS POLONICH Dennis Polonich wasn't often mistaken for one of the NHL's all-time leading scorers. But it did happen—once.

"I'm trying to make the team and there's Red Berenson, Marcel Dionne, and Alex Delvecchio at centre ice; well, good luck," Polonich said of his first training camp with the Detroit Red Wings.

So deep were the Wings down the middle that Polonich was scheduled to sit out a pre-season game against St. Louis in Lansing, Michigan. Dejected over being omitted from the lineup, Polonich hung around the rink, stretching, working out and showering more slowly than he normally would. When he returned to his room, the hotel phone message light was flashing. It was the coach: Dionne couldn't make it, and Polonich was coming after all. Quickly packing his gear, Polonich rushed to catch the team bus. But after arriving in the dressing room, it became apparent that someone forgot to tell the trainers about the change of plans.

"I walk in with my equipment and tell them I'm playing. They'd only brought 20 sweaters; they didn't bring an extra sweater. So I get to wear [Dionne's] No. 5."

At the time, there were no names on the backs of sweaters, and given Polonich was a right-handed shot like Dionne and both were relatively diminutive in size, the Lansing fans were convinced they had the genuine article on their ice. They would soon see a side of the Lady Bynger they'd never seen before and probably never believed they would.

"Back then they had the Plager brothers, John Wensink, and Battleship Kelly: real tough, character guys," Polonich said of the Blues. "And this is training camp and everybody's trying to make the team. And the little farm boy from Foam Lake [Saskatchewan] thought, 'This is my chance to make an impression, so I've got to do something.'"

A fight started on the ice and although he was on the bench, Polonich tried to get involved. His coach grabbed him to pull him back, but Polonich shook him off and pulled away to kick off a bench-clearing brawl between both teams. "I grabbed a guy by the name of Howie Heggedal . . . he was a pretty good player from the Central League; he wasn't a fighter, but he was like 6-foot. I just started whaling on him and I knocked him out—totally knocked him out. Well, the crowd went crazy: 'MARCEL! MARCEL! MARCEL!'"

When not impersonating celebrities, Polonich demonstrated an unparalleled skill at driving opponents to distraction and knocking them off their game. "I have a picture of me holding three, four or five trophies at awards night . . . I was 5-foot-4, 5-foot-5 back then, playing midget hockey, and pretty skilled," said Polonich of his Moose Jaw days, when he was an All-Star and winner of the Most Gentlemanly Player award. "Then I went to Flin Flon."

"Junior hockey was a jungle where the animals were fighting for their lives and nowhere was tougher than Flin Flon," said Tiger Williams.

Paddy Ginnell coached the Bombers and was notorious for recruiting character players who had few qualms about mixing it up. "[Ginnell] saw this raw farm kid who was willing to do anything to win and he kind of moulded me into what I became," Polonich said.

Teams would travel up to Flin Flon, Manitoba, for weekend doubleheaders, playing Saturday nights and again the next afternoon in order to arrive wherever they needed to be by Monday. "We would play like hell on Saturday, trying to get the score up and get really physical to make it a little bit easier on Sunday," Polonich explained.

He seemed a long shot to make the pros, getting selected in the eighth round (118th overall) by Detroit in the 1973 amateur draft.

Polonich signed his first pro contract—sans agent, of course—when Red Wings draft picks converged for camp in Winnipeg: "They just slid the contract in front of me, offered me a $7,500 signing bonus and $29,000 to play in the NHL and I signed," he recalled. "I came home and told my parents and friends that I just got a $7,500 signing bonus and a three-year NHL contract and my Dad said, 'Where's the money?' I said I'm going to get it when I go to training camp and he said, 'No, you get it now.'" Polonich spent his professional year with the Lions of London, England, a European touring squad owned by Red Wings chief Bruce Norris. When Polonich returned, he bought the cottage he still owns and a new Trans Am: "I was in heaven."

After another year's apprenticeship, this time with the AHL's Virginia Red Wings, Polonich was NHL-ready.

"Dennis could really skate and he was a good forechecker and obviously a very tough player," Dan Maloney said of his 5-foot-6 teammate. "He had a lot more skill than people give him credit for; he could really shoot and skate, and he was a hard-nosed guy."

"Polo was a good teammate and always worked hard and came to play," added Dennis Hextall. "I don't care where you were playing, he was going to show up. His stature didn't have anything to do with his intensity."

Blair Stewart remembered watching Polonich through many stages of his hockey development and recalled one thing in particular being the constant: "I played against him in junior when he was with Flin Flon; I played with him in Virginia and a little bit in Detroit. He was an agitator, a dirty little prick sometimes. . . . He's the kind of guy that you would have wanted on your team, kind of like [Dale] Hunter. He'd get under your skin but he played hard . . . I've never seen him back off [a fight]."

Kurt Walker, no fan of Polonich during their playing days, would beg to differ, but the fact that it still irks him demonstrates how much Polonich succeeded in getting under his skin.

"When he cut me in the head, he took his stick and jumped up and slammed the butt-end of his stick down on my head," Walker said, noting his gash required seven stitches to close. "And every time I ever went to fight Polonich, he turtled on me—at least three different times. And I wanted to stand him up and just hammer on him!"

SportsCentre ranked another Detroit Red Wing, Bugsy Watson, as the number-two pest of all time and left Polonich off the top-ten, but Walker actually believed Polonich was the greater agitator of the two. "Bugsy was just a lot of talk. Polonich, he was just a real little pain in the ass. And I'm sure he's a good guy, like most of us. But he used to piss me off and he wouldn't fight me, and that just killed me."

Nobody suffered more from Polonich's psychological warfare than Philadelphia Flyers head of security Dave Schultz.

"We've finished our morning skate and Polonich walks out, steps right onto *their* bus and starts yelling at Schultz," Hextall said. "This is at 10 o'clock in the morning. That's the kind of pain in the ass he was. You know it's going to go on the ice that night, but that's the way Polonich was. You never knew what he was going to do."

Polonich still gets a laugh over his long-running feud with Schultz, especially the day he tormented Schultz so much that he took three penalties against him in one shift.

"The morning skate before he took the three minor penalties, Detroit skated at 10:30 or 10:00 and Philadelphia was going on the ice at 11. For whatever reason that day, I had left the ice early and was leaving the Olympia and the Philadelphia bus pulled up. The players started coming off the bus and Schultz saw me going to my car," he said. "The Hammer" made threatening gestures at Polonich. "I pointed to my watch and said, 'Hey, it's only 11:00; the game doesn't start till 7:30 . . . go for your skate, have your six pack of bananas and I'll see you tonight.'"

Polonich recalled Philly captain Bobby Clarke and others having to come over and drag a livid Schultz away. "Those were fun days. You had to have that attitude; you had to have that swagger. When you played that game, when you lived on that edge, you had to be alert on the ice. You didn't let your guard down. I tried to use it to the team's advantage," he said, noting legendary Flyers coach Fred Shero credited Polonich for distracting teams more than anyone else. "They were so intent on going after me, they forgot what their other purpose was," explained Polonich.

Not even getting traded to Pittsburgh could save Schultz from Polonich's taunts. At home at the Old Red Barn, the Detroit Olympia, Polonich had his back to the Penguins' bench during an offside faceoff, and Schultz made the mistake of starting a war of words.

"I looked over my shoulder and I said, 'Schultzie, how're you gonna kill me? You never get on the ice!' [Coach and Red Wing alumni] Johnny Wilson, he just had to turn the other way, he was about to bust up laughing."

Polonich didn't pick his spots either, taking on noted heavies Schultz, André Dupont, Tiger Williams, Larry Playfair, and Jimmy Mann.

"The reason I ended up against the enforcers was because I played against the other team's top line," Polonich said, calling himself "a real bastard to play against."

His coaches regularly sent him out to check the likes of Montreal's Steve Shutt, Guy Lafleur, and Jacques Lemaire; the French Connection in Buffalo; L.A.'s Triple Crown line; Darryl Sittler and Lanny McDonald in Toronto; Islanders Mike Bossy, Bryan Trottier, and Clark Gillies; and Bobby Clarke, Reggie Leach, and Bill Barber of Philadelphia. Polonich explained:

So I'd have to face all those guys, do my job and get under their skin. When I'd go into Philadelphia, off goes Bobby Clarke, in comes Mel Bridgman. Or off comes Bill Barber, out comes André Dupont or Dave Schultz. So you gotta face the music, 'cause back in those days, they didn't have hired guns. I couldn't turn around and say, 'Okay, Georges Laraque, or okay, Colton Orr, or okay, [Steve] MacIntyre, go look after this for me.' You had to do it on your own. Because of my size, I lost fights, but at the same time, I surprised a lot of people too because I was very strong and fearless.

Polonich was one of the few bright lights of the Red Wings in the '70s. As much as he was hated everywhere else in the league, Polonich had a great following in Detroit. Fans in the balconies of the old Olympia unfurled banners that proclaimed them members of the "Polo Club."

Unfortunately for him, his fans and the Red Wings, Polonich never reached his full potential. He showed his promise in his second year, scoring 18 goals and 46 points to become the club's number-two scorer while still winding up with 274 penalty minutes. But early in his fourth season, a confrontation with Wilf Paiement started his decline.

Polonich has never been able to recall the details—he was immediately rendered unconscious and didn't come to until just before being taken from the dressing room to the hospital. But he's since been filled in: "Apparently, Wilf Paiement and Paul Gardner had a two-on-one on Rogie Vachon, and Paul Gardner shot and deflected the puck into the corner. I went into the corner to get the puck on my backhand and ice it," he said. "When I backhanded the puck, Wilf Paiement went to hit me and my stick came up. And that was his claim, that I provoked him, that I had high-sticked him. And he turned around and took a baseball swing at my face and hit me across the nose."

The set-to wasn't captured on film as television cameras had followed the play, which had gone up ice. While Paiement didn't want to relive what had happened, when Polonich filed a civil suit against him, Paiement testified in 1982 that Polonich had intentionally high-sticked him, cutting him above the mouth. Paiement said he raised his stick instinctively to protect himself.

Although no criminal charges were filed, Polonich was awarded $850,000 in damages by a federal jury after taking Paiement to court. Polonich believed the lawsuit led to him being blackballed

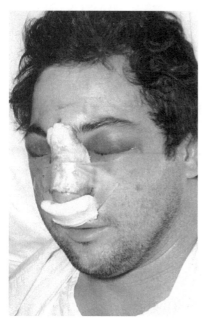

Dennis Polonich after a shot to the face with Wilf Paiement's hockey stick. (Courtesy Dennis Polonich)

in the league, but he has said he'd still sue if he had to live it all over again, with the only difference being he'd ask for more money.

"Because of the pain and suffering and because of lost wages. I was never the same player; my record and stats show that," said Polonich. "There's no question. The severity of it, if I showed you pictures, my facial injuries and the pool of blood. I didn't play again for a month-and-a-half and I've never been the same player since."

Polonich's injuries included breathing difficulties that never fully subsided. Two years later, he was in the minors.

But toiling there didn't prevent Polonich from enjoying success, as he was a member of the 1980–81 Calder Cup–champion Adirondack Red Wings, as well as the 1986 Turner Cup winners, the IHL's Muskegon Lumberjacks.

When his playing days were over, he coached and managed for 12 years, with stops in Yorkton—where he coached the Terriers to a championship in the Saskatchewan Junior Hockey League and won Coach of the Year honours—as well as Medicine Hat and Prince George of the WHL. Polonich became a certified NHLPA player representative after his coaching and managerial career ended in 1998.

GEORGES LARAQUE
Georges Laraque spent much of his career as hockey's dominant heavyweight, despite abhorring violence.

"I don't like fighting. I never talk about fighting. The fact we're talking about fighting is the most that I've talked about fighting to anyone. I'm not a fan of fighting. I did it because it was my job, not because I liked it," he said.

And he is no advocate of fisticuffs, believing kids too easily emulate the pros they see live or on TV: "I never liked that image of 'goon' and promoting violence. It was never me."

His hockey background is as nontraditional as his attitude. His parents moved from Haiti to Montreal when they were 20 years old: "That decision probably saved my life," said Laraque.

Like many Canadian boys, he grew up with a burning desire to play hockey, but he faced more hurdles than just learning how to skate and shoot; he was chastised by other boys and even adults watching in the stands, becoming a target for being a visible minority playing a so-called "white man's game." He would fight then, as he would later on, sticking up for himself. Baseball's Jackie Robinson would prove to be an inspiration—the Hall of Fame trailblazer never gave in to the taunts. Laraque, too, wanted to play with the pros.

If he could have, Georges Laraque would have realized his childhood dream with a more aesthetically pleasing game, but he simply didn't possess the skating or puck skills. Like many others before and since, he took the route of the uppercut, and it served him well.

Luckily for anyone who dropped the gloves with him, Laraque didn't hit the gym to add to his already immense 6-foot-3, 255-pound frame: "All I would do is cardio. I've never been a weight guy because I would become way too big."

"He didn't hit me—thank God," Bob Probert wrote of his fights with Laraque. Neither player was able to get loose to throw a big haymaker. "Laraque was strong."

In retirement, Probert judged Laraque to be the top enforcer, and his former peers agreed. A 2007 ESPN survey of players selected Laraque as the toughest player in the league. But like any great actor, Laraque was only playing a role.

"Off the ice, I'm the opposite—I'm so not aggressive," said the pacifist pugilist, whose ideals away from the rink more closely resembled Gandhi's than Attila the Hun's. In fact, one of the knocks against Laraque was he didn't have a mean streak. "I'm approachable, and one of the nicest things that I've had people say was that as a tough guy in the NHL, I was too nice. If somebody says you're too nice—but at the same time by my peers the last 10 years I was one of the most respected guys—that to me is worth more than money. That reputation to me was everything."

So thoughtful was Laraque that he even wished his counterparts good luck before every fight.

"I never fight mad, I never want to hurt anyone. I can't, it's not in my nature," he said, adding, "I always feel bad after every fight, always talk to the guy, ask him if he's okay."

Even now, Laraque has nothing but good things to say about his former opponents. Ask him about guys like Probert, Tie Domi, Stu Grimson, or any of the scores of heavyweights with whom he tangled, and Laraque just thanks them for giving him a chance.

"I respect [Grimson] a lot because I can't believe he was still fighting at 38 years old," said Laraque. "The older you get, the harder it is. And he was one of the toughest guys to play the game. And for a guy like that to give a chance to a guy like me, that was an up-and-comer trying to make a name for himself, that's always greatly appreciated because he doesn't have to. . . . All those guys, I'll never forget. No one would know me if it wasn't for the way that those guys gave me a chance," he said. "Once I became a veteran, I remembered what they did for me and I did the same for others, always giving everybody else a chance."

Tony Twist was struck by Laraque's gentlemanly manner following their only fight, early in Laraque's days with the Edmonton Oilers.

"I knew we were going to fight because he had just fought Stu Grimson a couple nights before. Georges is trying to make a name for himself and he gave Stu a pretty good beating. So coming into Edmonton, I knew the first shift we were going to go," Twist said.

But it wasn't so much the fight as the aftermath that was most memorable. "After the game, I talked to him," said Twist. "He actually said, 'I really appreciate you fighting me.' And I asked him why he would say that. Well, because a lot of guys weren't giving him a chance because he was just a rookie and you have to earn your stripes. I didn't really care. I took the Bob Probert route: I'll be your measuring stick. I have no problem with that."

Laraque was "The Next One" in a series of top heavyweights in Edmonton. Like Dave Semenko before him, Laraque donned the No. 27 and didn't need to get into many scraps to earn the respect of others. After eight seasons with the Oilers, Laraque signed as a free agent with Phoenix when general manager Kevin Lowe declined to give him a no-trade clause.

Phoenix players were thrilled that the team was adding some beef, and Coyote Mike Comrie, who played with Laraque in Edmonton, welcomed him to the team: "He puts the fear of God into the other team," he told the *East Valley Tribune*.

"He's a mountain that moves," 6-foot-2, 216-pound Shane Doan added.

Laraque, however, didn't last the season. Playing in front of numerous empty seats in Phoenix, he missed hearing the roaring crowds he'd become accustomed to in Edmonton. He also wasn't impressed with the coaching of Wayne Gretzky, whom he called "the worst coach I've ever played for." Although he'd later claim the quote was taken out of context, it's hard to confuse what he wrote in his memoir, *The Story of the NHL's Unlikeliest Tough Guy*:

"We could lose five or six games in a row and it didn't seem to matter to him," Laraque wrote, explaining Gretzky inexplicably never yelled at the players or tore into them to motivate them. "He sure didn't have any special system he wanted us to play. He wasn't a strategist. He wasn't a tactician. He would sometimes just throw the first three players closest to the door on the ice even if there was no centre among them."

Laraque was moved to Pittsburgh after requesting a trade, and the next season they made it all the way to the final before bowing out to the Detroit Red Wings. The Pens would win it all the following season, but without Laraque. GM Ray Shero couldn't afford to keep him, and a lowball contract offer convinced Laraque to look elsewhere.

Nashville offered the biggest deal, and Edmonton came calling as well, offering him a raise and the no-movement clause the team had previously refused him. But given how fans and reporters there hyped his possible return, Laraque balked at going back, doubting he could live up to their expectations.

Shockingly, he decided instead on Montreal, even though they offered him a shorter-term deal and despite the fact that he'd never before wanted to play for his hometown Habs. What had changed? He felt ready to handle the pressure and scrutiny that came with being a Canadien. More importantly, he wished to play in front of his friends and family, particularly his mother.

A top enforcer like Laraque seemed like a perfect fit for the team and its small forwards, who'd been derided as "Smurfs." But it was not to be: A bad back hampered him, and although he was playing through the pain, he felt coach Jacques Martin had little use for tough guys and kept him sitting on the bench for most games.

General manager Bob Gainey ended up buying out Laraque's contract, saying he was unproductive and a distraction to the team. Laraque, however, pointed out he was only playing three or four shifts a game, and that the distraction in question was the media pressing Martin about why Laraque was riding the bench.

During one particular contest, a game against St. Louis in which Blues tough-guy Cam Janssen was running over Montreal players, TSN's Pierre Maguire asked on the air why Laraque wasn't being used. "He was between the benches. Jacques could hear him. After the game, all the media were asking why I wasn't playing. I got released the next day," Laraque told OilersNation.com.

Laraque retired in 2010, his resume including a Memorial Cup win (with the Granby Prédateurs in 1996) and two trips to the Stanley Cup Finals, one each with the Oilers and Penguins. In 695 games, he accumulated 153 points and 1,126 penalty minutes. During those 13 years, Laraque estimated he got into about 130 fights, of which only five or six were losses—and none of those were knockouts.

Diagnosed with two herniated discs, Laraque decided to hang up his skates for good after being released by the Habs. Hockey is now behind him and will probably remain there. The spotlight returned, however, when Elizabeth May, leader of Canada's very left Green Party, offered him the position of deputy leader. Laraque accepted and helped get May elected in the 2011 federal election, and he is even considering running for office himself down the road.

He would also pursue his humanitarian efforts in retirement. Laraque, who had received the Oilers community service award for three consecutive seasons, would work with World Vision and the NHLPA to rebuild the Grace Children's Hospital in his mother's birthplace, Port-au-Prince, Haiti.

He is also a spokesman for animal rights group PETA.

Laraque, a convert to veganism during his last year in Montreal, has since opened two raw vegan restaurants: "I promote veganism across Canada and try to be the voice for animal welfare." Laraque would don the skates again for televised charity figure-skating contest *Battle of the Blades*. He may have taken more lumps practising with his 97-pound partner, Anabelle Langois, than he ever did in his previous bare-fisted confrontation, as practice mishaps resulted in her accidentally punching him in the nose and lips, kicking him with her heel, and even slashing his face with her skate, which cut him for 12 stitches.

Laraque was sent reeling again after lending his time, money, and name in an attempt to unionize players in Canada's three major junior leagues, only to see those efforts wasted. Laraque briefly became the face and executive director of the Canadian Hockey League Players' Association (CHLPA), intending to fight for better educational standards, but he stepped down when the CHLPA bizarrely unravelled amid uncertainty about the true identity of one of its officials and allegations a convicted fraudster was involved in the union.

When Goalies Fight

"That has to be the best fight of the year. This is old-time hockey," cried Gary Dornhoefer, thrilled by the epic battle on November 10, 1996. However, it wasn't between the usual suspects on the Leafs (Tie Domi, Wendel Clark) or the Flyers (Dan Kordic), but between the goaltenders, Felix Potvin and Ron Hextall.

At the conclusion of the game, a 3-1 Flyers win, Potvin slashed Daniel Lacroix, prompting Hextall to sprint the length of the ice.

"The two goalies ripped off each other's masks and traded perhaps two dozen punches," reads one report. "If the amount of blood spilled separates the winner from the loser, Hextall, leaking from a cut above his left eye, did not get the decision."

For its length, intensity, bloodiness, and the fact that it involved the reigning heavyweight champion of goaltenders, Ron Hextall, *The Hockey News* named it the greatest goalie fight ever. (Disagree? There are many similar lists compiled by fans and bloggers.) The players seemed convinced, as many who'd paired off stopped paying attention to their partners and watched intensely to see who'd come out on top.

The day after the fight, Hextall met with reporters, his eyebrow still puffed up after stitches and his record 29 penalty minutes in the books. He had ignored his daughter's advice: "The last thing my daughter said to me was: 'Good luck and don't fight,'" he told the *Philadelphia Inquirer*.

Goalie fights still make the news on the rare occasions that they happen. It usually indicates that a game has gotten out of control. The sight of one keeper in full gear skating to confront another always brings the fans out of their seats.

Gerry Cheevers of Bruins fame may have been netminding's first NHL and WHL goalie bad boy, a point hard to argue considering he twice tangled with the Leafs' Forbes Kennedy in a single game. It happened to be the night Pat Quinn knocked out Bobby Orr and Kennedy's last game in the NHL. But "Forbie" went out with a bang, setting penalty records for a single playoff game and punching a linesman, and Cheevers did show some remorse, pleading Kennedy's case to the NHL. "I told them I'd started it all, I was the instigator, and it was unfair that Forbie was suspended," Cheevers said in 2009.

Four-time Stanley Cup–champion Billy Smith would inherit the tough goalie mantle from Cheevers. "Battling Billy" was less a fighter than a stick man, chopping down opponents cruising too close to his crease by swinging his big goalie stick like a scythe. The most notable of his victims was Wayne Gretzky in the '83 Cup Final, but Smith didn't limit himself to league-leading scorers, having also got into brouhahas with fellow shit-disturber Tiger Williams, among many, many others. Long-time L.A. King Dave Taylor summed up Smith's intensity. "We've had a couple of run-ins over the years, but it's because Smith plays hard and protects his crease," he said in 1986, Smith's 14th year in the league. "He's put a couple of guys down with his stick, but I don't think that's the wrong way to play, either."

Ron Hextall would take protecting his zone to new levels, earning over 100 penalty minutes in each of his first three NHL seasons and finishing off with a career 584 PIM, plus another 112 in the playoffs. While disciples like Dan Cloutier and "Sugar" Ray Emery never came close to breaking Hextall's goaltending penalty-minute records, they both proved extremely handy and willing with their fists. Emery attained notoriety (infamy?) one February night in 2007 in Buffalo as an Ottawa Senator. After laying out fellow netminder Martin Biron during a line brawl, he scrapped with Sabres resident enforcer Andrew Peters. At no point during either event did Emery's grin get wiped off his face. "It's a fun part of the game," Emery said the day after the brawls. "But my Mom got mad at me. She was at the game, so I can't do that for awhile."

THE REAL LIVE WIRES

Few can doubt that the enforcers featured in this section were among the most feared, the ones who could get many agitators, instigators and toughs to back down with a just a glare. Annoying them was akin to poking a junkyard dog with a stick.

JOHN WENSINK Nicknamed "Wire," John Wensink caused many sleepless nights for opponents in the wild and woolly 1970s.

"He was called Wire because he was known to be a little crazy on the ice; unpredictable. You didn't know what he was going to do. So that kept players honest," said defenceman Ken Daneyko, who was trying to crack the New Jersey lineup when Wensink was a Devil.

One can't thoroughly examine Wensink's career without considering Don Cherry, his coach and greatest supporter. Their student-teacher relationship would eventually evolve into a close friendship that lasts to this day.

Without Cherry, Wensink likely never would have made it to the NHL, and maybe not even to the AHL. Disappointed by his poor skating, the St. Louis Blues, who'd drafted Wensink, had pegged him for the International League, two levels removed from the big time.

Enter Cherry, then coach of the AHL's Rochester Americans. He needed an enforcer to replace the recently promoted "Battleship" Bob Kelly, and he first caught a glimpse of Kelly's potential substitute at the Blues training camp before the 1973–74 season.

"His skating was so atrocious, I had half a mind to buy him a pair of double-runners. Yet there was something about him that I liked," Cherry said in *Grapes: A Vintage View of Hockey.*

Wensink had won a Memorial Cup with his hometown Cornwall Royals in 1972, contributing to the win by terrorizing opponents. After making a deal with the Blues that saved him from the IHL, Wensink became Cherry's personal project, and, not unlike Dr. Frankenstein's monster, he proceeded to cut a path of terror when set loose. Cherry would soon discover that his gut feeling about Wensink's ferocity was right, when his charge fought Len Cunning of the Nova Scotia Voyageurs.

"Wensink flattened him and once Cunning was down, he wouldn't let up. By the time the officials separated them, Cunning was in such bad shape that he had to be taken to the hospital," Cherry said.

Cherry's daughter, Cindy, explained that her dad had previously told Wensink to never hesitate in any fight because doing so could mean getting clocked. And despite knocking Cunning out with his first punch, he kept punching him while he was down.

"It was so bad, I was rooted," Cherry said in *Hockey Stories, Part 2*. "My toes actually curled. I thought he'd killed the guy. They had to carry the guy off. It was so bad that, after the game, a detective came, put John in handcuffs, took him in a room and questioned him. The detective told me after that while they were questioning him, John was eating a sandwich that was left over from the press room."

"He was eating one of the leftover sandwiches that I made for the guys in the press box . . . and he commented on how delicious they were," Cindy added.

But Cherry did more than just unleash a madman. He worked with Wensink after practice on both his skating and hockey skills, and he even protected him the way a fight manager would. When the Blues called him up, his debut was scheduled against the Pittsburgh Penguins, the same team for which Battleship was now plying his trade. Knowing the Blues' intention was to send Wensink out just for combat, Cherry tried to ensure that a fight with Kelly wouldn't happen, believing it was too soon for Wensink to take on such an experienced and dangerous brawler.

"It was after the morning skate and Don wanted to know if I'd have a pre-game meal with him, and Bobby shows up," Wensink remembered. "[Kelly] was staying at the same hotel, because St. Louis and Pittsburgh had just made the huge trade—they sent [Steve] Durbano and Bobby to Pittsburgh. Don came from Rochester to watch the game and we all had lunch together."

After Wensink left the table, Cherry asked Kelly for a favour—avoid getting into it with his new charge.

"I remember facing off against Bobby and Bobby says, 'I guess they're sending you out here.' And I said, 'Let's just play and see what happens.' I really didn't know Bobby that well," Wensink said, noting they'd first met at the Blues training camp that year when both were trying out for the team.

Wensink ended up checking Kelly a couple times, but Kelly never responded. "Don and Bob helped me along a little bit," Wensink said. "When you're 20 and you're coming into the pro ranks, you have to have a little bit of guidance, and Don definitely supplied that. If you're one of his players, you're one of his friends for life."

Not long after this Cherry got the call to coach the Bruins, and Wensink's physical health began deteriorating. He struggled in the minors, finding himself unable to play much more than a period or two because of back pain. He sat out a month and ended up calling it a season in February. By around the third or fourth day of training camp the next season, his back was acting up again. This time, the club sent him to a doctor in New York, who suggested a spinal fusion. It was done in October, and Wensink was done for another season.

When he returned to the St. Louis camp, the team gave him a couple minor league options: Providence or Rochester.

"I'd been in Providence, but the problem with Providence was that's where I'd had my spinal fusion and I never even played a shift.

So the logic was to go to Rochester, not knowing that Rochester was Boston's farm team."

After Wensink had played most of the season in Rochester, Cherry succeeded in convincing Bruins GM Harry Sinden to get Wensink under contract. "I started in Rochester that year and he called me up, so Don has been and is a big part of my life."

With Boston, Wensink's primary role was to keep the heavies and pests away from teammates like leading-scorer Jean Ratelle, who'd had a chronic bad back ever since the Bruins acquired him from the Rangers. The unwritten rule was to lay off him. One night, Islanders defenceman Gerry Hart made the mistake of violating that law by cross-checking Ratelle. According to Cherry, Wensink rammed Hart's head into the boards in retaliation.

"Next time you touch Mr. Ratelle, your head will go *through* the boards," Cherry paraphrased Wensink's words of warning to Hart. From then on, Hart avoided bothering *Mr.* Ratelle.

"He was very valuable to that team," said Islanders broadcaster Jiggs McDonald. "He was there to keep things peaceful—law and order. If it got out of hand, if there was something going on, then he would take matters into his own hands. Had a decent skill-set, not the skill-set of a [Bob] Nystrom or even a [Gary] Howatt, in my opinion. But he was a tough, hard-nosed kid."

Wensink, however, could on occasion get out of hand—sometimes becoming a veritable one-man riot squad.

On December 1, 1977, the Bruins knocked around the Minnesota North Stars at Boston Garden. During one particular skirmish, Terry O'Reilly clobbered one of the Stars while Wensink smacked another. Finished, Wensink skated over to the Minnesota bench and challenged everyone there. When there were no takers, Wensink threw up his hands in disgust and skated away.

"I gotta say, there was no lead up to it other than a spontaneous energy. There was a lot of energy built up and I was rarin' to go," Wensink said.

"If somebody did that to our bench, all of us would go," O'Reilly said at the time. "They were probably shocked by Wensink."

Sometimes even if opponents were through fighting, he wasn't.

"We were grappling with each other," said Ric Seiling in 1979. "When the ref said stop, I did. Wensink suckered me with a shot to the side of the head. All I could do was cover myself up the best I could. . . .

"Next thing I knew I was at the bottom of about 20 guys. Somebody had hold of my arms and somebody was biting my back. I showed the teeth marks to one linesmen, but he said nothing could be done about it because he didn't see it happen."

Off the ice, however, Wensink appeared far more reticent. Woodworking has been a particular love of his, and he's created everything from model boats and airplanes to intricate dollhouses. (His abilities transferred nicely into a post-hockey remodelling career that lasted 30 years.)

And when it came to on-ice action, what really got Wensink going wasn't mangling opponents or charging into bench-clearing brawls against the likes of the Philadelphia Flyers. Rather, it was the challenge of competing against the best and playing under pressure.

"If you went into Montreal, you were in for a tough game; maybe not the dropping of gloves stuff, but you were in for a tough game. You go into Toronto, here's hockey heaven, the place to play hockey, and there's pressures other than the physical part, there's the pressures of performing well on *Hockey Night in Canada*," Wensink said. "You go to L.A., you've got to face the Triple Crown Line. Or Buffalo, Gilbert Perreault, Jim Schoenfeld, [Jerry] Korab on defence . . . The fact we were playing against certain players pumped me up."

Scoring goals was another treat, and Wensink enjoyed a career year in 1978–79 when he lit the lamp 28 times. His reputation had grown to the point where opponents were giving him plenty of room to manoeuvre.

"I wish I would have known some of this stuff before I ended up retiring because now I'm back and I see some guys, and they're telling me stories about their pre-game chat. Instead of talking X's and O's and power plays and penalty kills, they were saying, 'Let's not bother him—leave him alone! Stay away from him,'" Wensink said. "I wish I would have known I had that much room. I might have been able to play a little bit better."

Cherry in fact believed Wensink could have surpassed that 28-goal total, especially considering he'd already scored 21 by Christmas.

"But I saw bad signs entering his game. I could see him saying to himself, 'Hey, this scoring stuff is all right, you don't get hurt hitting or bang your hands up in a fight. And look at my name in the headlines!'" Cherry told the *Vancouver Province*.

To Cherry, Wensink had been hitting and fighting less in his pursuit of goals. Cherry took him aside and told him that if he kept it up, it would get around the league that he'd turned into a pussycat. When he saw Wensink didn't believe him, he told him he wouldn't score 10 goals from that point on. He was right.

Unfortunately for Wensink, it would be Cherry's last year with the Bruins. It was a sad time for Wensink, who'd been to the finals twice and semifinals once with Cherry and the Bruins in the four years he'd been patrolling for Boston. "When he left, first of all I'm losing a good friend, he's going to another team. I don't know who the new guy coming in is, what he's going to do, or the team he wants. It was a tough deal."

Wensink played one more season with Boston, and the next year the Quebec Nordiques claimed him off waivers. A season there was followed by one in Colorado and another in New Jersey when the Rockies moved.

"He was one scary guy," said Ken Daneyko, adding, "When he came to Jersey, we weren't a very good team and we weren't even an overly physical, tough team. So John was one of those guys that gave us some credibility in that regard."

But after leaving Boston, Wensink found it harder to play his role. Having dressed for four NHL organizations in five cities, he found the longer he played, the more often he'd line up against friends and ex-teammates.

"Having played in Boston with some great friends—not just teammates but great friends—you go back to play against them, it always makes it tougher," he said, adding the same was true when he played against pals from the Blues and Nordiques. "For me, it was a tougher deal as I went on, it really was. But I also knew that that's what I had to do. But it made it tougher, no question."

DAVE SEMENKO A shy figure off the ice, Dave Semenko's glower alone caused alarm.

The World Hockey Association edition of the Edmonton Oilers signed a 20-year-old Semenko in 1977 after topping the offer made by the Minnesota North Stars, the NHL team that drafted him. "We wanted some aggressiveness," Oilers coach Glen Sather said at the time.

"We're definitely going to miss him," said his Brandon Wheat Kings coach Dunc McCallum, "and we won't be able to replace him overnight." It was in Brandon where Semenko had first gained his noteriety.

"It was something where I went into Brandon without any sort of reputation," said the Winnipeg-born Semenko. "It happened that somebody challenged me and I did surprisingly well and it sort of laid the foundation."

As a pro, he fought fewer times than most enforcers, which spoke volumes about the respect he got on the ice. Wayne Gretzky would explain that Semenko's look alone was usually enough to break most opponents' spirits.

"He is just so huge and has such a wild look in his eye that nobody would dare test him. All he usually had to do was issue his famous line: 'Maybe you and I should go for a canoe ride,' and the guy would start backing off," Gretzky said in *Gretzky: An Autobiography*. Semenko produced a mere 1,175 penalty minutes in

575 regular season NHL games—or an average of a shade over two minutes a game. According to hockeyfights.com, he engaged in only 70 scraps in his entire NHL career.

"Nobody wanted to tangle with him," said Curt Keilback, who watched Semenko take on the Winnipeg Jets on numerous occasions from his radio broadcast perch. "He intimidated just by his presence."

Semenko's aura made him seem even larger than his listed height and weight of 6-foot-3 and 215-pounds. And while his eventual full-time replacement, Marty McSorley, was "a tough hombre" in his own right, "I don't think he was any Semenko," Keilback said.

Semenko explained he got as much if not more mileage out of glaring at or talking to opponents than he ever did fighting them.

"I'd like to think that I stopped a lot of fights just by looking at people," he said in *Looking Out for Number One*. "I'd glare at some guy, and if I got the impression he didn't really want to go, then I'd just keep glaring. Almost always, he'd back off, and we could get on with the hockey game."

Although by no means a fan of fighters, referee Bruce Hood respected Semenko. Hood said Semenko's form of intimidation was merely being present, and that he didn't feel the need to resort to cheap shots or otherwise make a nuisance of himself like many others who filled the same role. Hood also saluted Semenko for never mouthing off at officials: "If enforcers have to be in hockey, that's the type they should be," Hood said in his autobiography.

Even in retirement, Semenko's icy stare could totally unnerve those who annoyed him in some way. Never able to completely shed his tough-guy image, he managed to scare the daylights out of a future pro wrestling heavyweight champion.

During one of the most memorable flights in the life of World Wrestling Entertainment's Chris Jericho, he sat among a number of Edmonton Oilers, including one older guy he couldn't quite place. When the rather large fellow left his seat, Jericho—who also happened to be the son of New York Ranger "Baby-Faced Assassin" Teddy

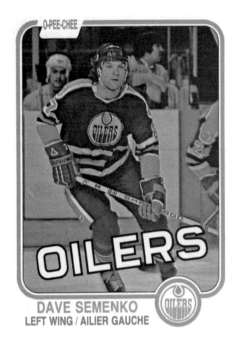

O-PEE-CHEE

OILERS

DAVE SEMENKO
LEFT WING / AILIER GAUCHE

Irvine—nosily checked the mystery man's carry-on bag for clues. He shared the story in *A Lion's Tale*:

I fumbled around until I found the name tag and a cold chill ran up my spine when I saw whose bag it was. Then a warm squirt ran down my undies when a pissed-off deep voice from over my shoulder said, 'Get your fucking hands off my bag' . . . I sat in silence, speechless and quivering in the face of death. Semenko leaned into my face with the power of 1,000 knockouts behind him . . . 'Don't touch my stuff, asshole.' When I began to retort he cut me off and said, 'Don't even think of talking to me for the rest of the flight either.' I stared at my suddenly quite interesting shoelaces for the rest of the trip and survived the trip to L.A. unscathed.

As an active player, when Semenko's reputation wasn't enough and he was forced to resolve disputes with his fists, few could stand with him.

"He was far and away the greatest fighter I ever saw," said Gretzky. "He'd knock guys out with one punch and then hold them up so it didn't look so bad."

But it would be off the ice where Semenko had one of his most famous fights.

In 1983, Muhammad Ali was overweight and years removed

from his drubbing at the hands of world heavyweight boxing champion Larry Holmes. But Ali still had enough left to give Semenko all he could handle in a three-round exhibition bout.

"Now I know why he's the greatest champion in the world," Semenko told the Associated Press in his dressing room after the fight, while wiping blood from his nose. "I'm glad I met him when he's over 40 years old."

Although boxing may have been something of a lark, the primary function of Semenko's fighting was to give his teammates the room they needed on the ice.

"He had a role and that was to protect Gretzky and anybody else, but in particular 99; you touched him, you had Semenko to answer to," said Keilback.

"He's big and mean, and he gives you the impression that he wants to hurt you," said Tiger Williams in *Tiger: A Hockey Story*, adding, "I know that he wants to get me, that he really hates me. This is probably because I take every chance I get to run at Gretzky."

Williams believed Semenko's bodyguarding was worth at least 25 goals a year to Gretzky alone, and that despite his limitations as a player, he was the most valuable Oiler after No. 99.

"And I'm not forgetting great talents like Mark Messier, Glenn Anderson and Paul Coffey. Without Semenko, there would be a competitive vacuum on the Oiler team," Williams said.

Known as "Sammy" by his teammates, Semenko was popular in the dressing room, and his teammates treated him like a 50-goal scorer, if not better—Gretzky gave Semenko the car he won as the MVP of the 1983 All-Star Game. "He was also a fine hockey player. The year we won our first Stanley Cup, Semenko played the best hockey of his life," Gretzky said.

But Semenko became less and less popular with Sather, who finally traded him to Hartford in his 10th year on the team. The beginning of the end may have come in the Oilers' 1985 playoff series against Chicago, specifically during a game in which Semenko tangled with the Hawks' Behn Wilson. A sore shoulder prevented him from exchanging punches with the big defenceman, and he simply held on, much to Sather's chagrin.

The trade, however, was unpopular with both Oilers and fans.

"[Sather] traded the funniest guy on the team," Gretzky said. "A hockey team isn't made up only of sticks and pucks and skates. A hockey team is a collection of people and the magic between the people has to be right. Semenko was a big part of that team for us, and not just on the ice."

Semenko only lasted a season in Hartford before being traded to the league's laughingstock Toronto Maple Leafs. It was not a marriage that would last, and Semenko walked out on the team before season's end, sick and tired of sitting on the bench most nights until coach John Brophy threw him out onto the ice to get into a fight.

No matter what other uniform he wore, Semenko's blood never stopped running Oiler copper and blue. Against his old team, Semenko said he would play the way he used to during Oiler training camps.

"I'd get in people's way but I wasn't going to hurt anybody. I'd been part of that organization and had spent nine years with some of those guys. How was I supposed to try to hurt Mess? Or Kevin [Lowe]? And if anybody was ever stupid enough to think I was going to try to hurt Gretz, they should have been locked up," he said.

Even when Messier cross-checked Semenko's Leaf teammate Dale DeGray in the face, knocking him out cold, the most Semenko felt he could do was skate over and chastise Messier for having complained to the referee about being given a five-minute major penalty.

"DeGray had been a teammate for a couple of months, but Mark had been a great friend for ten years. I wasn't going to fight him," he said.

Semenko's friendships transferred to the ice, and sweater colours didn't enter the discussion. Even as an Oiler, he refused to go after Nick Fotiu, who'd been obtained by the Calgary Flames during the peak feud years of the Battle of Alberta. During a game against the Flames, Semenko tried to get a piece of Neil Sheehy, but Fotiu grabbed him and told him not to waste his time and take a penalty for a guy who wasn't going to fight him anyway.

"While all this was going on, there were thousands of people in the stands thinking that Nick and I were about to drop the gloves and go at one another. Never happened. We were pals."

Fittingly, Semenko would return to the Oilers organization. After becoming an assistant coach in 1996, he went on to join the scouting staff.

DAVE BROWN
If not the best overall fighter, Saskatoon's Dave Brown may have been the most feared.

"He was frickin' crazy," said Bob McGill. "And he's so big—6-foot-5, long reach and left-handed. . . . He'd string you out there and tag you and you couldn't reach him and it was a little unfair. He was a pretty scary dude, for sure."

Speaking of his reach, one wag half-jokingly said Brown could strike a match on the ground without tilting. And it was a dangerous left at that.

"You didn't want to piss him off," said Tony Twist. "He was big, he was tall, he knew his assets and his strengths. Brownie never fought not to lose, he always fought to win. . . . If you're trading punches with him, you better be able to take one because if you can't, you're not coming back from him."

Even one of the best at taking a punch, Tie Domi, was shaken by Brown.

"The guy that hit me the hardest was definitely Dave Brown," Tie Domi said in his *What It Takes* video. "Dave Brown said to me, 'Tie, I don't want to fight you, I can't hurt you.' Meanwhile I'm smiling, but I'm dazed, because he hit me hard. And that's the hardest I've been hit."

Before Brown employed his left for knocking hockey players silly, he used it to throw fastballs in Saskatchewan. The talented pitcher even turned down a partial scholarship from Georgia Southwestern College to pursue hockey.

"I was a better baseball player than hockey player, but I figured I had a better chance in hockey," Brown told the Philadelphia *Daily News*.

After a fight-filled season with the Saskatoon Blades, Brown was drafted by the Philadelphia Flyers in 1982 in the seventh round, 140th overall. His physical play in the '82 camp impressed Flyers brass enough for them to give him a 25-game AHL trial. Brown earned a permanent spot with the Maine Mariners and put up 377 penalty minutes before getting called up by the parent club. In his second NHL shift, he jumped Gord Kluzak in Boston Garden—apparently retribution for Kluzak having snubbed him in the juniors—and put him in hospital. He'd return to Maine to add to his penalty totals and set an AHL record of 418 minutes.

Brown proved he was tough enough, but he wasn't NHL ready, lacking the skating ability to keep up with major leaguers.

"Dave fought every game. Every single game," Brown's Maine linemate Dave Poulin said in an interview with the *Daily News*. "You could see he had an idea of how the game should be played, but he was just so slow you just didn't see any way he would be an NHL player."

To alleviate his deficiencies, Brown spent his summers taking power skating lessons. On top of that, he went to Flyers assistant coach Ted Sator to work on hockey basics. "He is usually the first guy out for practice and always, I mean always, the last guy off," Sator said at the time.

In his first Stanley Cup Final, Brown had improved enough to see the ice during critical situations.

"Mike [Keenan] put Dave on the ice in the last two minutes of a playoff game against Edmonton," said Sator, calling Brown a solid defensive player. "The Flyers were protecting a one-goal lead. To me, that's the measure of an NHL player. . . . All a coach can ask from an athlete is that he shows up every day and gives 100%. Dave does that."

Dave Brown of the Flyers gets his team going during a game with the Penguins.
(Paul Bereswill/Hockey Hall of Fame)

"The difference between then and now isn't night and day. It's three days and two nights," said Poulin, by then the Flyers captain.

But no one, Brown in particular, ever doubted Brown's primary asset.

"What I contribute is part psychological. I think they [opponents] are intimidated. If I get the puck, they lay off. They don't come after me as hard. They give me more room, because they think I'm going to clobber them. There's a respect there. If they try to take the puck off me, maybe somewhere I'm going to remember that and do something about it," Brown told the *Philadelphia Inquirer*.

If that sounds rather calculating, then it shouldn't come as a surprise that Brown also tried to keep his cool during fights.

"I don't know if I ever really get all that mad. You have to have a clear head when you fight," Brown told *Sports Illustrated*, adding he wanted his punches to be as accurate as possible and cause the most damage. "Broken nose, broken jaw—that's the quickest way to get the point across. There's no sense getting into a fight if you're not trying to hurt them."

And he didn't only target enforcers; if *anyone* dirtied one of his teammates, he'd dirty them back.

A player with a reputation for being one of the dirtiest of them all, New York Rangers forward Tomas Sandstrom, learned that lesson—twice. In their first confrontation, Brown received a five-game suspension for hitting Sandstrom on the head with his stick after Sandstrom clipped Flyers All-Star Mark Howe.

In a return engagement at Madison Square Garden the next season, Sandstrom speared Howe in the groin and later ran and jabbed at goalie Ron Hextall. As play was whistled down, Brown calmly cruised near the crease and cross-checked Sandstrom in the neck.

The infraction drew gasps from players, the crowd, and management. An incensed Rangers head coach Michel Bergeron cried, "If he did the same thing on the street he'd get 10 years in jail. He didn't just try to hurt him; he tried to kill him!"

Even Brown's parents were taken aback. "I got a sinking feeling," his mother, Eleanor, told the *Daily News*. "I was hoping, first of all, that [Sandstrom] wasn't hurt. Then I thought about David, what this would mean for him."

"I said, 'Oh, David, oh, David,'" Brown's father, Phil, added. "I played a lot of hockey myself, and I knew what he had done was wrong. There's no sense arguing. I don't think David went out to hurt anyone. I think it was just the spirit of the moment. He blew his cork. Used too much muscle."

By 1988–89, Philadelphia had a glut of tough customers with the likes of Craig Berube, Rick Tocchet, Jay Wells, Jeff Chychrun, and

Terry Carkner. The same was not true in Edmonton, where the Oilers were desperate for a replacement for Marty McSorley, who had followed Wayne Gretzky to Los Angeles. Edmonton would alleviate the enforcer gap by acquiring Brown for Keith Acton.

"If we didn't get him, Calgary would have," Oilers GM Glen Sather said at the time. "One of the reasons why our hockey club has had so many injuries this year is that we've had a lot of people take advantage of us."

Calgary's Tim Hunter called Brown "a serious threat to break your face" in an interview with hockeyfights.com. Hunter fought him very cautiously and urged other fighters to do likewise. But his warning wasn't well heeded by teammates Stu Grimson and Jim Kyte, who both had orbital bones crushed by Brown.

Grimson was making his way in the minor pro ranks when the Calgary Flames called him up in January 1990 for a home-and-home series against their provincial rival, the Oilers. "The Grim Reaper" understood he'd need to hold his own against Brown to have a chance of sticking with Calgary. In Edmonton, Grimson got a piece of Brown off the draw, hit him with a couple of solid rights, and ended up putting him down on the ice.

"I always tell folks it was at that moment I realized I had achieved the single greatest moment of my career, and probably made the biggest mistake of my career at the same time, because you don't get the best of Dave Brown and not have to answer for it soon after," Grimson said.

When the Flames returned to Calgary for the return match, Brown went after Grimson and was looking for revenge. He got it: "He ended up breaking a bone underneath my cheek and orbital in three different places; kinda put me out of commission for about five weeks. I had a whole new level of respect for Dave Brown."

Grimson fought all the top heavyweights in the NHL—Bob Probert, Joey Kocur, Tony Twist, and Georges Laraque to name a few—and concluded no one could match Brown's devastating power. "Dave Brown was far and away the hardest hitter I've ever fought. That was a guy, he had a left hand that hit like a thunder cloud. He was unbelievable," Grimson said.

In the spring of '91, Brown left Jim Kyte's face a swollen mess in a one-sided affair.

"It was a given, we were going to fight," Kyte said after the game. "You know you have to hold on to it [Brown's left] but I couldn't do it."

So feared and respected was Brown that even a draw against him amounted to a major moral victory for the opposition.

Jim McKenzie remembers his first big-league fight against Brown—even though he wasn't aware of its importance at the time.

The Hartford Whaler was out for the first shift of the game with Brown, and they didn't hesitate to exchange hostilities. McKenzie held his own, but having dominated the minor leagues, he felt he should have done better. After brooding in the penalty box, McKenzie skated back to a bench full of ecstatic Whalers. Backup goalie Daryl Reaugh complimented McKenzie on the great job he'd done, but McKenzie was unconvinced. He even tried for a rematch with Brown, who demurred and told him the issue was "settled."

Back on the bench, McKenzie commiserated with Reaugh, believing his showing would result in him being sent back down to the minors. Reaugh looked at him as though he were an imbecile and asked him if he realized whom he'd fought.

"Some Brown guy," McKenzie answered.

When Reaugh filled him in—that "some Brown guy" just happened to be the same dreadnought who'd cruised for the Philadelphia Flyers but was now searching and destroying for the team they were playing, the Edmonton Oilers—McKenzie's stomach dropped. There were still 10 minutes on the clock, and he remembered he'd challenged Brown to another fight just moments before.

"I'm kind of hoping the clock runs out," McKenzie said while laughing in an interview with hockeyfights.com. He couldn't even remember if Hartford was winning or losing by that point. "I just knew that if we scored one more goal, then I'd be back out there, and I would have my chance to fight him again . . . I wasn't sure that I wanted to fight him again. For me, it was easier fighting him not knowing who he was. It turned out nobody scored, and the game stayed the way it was. That was my introduction to Dave Brown."

After winning a Stanley Cup with Edmonton, Brown returned to Philadelphia and wound up his career with the San Jose Sharks. There, he nearly scared future champ Georges Laraque out of hockey. Most fans would think Laraque is the last person who could be shaken by Brown, but as a rookie, even his knees trembled when lining up against the notorious tough guy.

In his first exhibition game, Laraque stood across from Brown at a faceoff, and the only thing going through his head was that second Brown-Grimson tilt. They never fought—Laraque took on someone else—but the thought of facing Brown so unnerved him that he turned down Edmonton coach Ron Low's offer to suit up for the team on opening night, asking instead to be sent back to junior.

"Dave Brown hadn't even had to look at me to intimidate me. I had to reconsider what I'd been aiming for all this time. Was I really built to be an NHL tough guy? Did I really want to spend my life fighting these guys? After facing off against Dave Brown, I couldn't even think about being one of them anymore," Laraque said in his memoir, *The Story of the NHL's Unlikeliest Tough Guy*.

Brown seemed to make a surprisingly easy transition into hockey management. After his last year in the NHL, in 1995–96, he became an assistant coach with the Flyers for a couple seasons before scouting for the Rangers. He returned to the orange and white of Philadelphia in 2006, when he was named Flyers director of player personnel.

"We have always liked Dave and felt that he was a Flyer," said GM Bobby Clarke in announcing Brown's return.

CHAPTER 5

MODERN-DAY WARRIORS

STEVE MACINTYRE A 6-foot-5, 250-pound forward/ defenceman with heavy hands, Steve MacIntyre has an edge over many of his peers that goes beyond his size and strength.

Many enforcers are forced to evaluate their own fight performances and scout their future opponents. MacIntyre has a specialist he can turn to—Doug "The Thug" Smith, the minor-league fighting sensation whose exploits were documented in a book he co-wrote, which was eventually made into the film *Goon*. If you're going to seek advice, you might as well ask an expert.

While playing for Providence of the AHL in 2007–08, MacIntyre came upon the rarest of creatures, an enforcer coach—Smith. Best of all, no one could reasonably question his credentials.

"He's been there, done that, and I take every bit of information all in and use it the best way I can," said MacIntyre.

It's a relationship that's lasted to this day, said MacIntyre, who still occasionally works in person with Smith. And when travel and schedules make personal instruction impossible, Big Mac just picks up the phone.

"I call him and ask how'd that look? And he's like, 'Try this, try that,'" said MacIntyre, adding he also uses Smith to scout the opposition. "I just call him up and say, 'Hey, Doug. What do you think of this guy?' 'Oh, well, he does this, or does that.' It's a nice tool."

Prior to Smith, MacIntyre was literally being educated at the school of hard knocks.

"I didn't do so well," he said of his initial hockey fight as a teenager at his first training camp with the WHL Saskatoon Blades. "I didn't do much winning for the first little bit, and then my dad gave me some pointers and told me to move my hands a little faster. He told me to move my head, but it seemed like I'd take a little bit more than I should."

The WHL graduated a number of enforcers from MacIntyre's class into the NHL, including marquee heavyweights Eric Godard, Derek Boogaard, and Colton Orr.

"It was tough. The Western Hockey League by far, I think, is the toughest junior league. . . . You better have your chinstrap tight."

MacIntyre kept improving, to the point where he actually seemed to enjoy getting into scraps: "It was exciting. I don't think you really worried, necessarily. Once I was into the fight, it was fine. I didn't have a problem with it. I felt like I was ready. The lead up to the fight, I still hate it. But I mean, once a guy's in it, that's where things got exciting, for me anyway."

MacIntyre had big shoes to fill, having followed Wade Belak as one of the club's heavies. He'd always looked up to Belak, and when he made the roster, they gave him Belak's old No. 33 to wear. The two would actually skate together briefly when both were Florida Panthers, and MacIntyre was honoured when, as an Edmonton Oiler, he got to drop the gloves against his old idol. He still has the memento of the collision. "It was probably one of my best fights ever. If you watch that fight, I come up smiling. I knew he hit me pretty good, but I think I got the win on that one," remembered MacIntyre. "And then when I looked at my helmet, he busted it. So I was like, 'Well, I gotta tip my hat and send it over to him and see if he'd sign it.'"

Belak did in fact sign the cracked bucket, and MacIntyre still has it, with plans to one day put it on his mantle, under the stick he used to score his first NHL goal. Not only will it serve as a reminder of that fateful fight, it will perhaps also serve as a reminder of his relationship with *both* Belak brothers, Wade and Graham.

"I grew up playing against his younger brother Graham, and I tell you what, they were two of the toughest SOBs. Man, they were tough! Long, lanky, his brother gave me a dirty lickin' one time. I always remembered that. He gave me a pretty good black eye. I didn't fare so well at the start of that fight and came out a little worse for wear. But I caught him a couple good lefts so I was pretty happy with that."

The WHL was where MacIntyre would learn that it might be better to rent than buy if he was going to pursue a career in hockey.

He'd bounce from the Blades to the Red Deer Rebels, the Prince Albert Raiders, and then the Medicine Hat Tigers before winding up in the northern Manitoba community of The Pas to play for the Opaskwayak Cree Nation Blizzard of the Manitoba Junior Hockey League.

"I had a blast there," he said of the town, located about 390 miles northwest of the provincial capital, Winnipeg. "It was probably one of the most fun years I ever had playing hockey as far as junior goes."

After winning the league championship, he was on the move again, this time to Michigan and the Bay County Blizzard of the now defunct Continental Elite Hockey League, a "glorified Junior B league" according to MacIntyre. He fit right in on the pro-pugilist team—perhaps too well, getting booted out of the league after accumulating too many suspensions.

The next few years would be a whirlwind for MacIntyre, who found himself patrolling the arenas of an alphabet soup of various minor leagues. By the time he landed in Moline, Illinois, in 2006 to suit up for the Quad City Mallards of the United Hockey League, MacIntyre had had enough.

After a handful of games and fights, his heart was no longer in it. Fighting the same guys and feeling like he wasn't going anywhere, he wanted to go home. When he did, he got to be home at Christmas for the first time in years, but he couldn't get hockey out of his mind.

Back in his hometown of Brock, Saskatchewan, he sat down with his father and a close family friend for a heart-to-heart. Did he quit on his own or for the wrong reasons?

"Ultimately they said you can only do this for so long and are you going to be able to look at yourself 10, 20 years down the road and say did you throw everything into it and give it one last try?"

After mulling over the matter and discussing it with his wife, MacIntyre ended up returning and finishing off the year with the Mallards. It was the right decision, as the next year he played a full season with the AHL's Providence Bruins and, the year after that, fulfilled his dream of playing for his boyhood favourites, the Edmonton Oilers.

He had signed as a free agent with the Florida Panthers in July 2008, and they assigned him to their minor league affiliate, but the Oilers, looking to insert some robustness into their lineup, and having failed to lure Georges Laraque back into the fold, picked MacIntyre off waivers.

He immediately endeared himself to Edmonton fans in an exhibition game against the hated Calgary Flames by dropping fellow Westerner Jim Vandermeer with a deadly right uppercut.

"That first game as an Edmonton Oiler, I mentioned to our captain Ethan Moreau, 'I can't believe that I get to pull this jersey over my head.' It was still exhibition season, but that was honestly a dream come true. To actually pull that jersey over my shoulders and to realize hey, I'm an Edmonton Oiler, it might only be for this game, but I can say I played a game for them and succeeded in my quest as a hockey player," said MacIntyre.

He'd play more than just the one as it turned out, making the squad for the start of the regular season.

"He has endeared himself to everybody, including our players," said Oilers coach Craig MacTavish. "You can't help but admire a guy like that who is so passionate. He knows his limitations and that's a real important part."

Things only got better as he played a rematch against the Flames at home, a Saturday night affair televised on *Hockey Night in Canada*. His mother, father, and uncle were in the stands, wearing jerseys from teams he'd previously been on. It was a night to remember. After hammering Dustin Boyd into the boards, he pasted Brandon Prust—who flew in to avenge his downed teammate—with heavy lefts.

"I went to the penalty box and the whole place erupted. That was when I knew I had arrived."

"SMACKINTYRE!" blared the following day's *Edmonton Sun*.

It wasn't all highlights, though, and MacIntyre would be sidelined after renewing his rivalry with Pittsburgh's Eric Godard. "They were all-out slobber knockers," MacIntyre said of his WHL scraps with Godard, whom he'd take on just about every time they played each other in junior. "We were trying to knock each other's heads off."

On this particular night, it was Godard who came out with his head intact after breaking MacIntyre's orbital bone.

"He hit me three or four good ones before I really kind of knew he hit me—he's got fast hands and he hits you like a sledgehammer!"

MacIntyre, initially unaware of the seriousness of his injury, stayed in the game, flattened defenceman Kris Letang with a body-check and sought a rematch against Godard.

"We didn't know it was broken. I knew the next period, because I blew my nose and my whole face exploded," he said in describing the extreme swelling. "I knew something was wrong. Thank goodness Sheldon Souray got between us because if I got popped again it would have been worse!"

He missed the next 26 games and scored his first NHL goal in his second game back, against Washington.

The following season was less kind to MacIntyre. Pat Quinn took over from MacTavish and soured on MacIntyre.

"I've always believed in a four-line concept where you involve all your players," Quinn told the *Edmonton Journal*. "For some reason, even when we had Steve dressed through circumstances, he didn't play much . . . either through a bad penalty, or the first time I put him on the ice he wanted to fight [Brian McGrattan]. . . . Fighting has a place in our game, but in that case he took himself out of the game early on. I wanted him to play and wasn't sure he could help us on our fourth line as much as I thought he should."

After only playing a minute or so in each of the four games he dressed for, Florida came and saved MacIntyre from demotion to Edmonton's farm team.

But MacIntyre would again dress in Oiler copper and blue, signing a one-year contract in July 2010.

He made early headlines after a massive punch-up with another Calgary Flame, Raitis Ivanans, during an October regular-season showdown. In the final minutes of a 4-0 game where Edmonton was leading, Ivanans hit the ice and started roughing up the Oilers. Enter MacIntyre, who took the next faceoff. Exit Ivanans, whom MacIntyre knocked out and needed help leaving the ice.

"He's going to go out and protect guys who can't protect themselves in certain situations," said captain Shawn Horcoff.

MacIntyre almost put himself out of a job with the fight, as there were far fewer takers willing to test him, especially after news emerged that Ivanans would be forced to miss the rest of the season with a concussion.

One of the only players who had no qualms about facing him was the league's heavyweight champ, Derek Boogaard. The two clashed twice during one November 2010 game at Madison Square Garden.

"I kind of felt like I didn't do so well in the first fight so I had to make sure he knew I was still around," MacIntyre explained. "My Dad, he's like, 'You lose, you make sure you pick yourself up and make sure everybody knows you're still there.' I kinda did that out of pride. Him and Storts [Zack Stortini] were kind of jawing at each other and I didn't feel that was right, so I said let's go again, big boy. I'm not gonna roll over and quit."

Faring much better the second time, MacIntyre earned positive reviews from new coach Tom Renney. But playing on a low-scoring team like Edmonton, whose victories typically came by the narrowest of margins, made it difficult for MacIntyre to get much ice time, especially as penalties could make the difference between a win and a loss.

"I want Mac to be a player, to the best of his abilities, I want him to be a player," said Renney. "Are there limitations there? Yes there are. That, at the end of the day, factors in how much I play him and whether or not he's dressing."

When the Oilers signed Darcy Hordichuk and Ben Eager in July 2011, MacIntyre became expendable, and the Oilers didn't offer him a contract. The matter remains a sore point: "I grew up watching them. I felt terrible. It was ultimately their decision. It's still a touchy subject. I didn't want to leave."

His disappointment was partly offset by the Penguins' interest in him, and he signed with them. "Getting picked up and offered a contract with Pittsburgh, that was pretty cool too, riding shotgun for the best player in the world."

Sidney Crosby welcomed the big winger's presence.

"He's a great guy, he's fit in really well and works really hard, that's something we've seen from Day 1," Crosby said, adding MacIntyre helped keep the guys loose. "You need different personalities on a team, but the one that he brings, he's happy every day and he's working hard and has a great attitude. Those are the teammates you love to have."

MacIntyre played a dozen games with the Penguins in 2011–12 and is a regular with their AHL affiliate in Wilkes-Barre/Scranton.

"It was a long journey and it still is. It's an ongoing process. It's great that I have such a great wife and family because they have supported me and put up with a lot of my BS to help me fulfill that. If it wasn't for my wife and family, I don't think I would be where I am."

BRIAN MCGRATTAN If you get to the top in your profession, chances are somebody along the way took the time to teach you. For Brian McGrattan, it was Dennis Bonvie, the all-time leader in penalty minutes in professional hockey.

McGrattan was a promising, though well-travelled, junior prospect, suiting up for six OHL teams in five seasons. At one point, he was captain of the Mississauga IceDogs, potting 20 goals in 2000–01. The Los Angeles Kings took him in the fourth round, 104th overall, in the 1999 NHL draft, but everything went off the rails when he hurt his knee in January 2001. The Kings declined to sign him, and he didn't catch on at a tryout camp with Detroit. His over-age year was pretty average.

The Ottawa Senators took a chance on him, inviting him to the team's rookie camp. Dropping the gloves a few times with the other wannabes, McGrattan determined that his fists could be his path to the NHL.

"I signed an East Coast/American League deal with Ottawa later on in the month after training camp. I figured being a bigger guy, I had to do something to stay around, so I started fighting," said McGrattan.

That first season and a half, McGrattan played with the Binghamton Senators but didn't win very often: "I got my ass kicked, I don't know how many times."

Enter Bonvie, a Binghamton teammate.

"He kind of showed me the ropes, pulled me aside, taught me some things that I could use to my advantage, like my height, my reach," said the 6-foot-4, 235-pound McGrattan. "But he told me it's the only way you learn is when you're losing and not to let it shake your confidence. The best thing to do when you take a real bad beating is to get right back in there again. I credit a lot to him. He taught me a lot as a young guy. I don't think I'd be where I'm at, in that part of the game, if it wasn't for him."

Like a proud papa, Bonvie can now look at his protege as one of the most-feared players in the NHL who can take a regular shift on right wing or patiently sit on the bench. "He was willing to learn, and I certainly helped him and showed him when and why to do it, how to do it, to the best of my knowledge," said Bonvie. "He went through some ups and downs. From where he was in the first month to going on a couple of years later, and now, he's done a tremendous job."

Perhaps more importantly, Bonvie, now a scout for Chicago, is pleased that McGrattan has turned his personal life around after a stint in the NHL's substance-abuse program in December 2008. "He's cleaned up his act, in great shape, and got a little zest for the game," said Bonvie.

"At the time, it was the hardest decision that I ever had to make. I was embarrassed. It was like the lowest point in my life, like I couldn't have gone any lower. I manned up and changed my life," confessed McGrattan of his battles with alcohol. "Of course, people react in different ways. Some people probably thought, 'This guy's a professional athlete, he has the world at his fingertips.' But I'm a normal person too, and I have normal people problems. That was a big issue that was affecting my life. It was affecting hockey, yeah, but it was affecting my life too. I needed a change."

On the ice, McGrattan has had up and down years—getting in 60 games in 2005–06 but only 34 with the Flames in 2009–10—and some memorable bouts. For beat writers, his practice tilt with goalie Ray Emery while with the Sens was gold, but for McGrattan, it was an overblown release of steam between two buddies.

A far bigger occasion for McGrattan was his October 2005 fight with Tie Domi, whom he had idolized, along with Doug Gilmour, while growing up in Hamilton, Ontario. Having been knocked

It's the Battle of Alberta, as Steve MacIntyre of the Oilers takes one on the cheek from Brian McGrattan of the Flames in October 2009. (Mike Drew, QMI Agency)

around in the playoffs by the Leafs, the Sens picked up McGrattan as an enforcer. In his second fight with the Sens, he took on Domi in Toronto. "He tied me up, and I got my right arm out of my jersey. I hit him with one and put him on his back," McGrattan recalled. The *Toronto Star* proclaimed the one-punch knockout was Domi's "most decisive loss in 10 years."

"I was still living in a hotel at the time, because I was on a two-way, whatnot. After that fight, I had the letter in my locker the next day to stay and get my own place."

Since then, McGrattan has had to find places to live in Phoenix, Calgary, Boston, and Anaheim, though he never suited up much for any of them. In the AHL with Binghamton in 2004–05, he set a single-season record with 551 penalty minutes, eclipsing his mentor,

Bonvie. Later, during stints with San Antonio and Providence, McGrattan found a distinct lack of "takers."

He does pride himself on being extra prepared. "I go on hockey fights.com quite a bit. You kind of see who the up-and-comers are, the young kids," he admitted.

Nashville was a pleasant surprise for him on many levels, and he was a celebrated part of the Predators, even if he didn't play every game. He could walk to the arena and enjoyed the atmosphere. "It's a hockey town. I was kind of shocked at first, because you're in a southern market," he said. "Home games are pumping from the minute that the puck drops until right to the end. People are going nuts."

Usually the 12th or 13th forward, McGrattan did not see a ton of ice time. "It's not necessarily fighting every night, but it's having that presence on the bench, knowing that if somebody does something stupid, they have me there to back someone up."

That positive attitude has to extend to the dressing room as well, and that is one of the reasons the Flames reacquired McGrattan from Nashville in exchange for defenceman Joe Piskula in February 2013. He said: "I'm not going to be one of those mopey babies around the room because they're not playing. . . . I just go to the rink every day, because my number could get called tomorrow. One of my bigger upsides as a player is the guy that I am in the dressing room. I'm always upbeat, joking around. Things could be a lot worse than being scratched for six games. You just have to find a way to stay upbeat, positive, go to the rink, work hard, put your time in, and stay as ready as you can to play," he concluded. "There are a lot of guys dying to be in the position that I'm in."

ARRON ASHAM
Arron Asham knew it looked bad the moment he got off the ice. The news reports on October 13, 2011, called it "the most memorable KO of the young NHL season," and

the TV news cycle replayed it constantly. Rookie Jay Beagle of the Capitals had provoked Asham of the Penguins to the point of no return. The youngster got a couple of shots in, until Asham got his feet set and nailed Beagle twice in the face, dropping him to the ice, blood pooling. Skating away, Asham played to the Pittsburgh fans, gesturing that Beagle was finished and off in sleepyland.

The veteran was called to the carpet immediately, apologizing to Beagle and calling his own actions "classless." The Pens coach, Dan Bylsma, said that Asham reacted in the heat of the moment: "Emotions got the best of him. He wishes he could have them back. He stuck up for a teammate but I don't think anybody liked what ensued after that."

In conversation, Asham tried to give the incident some perspective.

"It was more him wanting to fight. I skated up to him and gave him a shot and told him to settle down. He was the one that was like, 'Okay, let's go.' But all the media thought it was me going up to this poor kid that hasn't had an NHL fight and challenging him. It was totally the opposite," said the 5-foot-11, 205-pound Asham. "I knew this kid didn't fight. . . . When I got to him, he looked at me, saw he was five inches taller and decided to have a go at it. He learned his lesson."

The heated atmosphere of a hockey rink and facing off against a team in your division can affect your decision-making, Asham said. "I got emotional and got carried away with the moment. We were playing one of our rivals, at home, there's 19,000 people screaming your name—you get revved up! It's unfortunate what happened."

In a way, it's unfortunate what has happened to Asham in the NHL. In junior hockey, Asham played in Red Deer and racked up 32, 45, and 43 goals in his last three seasons with the Rebels. He was drafted 71st over-all in 1996 by the Montreal Canadiens and assigned to the team's Fredericton, New Brunswick, farm team upon graduating from the WHL.

"It's almost like he's been pigeon-holed to a certain style of play or something. He's got some offensive talent there, and it's just the way it's worked out these last few years for sure," said Todd Blight, who was Asham's minor hockey coach and worked with him for five seasons. He has remained close to his protege. "You feel for him, and you'd like to see him play, not to take anything away from the guys he's played with, but you'd like to see him play with some more offensive-minded players, where he could step up and play a little bit better offensively."

Feeling sorry for him is the last thing Asham wants anybody to do.

"I had my first junior fight when I was 16 at camp. I just fell in love with that aspect of the game, but continued to score and stuff," Asham said. "Once I made it to Fredericton and eventually to Montreal, my roles were kind of combined. I think they wanted me to be a power forward, a guy that has to drop the gloves. I ran with it. Though I enjoy doing it, I'd much rather be playing a regular shift and scoring goals than doing the fighting. It's my way to stay in the league and it's been working ever since."

He's had his moments on the scoreboard for sure, potting 15 goals in his first year with the Islanders and playing on the third line with the Flyers as they made the 2012 Stanley Cup Final, lining up on the right wing alongside winger Claude Giroux and centres James van Riemsdyk or Mike Richards. "Ash has shown the ability to play with offensive guys. He has great hands, good vision, and he's a bigger guy on the line who can get to the net," said then–Flyers coach John Stevens in October 2009.

Growing up in Portage la Prairie, Manitoba, and of Métis heritage, Asham remembers a lot of fights with his two older brothers and one younger one. A fan of Mario Lemieux and Wayne Gretzky, Asham has said he didn't study the fighters and learned on the fly once he was in Red Deer. "I never really was shown a proper way to fight. I fought a little bit on the streets when I was younger. My first fight, I was basically throwing with two hands and realized I had better tie this guy up, because he kept punching me in the face, and it wasn't feeling good. Basically, I just came up with my own little style of fighting. It seems to be doing alright."

Having been in the spotlight following the Beagle fight, Asham can truly appreciate how the media, with its 24-hour news cycle, is driving a lot of the campaign against fighting in hockey. He said it still serves a role and that fisticuffs should be allowed.

"If you ask anyone on a hockey team if they think the team should have a tough guy, I'm pretty sure that everyone is going to say yeah, because you need that presence, you need that somebody that's going to stand up and go and protect your skilled player," explained Asham, who signed a two-year deal with the New York Rangers in July 2012. "I'm pretty sure that Sidney [Crosby] and Gino [Evengy Malkin] appreciate having a tough guy around, like Mario and Wayne did. They had their tough guys. It just makes the game a lot easier for the skilled guys knowing that they've got a guy that's going to stick up for ya and fight for your team."

DEREK DORSETT There's an entertainment factor that is impossible to deny: The fans love fighting in hockey, and players like Derek Dorsett of the New York Rangers know how to deliver. He has also heard all the criticisms about staged fights.

I don't think there's so many staged fights where it's just, "Let's fight." There's usually a reason behind it. Sometimes there's two heavyweights that know they're going to fight at some point in the game. . . . Sometimes they're like, "Let's get it out of the way. Let's start this game off with a bang. Let's get the fans into it." Me and Jordin Tootoo fought right off the start of the game in Nashville. Me and him don't really have bad blood, but at the same time, we got the fans into it, both teams into it and it was a great game right there from the start.

Learning the time and the place to fight is a skill picked up by watching veterans and listening to advice from players and coaches. "For example, if you're in the offensive zone and someone asks you to fight, well, let's see if my centreman wins the faceoff first. If my centre wins the faceoff, I'm not going to fight because there's a good chance we're going to get a chance on goal. But if the puck leaves the zone, 'Okay, I'll fight you.' There's things like that," explained Dorsett. "The score reflects whether you fight. If you're down 2-0 right away, early in the game, maybe you fight to try to get a spark into your team. There's times I fought three seconds into a game. That's more or less coming off a tough couple of games and we haven't responded very well. That's trying to send a message to the team, 'Come on boys, let's go.'"

For Dorsett, the lessons really came growing up in Kindersley, Saskatchewan. His family billeted players from the Klippers SJHL team, and the three Dorsett boys learned to love the game. Jon Mirasty was of particular help, both when Dorsett was a junior in town and a couple of years later when, having excelled for the Medicine Hat Tigers—WHL champs in 2007—he landed in Syracuse alongside Mirasty to further his trade in the AHL.

It was "Nasty" Mirasty who nicknamed Dorsett "Shifty" because "he's a little guy and he's hard to hit." Mirasty said, "He was a little fan of mine. It was pretty cool and pretty ironic that I'd end up playing pro hockey in Syracuse, New York, with him."

His career as a fighter started in the WHL, where Dorsett played three seasons in Medicine Hat and ranked the 18th highest total of penalty minutes in the history of the team, with 593. The "über-pest" showed the ability to bounce back in the juniors. After being suspended a game for biting Kenndal McArdle of the Vancouver Giants in the WHL final, he fought through all the boos by the Vancouver crowd in the Memorial Cup, scoring a game-winner during the round-robin.

His higher point total in junior (19 goals, 45 assists in 2006–07) never translated to the pros, though he notched a career-high 12 goals in Columbus in 2011–12, which drafted him 189th overall in the 2006 NHL Entry Draft.

In the game's vernacular, the yappy Dorsett is a gritty, blue-collar right winger who can protect his teammates and occasionally contribute to the scoresheet. "I like to play a physical game. I like to put the other teams on their toes, so when I do get on the ice, people know that I'm on the ice. I try to create room for my teammates," he said. "I'm not afraid to fight. I like it. It's part of what's made me successful, to get me to where I am today."

A lot of his work gets noticed in the box scores. In the 2011–12 season, Dorsett led the league in penalty minutes, including 19 majors. "Just the style I play, I've always had high numbers of penalties—in the Western League, in Junior A, the AHL I had a lot. I've always been a guy that gets a lot of penalty minutes with majors and coincidentals, and penalties, charging, boardings and stuff like that."

Aaron Portzline, the beat writer on the Blue Jackets for the *Columbus Dispatch*, said that while other higher-profile players, like Rick Nash, might get the attention,

> Dorsett was, without question, the club's most consistent performer. His career-high offensive output was an unexpected bonus, but it was his energy and competitive fire that really stood out. On a club that barely registers a heartbeat in too many games, Dorsett's fire and battle helped drag many of his teammates along this season. Because of the role he fills, Dorsett is quick to draw the ire of many fans around the league, and he's on the radar of every opponent the Blue Jackets face. But there's a healthy dose of respect present, too. He's a gritty player, not a dirty one.

The Rangers thought enough of Dorsett, an assistant captain in Columbus who had signed a three-year deal in May 2012, to acquire him at the trade deadline 2013, even though he was on injured reserve with a fractured clavicle.

At just a shade under 6-foot and weighing in around 185 pounds, the middleweight finds himself lining up against some of the game's giants. In February 2012, he took a memorable beating from Chicago's John Scott, who is 6-foot-8. The *Chicago Tribune* described the fight: "More comical than brutal, this dust-up features Dorsett facing a decided height disadvantage, but he gets the first hit on an unsuspecting Scott. When Scott finally gets his gloves off, he lowers the boom, delivering a series of rights before the two are separated. Scott skates off the ice, laughing."

Portzline found Dorsett's fight with Scott hard to forget. "It was a comical scene, with Scott towering over Dorsett and hammering his head like a railroad spike. Dorsett knew his chances weren't good to win a fight versus Scott, but the Blue Jackets needed a spark and he was the one who stepped forward. He'd do it again, too, you just know he would."

In retrospect, Dorsett was in over his head. "That was unnecessary," Dorsett said, admitting it was a stupid move. "It's never a good thing when I'm fighting with those guys."

CHAPTER 6

TODAY'S GAME

THE RISE OF THE RATS

"IF VIOLENCE CEASES to exist, it will not be the same game."

That's not a quote from some knuckle-dragging, bloodthirsty fan, nor a pugilist whose living depends upon being given free rein to loosen teeth. The words belong to an Oxford University Rhodes Scholar, 30-year president of the NHL, Clarence Campbell.

Campbell had numerous clashes with bruisers, whom he called upon the carpet on multiple occasions in order to hand out disciplinary action. Ironically, those same rule-breakers and their successors would be in full agreement with him in this case.

"I have this philosophy on the game of hockey: It all comes down to the fans liking the three Gs—they really get behind your goaltender, your goal scorer, and your goon. Those are the jerseys you see in the stands," said Todd Ewen, who patrolled NHL rinks in the 1980s and '90s. "Once you change the game, like they have, to do nothing but benefit the goal scorer, [you lose] two-thirds of the fans and two-thirds of the game."

"[Enforcers] were all over the place back then—every team had two. That's why they had 17,000 people in the stands," said Jay Miller, who played for the Bruins and Kings around the same era. "They don't sell out as much as they used to. It was part of the game. Doesn't seem like that anymore."

Debate about the extinction of the enforcer picked up considerably following the Toronto Maple Leafs' demotion of Colton Orr, their top gun, after he'd been a healthy scratch for 34 of 39 games. Maple Leafs then-GM Brian Burke, who'd signed Orr, a free agent, to a four-year contract a couple a seasons earlier, saw Orr's lessened importance and role as a bad omen.

"I have this fear that if we don't have guys looking after each other that the rats will take this game over," Burke said. "I see guys running around and starting stuff and won't back it up. It makes me sick to my stomach."

Burke believed enforcers' waning capacity to make others accountable gave agitators *carte blanche*. "You never have to answer for that in the game anymore. You used to have to answer that in the game. Players used to police the game and now it's [league discipline chief] Brendan Shanahan," he said. "But I'm not being critical of him. It used to be that if you were going to cheap shot a guy, you had to fight him or fight someone else on his team who was tougher than him. That seems to be gone. There are no checks and balances."

All-time AHL penalty-minute-leader Dennis Bonvie said hitting can be even more dangerous than fighting. Whereas fighters are on guard and can typically diminish the blows launched at them, bodychecks can be devastating, especially when someone's caught unaware and in a vulnerable position.

"You can hurt a guy so seriously by just elbowing him in the head—or any headshot," added Bob Nystrom, who played for the great New York Islanders teams of the late '70s and early '80s. "I'd just as soon see people be able to drop their gloves and fight."

When the league introduced the instigator rule in 1992—which allowed referees to issue a two-minute minor to anyone starting a fight—it marked the beginning of officials shouldering more of the justice load. The onus on referees and not the players to police the game grew when additional rules to eliminate interference, obstruction, and hits that targeted the head were implemented.

"The referees are like policemen—they can only do something *after* somebody gets hurt," said Ewen, adding that with the changes came a rise in injuries. "What they asked of us was to stop it before something happened. Now it's just reactionary hockey, which is not what our game's about."

Steve MacIntyre, an enforcer who's played over a decade of minor pro and NHL hockey, thinks discouraging players from sorting out their own problems was a step in the wrong direction. "It's almost like we're a dying breed. It feels like we're the last gunslingers," he said of himself and his peers. "They think if we take fighting out and penalize the guys, suspend them, and all this other baloney . . . I'm old school: If we could police our own selves and take care of our own matters internally, I think the game will be a lot better."

Legendary Broad Street Bully Dave Schultz also argued suspensions and fines aren't enough of a deterrent to stop players from taking liberties.

"What's $10,000 to a $3 million hockey player? Or a suspension? Three days off? Really?! Can I? Hey, thanks!" Schultz said to the *Calgary Herald*.

Schultz seethed about the lack of accountability. Pointing to Scott Stevens's devastating open-ice hit on Paul Kariya in Game 6 of the 2003 Stanley Cup Final, he asserted Anaheim's coach should have sent his players over the boards to exact revenge. Clean hit or dirty, a franchise's top player can't be laid out unconscious without someone to answer for it. "In my day, when Scott Stevens hit Paul Kariya, the coach would send the bench on the ice and say, 'Let's get him.' Now there's nothing. I don't think anyone even talked to him. I don't understand it, but that's the way it is."

Instead of reducing violence, anti-fighting rules like the instigator penalty helped contribute to Todd Bertuzzi's 2004 attack on Colorado Avalanche player Steve Moore, according to Schultz. Bertuzzi sucker-punched Moore from behind after failing to goad him into a fight in retaliation for a blindside hit Moore laid on Markus Naslund in an earlier game, which concussed the Canucks star forward. Schultz argued that merely penalizing an offender who's delivered a spear, elbow, slash, or hit from behind won't necessarily wipe the slate clean.

"Hockey players are human, and a cheap shot is nothing less than an act of disrespect that will not be forgotten. Players are forced to carry the frustration, resentment and anger from game to game, leading to a Bertuzzi-style attack," he told *The New York Times*.

Wendel Clark claimed that prior to the instigator penalty, anyone running around hitting guys but refusing to fight would still get slugged. "It's not that way today. Back then, I either had to stop running around or answer for it. The way the game's played now, I could run around all night and nobody would stop me. I wouldn't have to answer the bell to anybody," wrote Clark in *Wendel: My Life in Hockey*. "The hitting is now more dangerous than ever. The game no longer polices itself, which is why I think the game was much safer when I played."

"The instigator rule has really, really made a big change and I don't think it's made a change for the better," said John Wensink, agreeing that rule changes have opened the door for players to take more liberties with one another.

Wensink recalled that Red Wing Dennis Hextall became a marked man after running Boston's Gary Doak into the boards. "Every time he played the Bruins, we were lined up to go after him. Nowadays, guys might get fined and suspended, but they don't have to worry about having someone step in and settle it," explained Wensink.

If a fight does occur to settle a violation, it's often between the two teams' enforcers rather than the actual perpetrator. "The other guys on both benches don't have to worry that one of those tough guys might come over and give them a slap or two," Wensink said. "That's the player I don't like—the player that's changed the game and made it cheap, the player that knows he's not going to have to stand up for himself because someone else is trying to stand up for his teammate. You've got a lot of cheap shot artists out there that don't fear the possibility that they might have to stand up for themselves."

Ewen said the league has altered the game to the point that agitators are dictating the flow of the game, and it's those players who tend to fly under the radar as they go after the top players. The tough guys are stymied in ensuring their club's stars survive not only the regular season but the playoffs as well.

Steve MacIntyre believes the stars are in favour of being taken care of, pointing out Sidney Crosby appreciated the kind of protection he could provide. "It's almost like an eye for an eye thinking . . . If something happened to Sid, then we have to go out there and either take the guy by the scruff of the collar and give him a licking, or make it miserable for the other team's skill guys," he said. "I don't think those guys [like Crosby] are untouchable, but at the same time, it sends a message to the other team, that if you screw around with Sid, somebody's coming after you."

The poster boy for agitators over the course of the last decade has been Sean Avery, a forward who'd use any tactic to drive opponents up the wall. But he would have had to change his game significantly if he'd have hoped to survive playing in the old "Chuck" Norris Division, where every team was loaded with players who would have licked their chops at the chance of getting their hands on him.

"He probably wouldn't be as flamboyant as he is because guys would be in his face and after him all the time. You'd have to be more accountable," said Bob McGill, who played in the Norris for most of his NHL career. "One thing about the guy is he can play. I don't understand why it has to be such a sideshow all the time. It bothers me because the guy can play and yet he wants to be a jackass.

The linesmen step between Cody McLeod of the Avalanche and Arron Asham of the Penguins in March 2012. (IHA/Icon SMI)

I've got no time for a guy like him—I'd like to play against him a couple times just to fricken try and give it to him, no question."

The instigator rule has also had the indirect effect of watering down rivalries. Wade Belak, who grew up glued to broadcasts of the Battle of Alberta and then played in the thick of the Battle of Ontario between the Leafs and Ottawa Senators, said there was no comparison between the two rivalries.

"Now what can you do? Tough guy fights tough guy—you're lucky if you're in the lineup. It's a rivalry as far as being in the same province. But as far as physicality, they used to drop the puck then drop the gloves. It was a lot more physical. A lot more violent. The game's changed a lot since then," Belak told the *Toronto Star*.

The ways in which enforcers have been forced to adapt to the new rules has affected the flow of the game as well. Todd Ewen said his role had been to make room for himself, bring his team emotionally into the game, or settle the other side down.

"You could do a lot for the momentum," he said, adding that fights today often seem to lack any motive at all. "Now it just seems like out of the blue they just go meet up at centre ice and they'll dance around for a while and throw their elbow pads. A little bit of WWF and put on a show. Before you fought for a reason—it was to win the game. Now it seems like you're making a name for yourself."

Dave Richter agrees there's far less spontaneity in how fights develop in games, which partly reflects the fact the enforcers aren't playing regular shifts like they once did.

"People seem to be doing it more for who's king of the mountain," said the one-time Minnesota North Stars defenceman. "Now you've got a lot of enforcers that are back to sitting, not getting a whole lot of ice time, so when they get on the ice, they're just having at 'er."

For Bob Nystrom, whose son Eric is in the NHL, having the two toughest guys on both teams squaring off in an impromptu match without any kind of lead up proves nothing. "I don't understand how two guys can be standing at the faceoff circle, and not have done anything to each other, and then they start fighting. The only time I ever fought was when I thought someone took a liberty with me and embarrassed me."

Where fighting was once a spontaneous act, Dennis Polonich only sees a meaningless staged contest: "Sometimes I don't understand the purpose, two heavyweights fighting at centre ice, other than entertainment purposes. If I'm on either team, those two guys on the ice fighting has nothing to do with how I'm going to play the next shift or five shifts later."

The OHL is the petri dish for a new experiment to discourage staged fights. To start the 2012–13 season, the league instituted a new rule deterring the frequent fighters. A player who gets into an eleventh fight that season will get an automatic two-game suspension for every additional scrap up until his fifteenth fight, on top of the penalty in the game itself. For fights past the fifteenth, it is still a two-game ban, but the team gets a $1,000 penalty as well. If the player is deemed to be the instigator of a fight and he is past his fifteenth bout, he sits out four games. According to the *Guelph Mercury*, the total number of fights fell from the previous year.

"When we brought in the rule, the intent wasn't to reduce fighting by 24%. That was a positive byproduct of it, but that wasn't the intent," said the league's vice-president Ted Baker. "The intent was to eliminate the one-dimensional player."

Comparing the seasons on hockeyfights.com, only four players fought more than 10 times in the 2012-13 regular season compared to 25 players the previous year; on a player level, Emerson Clark of the Windsor Spitfires had 13 fights, and the year before, Windsor's Ty Bilcke had 37 fights.

KEEP YOUR HEAD UP

Modern regulations have changed the game, making it unrecognizable to some.

Formerly clean bodychecks can now garner a minor penalty, whereas in his day, Blair Stewart said it was commonplace for cross-checks and stick hacking in front of the net to go uncalled. Stewart recalls how, in a game against St. Louis, Larry Patey slew footed him and his own vicious retaliation.

"I got up and I just beelined for him. I had a wooden KOHO and I cross-checked him in the back of the neck. Next thing you know, I have two pieces of lumber in my hand. We dropped the gloves and we fought. I got two minutes for roughing and five for fighting. Today, I'd be in jail," Stewart said.

Stewart also recalls trying, but failing, to get around Buffalo Sabres defenceman Jim Schoenfeld.

"He put his arms around me from behind and basically picked

me up—my skates were off the ice—and drove me into the glass. He got like two minutes for holding. More like two minutes for trying to put me into the stands," Stewart said.

The new rules, however, have had a particularly stifling impact on defencemen, according to Dave Manson. Players like himself and many of his peers wouldn't even be allowed to step on the ice in today's game because every time they did, they'd wind up in the penalty box. He explained, "You look at Denis Potvin, Kenny Morrow, Scott Stevens, Derian Hatcher, myself, every team had the defencemen or forwards that put back pressure on the puck and caught players coming into the dangerous part of the ice, which is between the dots," adding, "Now, there's no consequence for those players coming through those dangerous areas with their heads down. . . . There's no accountability on the forwards' part to carry the puck with their heads up."

Manson coaches young players and tries to impart on them lessons about both avoiding and throwing hits. He recognizes the NHL has implemented a series of rules in order to curb injuries but suggests its actions also punished physical players for what had always been a staple in the NHL: hitting. "We had an instance with our Triple-A team. We had a defenceman who timed it perfectly, he arrived when the puck did. The player receiving the puck turned up ice and our men arrived there and bang! And they called him for interference," lamented Manson. "Well, it's a hard play as a coach to say don't do that because everything was perfect. So you have to encourage that [hitting]."

The onus now is on the hitter, instead of on the puck carrier or the player waiting for a pass. The old lessons of sensing danger coming or bracing yourself against the boards are being taught less.

"I'm going over it with kids in my youth hockey. Somebody's coming to hit you, get against the boards: protect yourself. And there's people actually teaching the exact opposite, to get away from the boards," said Dave Richter.

"Now I coach St. Louis University, and I'm going boy, they've got to get checking in a lot sooner. There's four corners to these rinks and these kids don't know how to do it at all—it's awful!" said Todd Ewen.

After taking in a few minor hockey games in Ontario, Marty McSorley expressed to the *Globe and Mail* his shock at how poorly players protected themselves, often leaving themselves totally vulnerable.

> I don't know how many kids were there, facing the forwards, or going to the boards and spinning, where they put their backs to the other players. I think that has to be addressed. There are coaches that teach their kids to turn their backs to the players to protect the puck. They'll say, 'If you're on the boards and you bobble the puck, just turn your back—they can't hit you and they can't get to the puck.' The one thing I'd like to see—you know how they penalize kids when they hit someone from behind? Well, I'd like to see them penalize a kid who turns to the boards to protect the puck.

Wendel Clark suggested some of the big, memorable hits he dished out in his career would no longer be permissible today. Perhaps his biggest hit ever was when he levelled Bruce Bell of the St. Louis Blues behind the net, knocking him out cold.

"I caught him not looking and with his head down. Sure, it was a hard hit, but it was also a clean hit, where my shoulder made contact with his head. I was never a head-hunter. But if it had happened today, I'd be suspended. They don't allow a check like that anymore," Clark said in his memoir.

"Pre-lockout and changes [of 2004–05], I think it was much more a grinding style of game and physical dominance played a much more important role," added Stu Grimson. "If you could dominate a team physically in the pre-lockout era, you were well on your way towards winning that night. I'm not sure that's necessarily the case any more."

Chris Nilan believed that by forcing the game open as the league has, it has seriously altered the style of hockey North America was always known for.

"All I know is when I was playing, the guys were worrying that the Russians and the other Europeans were going to take our jobs. They took our jobs, all right, and they took our game, too," the man known as "Knuckles" told the *Montreal Gazette*. "The rules were changed to help the European guys. Now it's more of a European style game than the North American brand we used to have and used to enjoy watching."

It's particularly irksome to Tiger Williams that today's players won't have to pay the same price he and his peers did in order to score a goal.

"Some snot-nosed little [punk] that isn't going to break a nail is going to score 50 goals and he's never driven to the net in his life. He's never stood in front of the net with Moose Dupont giving him 89 cross-checks in the back of the head," Williams said. "To have today's players score 400 goals in a no-touch pond hockey league is garbage. Getting in another guy's face is part of the character of the game."

CONCUSSIONS

In spite of the instigator and obstruction rules, players are still getting seriously hurt, some even retiring prematurely, often as a result of concussions.

"I'm of the mind that the rink's the same size, and the men are much bigger and much faster today, and there's no doubt why guys are getting hurt," said Dan Maloney.

"The guys are so fast today, it's incredible . . . I look at our videos, and it's like we're skating in quicksand," said Bob Nystrom. "The players are better conditioned now, they're bigger, faster, stronger. It's the same in every sport. The training, it's very scientific now compared to when we played. We were probably the first team ever to start riding bikes and work on our conditioning that way. But nowadays, it's a 12-month training process."

The removal of the centre ice red line post-lockout in 2004–05, done to foster greater offence, sped up the game even more—perhaps making it *too* fast.

"They took the red line out of the game and now you get guys who are 220 pounds skating 30 miles an hour just getting ready to drill you," said Kurt Walker, who decried that the rules were being changed by those who had never played the game and didn't understand players' psychology. "As much as [NHL commissioner Gary Bettman] wanted to improve the game, he may have harmed the game. . . . Once that red line was gone, you know the kind of speed the guys could start to travel, and quite honestly it made it a lot easier for some of those open ice headshot hits."

A whole new set of rules had to be created to stem the rash of devastating blindside hits, as well as hits that targeted the head. But even those actions weren't enough to eliminate checks that left players unable to leave the ice under their own power.

"The speed of the game, I don't know how we control it without allowing clutching and grabbing, and maybe putting the red line back into the game," said broadcaster Jiggs McDonald. "The tempo, the speed of today's game, and then the collisions that occur at that speed, you're bound to have injuries."

The changes to equipment have also contributed to injuries, giving many a false sense of near indestructibility.

Canadiens enforcer John Ferguson said stick swinging became more noticeable when players started wearing helmets, and even more so when face guards came into being.

"It starts with kids in the lower ranks and continues through the colleges. As long as players wear all that face protection—and as long as they start doing it from the very beginning in the lower leagues—there will be less respect in using the stick," Ferguson said in *Thunder and Lightning*.

Dave Richter, a collegiate before turning pro, saw proof of

Ferguson's words as an amateur. During his first two years with Michigan, players weren't required to wear facial protection, but in his final season, full cage masks became mandatory.

"That definitely changed the way the game was played," Richter said. "It was just terrible. Everybody just started using their sticks more. . . . They swing their sticks, nobody is worried about getting hit, and to me, the worst thing that ever happened to hockey is the face mask. And then you take that into the pro level."

The sense of security helmets and shields created also brought forth a lack of respect.

"I started off playing without a helmet. Nowadays, people say, 'Oh, you're crazy,'" said Bob Nystrom. "Yep, but people had respect around me, because they knew they could really hurt me."

"When you think about our era, we didn't wear helmets. But there was a mutual respect. Guys kept their sticks down," Walker added.

More protective body padding has also contributed to the greater number of injuries, said Dennis Polonich, arguing that the hard plastic elbow and shoulder pads are particularly dangerous and that the changes that have been made to equipment need to be examined. "The athletes are bigger, stronger, faster, so what do they do? They dress them in Kevlar. They dress them in plastic. They dress them in fibreglass," said Polonich. "Well, I guess the athlete's going to feel invincible. I'm not saying they need to go back to the olden days and dress in cotton, but certainly look at the equipment and revisit that."

Richter agreed that reckless play is a direct result of lighter and more protective gear.

"Everybody is worried about the concussions and the hits to the head. Well, if you weren't wearing a mask yourself and you didn't have all this high-tech padding—and there might be a possibility you might get hurt just as much as you hurting somebody else when you go to hit them—you might not be going headlong at them," Richter said. "It's frustrating to watch a lot of the NHL games, and definitely youth hockey, because nobody cares about anybody else and they're all like bullets running around, feeling they're not going to get hurt because they're in their suit of armor."

Former Edmonton Oiler Dave Hunter found the modern equipment to be dangerous enough to cause unintended injuries. "You wouldn't have to hit a guy very hard and you'd knock him senseless," he said to the *Edmonton Sun*. "I've seen some checks that weren't dirty, but the chin hits that pad on the right spot, you're gonna get a concussion."

The issue of concussions has grown across all sports, and knowledge about their effects on the brain has advanced considerably. Long-time New York Rangers star Harry Howell believed he was concussed more than once back in the Original Six days.

"I was told I had a lot of headaches," Howell laughed. "You get dinged, you get hit in the head, one way or another, and you go down. The trainer used to run out and say, 'Open your mouth.' He'd pop an aspirin in. That's it. Get up and play. Nobody ever complained, not that I know of. They were all hockey players. You didn't have a doctor following you around like they do now."

Kurt Walker said he had at least four or five concussions: "And what trainers would do is say smell the smelling salts, how many fingers, take a five-minute break, go back and play."

Little changed even in the 1980s and '90s.

"A concussion for me back when I played was a headache: 'Here, have some Tylenol, see you in the morning,'" said Kevin McClelland, another Oiler from their glory years.

While acknowledging one can carry the effects of a concussion for the rest of one's life, ex-defenceman Dave Manson said that when he played, he gave it little consideration. Once the adrenaline kicked in, he worried about the game: "It's one of those things you didn't really think about, but now that you're 45 years old, you're thinking, aw jeez . . ."

How the NHL treated players with concussions began to alter following the study of Reggie Fleming's brain after his death in 2009.

His brain was found to have chronic traumatic encephalopathy (CTE), a degenerative brain disease. His family estimated he suffered 20 concussions in his 20-plus seasons in professional hockey.

Chris Nowinski, the president of the Sports Legacy Institute, has been front and centre in the debate about concussions in all sports and sees progress.

"The hockey community has really embraced this research, led by people like Keith Primeau," Nowinski said. Athletes and their families have committed to donating their brains to research following their death, and Fleming's findings have led to the increase of hockey players on file.

But brain injury science is still relatively new, and not everyone is on board with what the Sports Legacy Institute and others are championing. "The NHLPA has not embraced the work like the NFL and NFLPA has, or even the Pro Hockey Player's Association, which is the minor league association," said Nowinski. "They've actually sent out a brochure to every player in minor league hockey, encouraging them to participate in our research."

In 2010, findings that Bob Probert too suffered from CTE really seemed to bring the long-term brain damage issue to the forefront.

"If he was playing blackjack, he could remember plays from years ago, and every player's hand and what the dealer had. But boy, if you asked him what he had for breakfast that morning. . . . It definitely makes you think," his widow, Dani, said to the *Globe and Mail*.

When Boston University confirmed Probert's CTE, many of his peers began having second thoughts about their own situations.

"There's no better comparable for me than Bob. We're two guys who suffered similar amounts of brain trauma," Probert's former sparring partner Stu Grimson told the *Toronto Star*. "I recognize I'm probably assuming too much if I assume I'm walking around with CTE just because Bob had it. But it definitely gets your attention."

Marty McSorley, who spent most of his 17 NHL years protecting Wayne Gretzky, has revealed he's experienced memory gaps in retirement.

"There are times when I'll walk into a room and I'll stand there and go 'Why am I here again?' And you just don't know," he told the *Globe and Mail*.

Tie Domi didn't even want to think about the possible side effects of his several hundred career fights.

"And if I get checked out, then what? What's that going to do for me? . . . I can't be thinking about this. I don't want anybody worrying for me. This [Probert news] has made people worry about me. I don't like that," Domi said to the *Toronto Sun*, adding he won't see a doctor. "I'm one of those guys who doesn't like to look in the past. I haven't read one article about what happened [to Probert] and I don't plan on reading one."

If anyone seemed untouchable, it was 6-foot-7, 270-pound Derek Boogaard. But even though his size and strength could annihilate opponents, he was in truth just as susceptible to human frailties as anyone else. He suffered a broken jaw in the juniors, and there were also concussions, bulging discs, a broken hand and teeth, and a busted nose over his career. He required shoulder surgery in April 2009, and on December 9, 2010, he suffered a season-ending concussion during a fight when he fell to the ice with Ottawa's Matt Carkner on top of him.

In the following months, light sensitivity issues drove him to spend hours in darkened movie theatres. Wherever he went, he wore sunglasses.

Perhaps most shocking were the syndromes he experienced the summer *before* the fight that ended his season. Boogaard had phoned sports author Ross Bernstein, insisting he pick him up. When asked where he was, Boogaard replied he didn't know.

"Turns out he was at a big home improvement store," Bernstein told ESPN. "This shit's real. It's progressive. I can't imagine that you heal up and then another shot to the head helps."

Boogaard's story became more tragic when he died of an accidental fatal combination of alcohol and the painkiller Oxycodone in May 2011.

REQUIEM FOR A GUNSLINGER

As much as the league is discouraging fighting as a tactic and limiting hitters, enforcers believe toughness will always be a vital component of the game.

"Hockey is a game of intimidation, there's no question about it. If I could get another second because someone was afraid to hit me, then it was to my advantage," said Bob Nystrom, stressing every club needs overall toughness to be effective. "We had team toughness. [Mike] Bossy was never a fighter, or Trotts [Bryan Trottier], but they still were able to play the game, even if guys tried to intimidate them."

Team mettle is most highly tested during the playoffs. Teams can use their size and force during the postseason to their advantage. The Los Angeles Kings pounded the opposition on their way to their first Cup in the franchise's 45-year history in 2012. They took a page out of the book of other modern intimidating teams. In 2007, brawny players like George Parros, Brad May, and Scott Thornton helped the Anaheim Ducks win it all, and Thornton would play an even greater role with the championship Boston Bruins of 2011.

"Boston intimidated Vancouver," Wilf Paiement said of the 2011 final. "I think Vancouver had a better team. But Boston intimidated them. Boston is a real tough team, and they probably have the top four toughest guys in the league. And three of them are stars. And then you had a goalie that was really hot."

Whether teams use an enforcer or not often boils down to the direction the coach and organization want to take.

"I played against Thortie [Scott Thornton] when he was in Norfolk and I was in Hartford [of the AHL], and he's come a long way," said Steve MacIntyre. "But he's had an opportunity where he can go play."

As much as he wanted to score 10 or 15 goals a year, Kurt Walker said he never had the opportunity to do so. When he was sent out onto the ice, it was to get into a fight more often than not.

"The first shift I took in Maple Leaf Gardens on a Saturday night, I hit the post," he recalled. "And [GM] Jim Gregory said, 'Glad you didn't score that goal.' And I was like, 'Why?' 'Because you would have thought you were a goal scorer and that's not what we brought you up here for.'"

There are a lucky few who've been allowed to do more than just swing their fists, like Chris Nilan and Tie Domi, as well as the roughnecks on the Lunch Pail Bruins.

"John [Wensink] was fortunate that he had Don Cherry as a coach. Those guys seemed to play more," said Walker.

The former Bruins coach and commentator has never budged from championing enforcers. When ex-Canadien and Maple Leaf John Kordic died in the early '90s, Cherry emphasized his stance against limiting players to fighting only, as Kordic had been pigeon-holed.

"It is demeaning for a human being to sit on a bench for most of a game and be thrown out there only to fight like a mad dog," Cherry told the *New York Times*. Kordic, he said, "always wanted to play the game of hockey, but everywhere he went he was considered just a goon."

Wensink said it pays to work with your fighters.

"Ice time's a great reward. And truthfully, that's all that anybody wants. You want to feel you're contributing, and one of the ways to contribute is to be on the ice," said Wensink. "Whether you score a goal or get an assist, or your assignment is to be the defensive player and you have to watch the other team's top player, it's ice time. That's what you play for—no one practices everyday to sit on the bench."

At a time when Colton Orr had fallen out of favour with Maple Leafs coach Ron Wilson, Wensink had suggestions for how Toronto could make better use of Orr, advising them to give him an assignment like helping shadow another team's player.

"Your job is not to get a penalty against him or knock him out of the game, but to skate and keep the puck away from him; you're assigned to watch him," Wensink explained. "If he goes for a crap, you go with him. . . . It's worth a try for Toronto. If nothing else, at least Colton's going to feel like a better part of the team. As long as he knows that that's his reward for doing the other things."

Apparently, Wensink's mind was one with Wilson's replacement, Randy Carlyle. Carlyle made liberal use of Orr's talents as a fore-checker and enforcer, playing him regularly and adding him to a mix of other competent toughs in Mike Brown, Frazer McLaren (whom Carlyle called a "George Parros–type" player), and Mark Fraser.

"Our players have to feel they're protected," Carlyle told the *Toronto Star* during the lockout shortened 2012–13 season. "When you have a 48-game schedule, the points mean so much more and those are the things that set the tone. I would say if you look at the league as a whole, I think there's been a revitalization of that role on various teams."

Carlyle was unapologetic about the fact his Leafs led the league in fighting in 2012–13, with 46 majors, and 776 total PIM. "I know there are people that want it out of the game," Carlyle said halfway through the lockout-shortened season. "But I don't think it's going as quickly as some people would like. It's a fact of life in the NHL."

Dennis Bonvie is all for coaches putting their tough guys in spots where they can be assets: "It's like anything, when you get some love and the coach shows you a little confidence, who knows what can happen."

He said the opportunities for a player like himself, whose role was very specific and centred on staged fights, have diminished. But that doesn't mean fighting will be totally drummed out. There will always be the chance of a scrap breaking out in a high-energy con-tact game like hockey between competitive players, stressed Bonvie.

The league's pendulum has swung widely, and whether or not it settles in the middle isn't a certainty to everyone.

"Respect is worth fighting for," said Dave Schultz, stressing, "Fighting is one of the more celebrated traditions of hockey." He expressed his difficulty in watching the league "stray so far from its roots."

"The way it's going, it's going to be a tough call in the future whether they're going to have us enforcers [or not]," added MacIntyre, "or if it's going to come full circle where they're going to say, 'Well you guys need to come back and take care of the game.'"

Bernstein, Ross. *The Code: The Unwritten Rules of Fighting and Retaliation in the* NHL. Chicago: Triumph Books, 2006.

Brewitt, Ross. *Clear the Track*. Toronto: Stoddart, 1997.

Cherry, Don, and Stan Fischler. *Grapes: A Vintage View of Hockey*. Scarborough, Ont.: Prentice-Hall Canada, 1982.

Cherry, Don, and Al Strachan. *Hockey Stories and Stuff*. Toronto: Doubleday Canada, 2008.

Cherry, Don, and Al Strachan. *Hockey Stories Part 2*. Toronto: Doubleday Canada, 2010.

Clark, Wendel, Scott Morrison, and Jeff Jackson. *Wendel: My Life in Hockey*. Burlington, Ont.: Jackson Events, 2009.

Cole, Stephen. *The Last Hurrah*. Toronto: Viking, 1995.

Frayne, Trent. *The Tales of an Athletic Supporter: A Memoir*. Toronto: McClelland & Stewart Limited, 1990.

Frayne, Trent. *The Mad Men of Hockey*. Toronto: McClelland & Stewart Limited, 1974.

Geoffrion, Bernard, and Stan Fischler. *Boom Boom: The Life and Times of Bernard Geoffrion*. Toronto: McGraw-Hill Ryerson, 1997.

Hiam, C. Michael. *Eddie Shore and That Old Time Hockey*. Toronto: McClelland & Stewart, 2010.

Hood, Bruce, and Murray Townsend. *Calling the Shots: Memoirs of an* NHL *Referee*. Toronto: Stoddart, 1988.

Ferguson, John, Stan Fischler, and Shirley Fischler. *Thunder & Lightning*. Scarborough, Ont.: Prentice-Hall Canada, 1989.

Feschuk, Dave, and Michael Grange. *Leafs AbomiNation*. Toronto: Random House Canada, 2009.

Fischler, Stan. *Ultimate Bad Boys: Hockey's Greatest Fighters.* Toronto: Warwick Publishing, 1999.

Gretzky, Wayne, and Rick Reilly. *Gretzky: An Autobiography.* Toronto: HarperCollins, 1990.

Imlach, Punch, and Scott Young. *Hockey Is a Battle.* Toronto: Macmillan of Canada, 1969.

Imlach, Punch, and Scott Young. *Heaven and Hell in the NHL.* Toronto: McClelland & Stewart, 1982.

Jericho, Chris, and Peter Thomas Fornatale. *A Lion's Tale: Around the World in Spandex.* New York: Grand Central Publishing, 2007.

Laraque, Georges, and Pierre Thibeault. *The Story of the NHL's Unlikeliest Tough Guy.* Toronto: Viking Canada, 2011.

Mason, Gary. *Oldtimers: On the Road with the Legendary Heroes of Hockey.* Vancouver: Greystone Books, 2002.

McDonald, Lanny, and Steve Simmons. *Lanny.* Toronto: McGraw-Hill Ryerson, 1987.

Plager, Bob, and Tom Wheatley. *Bob Plager's Tales from the Blues Bench.* Champaign, Ill.: Sports Publishing L.L.C., 2003.

Probert, Bob, and Kirstie McLellan Day. *Tough Guy.* Toronto: HarperCollins, 2010.

Robinson, Larry, and Chrys Goyens. *Robinson for the Defence.* Scarborough, Ont.: McGraw-Hill Ryerson, 1988.

Salming, Borje, and Gerhard Karlsson. *Blood, Sweat and Hockey.* Toronto: HarperCollins, 1991.

Semenko, Dave, and Larry Tucker. *Looking Out for Number One.* Don Mills, Ont.: Stoddart, 1989.

Sittler, Darryl, Chrys Goyens, and Allan Turowetz. *Sittler.* Toronto: Macmillan Canada, 1991.

Tretiak, Vladislav. *Tretiak: The Legend.* Edmonton: Plains Publishing Inc., 1987.

Williams, Tiger, and James Lawton. *Tiger: A Hockey Story.* Toronto: HarperCollins, 1986.

Young, Scott. *The Leafs I Knew.* Toronto: Ryerson Press, 1966.

ACKNOWLEDGEMENTS

DON'T CALL ME GOON had its genesis over lunch with ECW Press senior editor Michael Holmes, who encouraged Greg to try something outside of the professional wrestling writing that had been his bread and butter for years. In Richard, Greg found an extra-willing co-conspirator who threw himself into the project, digging out names, conducting interviews, and writing up a healthy chunk of this book.

We both want to thank the many people who took the time to share their memories and recollections. There were times when we couldn't believe we were talking to these great players we had watched for so many years. It is especially unnerving to move into a new "beat" and build up a new set of contacts. A special shout-out goes to Jeff Marek, formerly of *Hockey Night in Canada* and now with Sportsnet.ca, whose friendship and support helped tremendously and who paved the way for the whole "wrestling guy moves mainstream" thing.

The unsung heroes of the internet age are the folks who maintain the websites and statistical databases that we frequented. Hockeyfights.com was essential, as were HockeyDB.com, the Hockey Hall of Fame site, and many more websites. And then there's YouTube, home to a surprising array of fights, brawls, and incidents from hockey's past and present.

Yet, even in this New Media age, there is nothing quite like a library. We pestered librarians in Winnipeg and Toronto and found treasures through online access to newspapers of the past.

The trips to the Hockey Hall of Fame's D.K. (Doc) Seaman Hockey Resource Centre in Toronto's west end were incredible experiences for Greg. After all, where else would one find a scrapbook kept by Joe Hall's family? Special thanks go to Craig Campbell and Miragh Bitove for their help. (Fair warning—Greg will be back!)

On a personal level, this is Richard's first book, and he wants to say thanks to his parents Alex and Sonja, who should be nominated for sainthood. When others would have happily abandoned Richard in a demilitarized zone, they stuck by him and supported him. Also, Richard thanks his dog, Max, for dragging him out every day for fresh air and exercise.

For Greg, this book marks the end of his true stay-at-home dad/writer phase, with his patient son, Quinn, heading into full-time school. Blame for any future afternoons wasted playing Wii or fighting with foam swords in the yard will be entirely his own. And patience is a good word for his wife, Meredith Renwick, who has supported him during the good and bad times. Thanks, Meppie!

Finally, we've enjoyed the discussion so far on our Facebook page for *Don't Call Me Goon*, and look forward to you joining the conversation too: bit.ly/DontCallMeGoon.